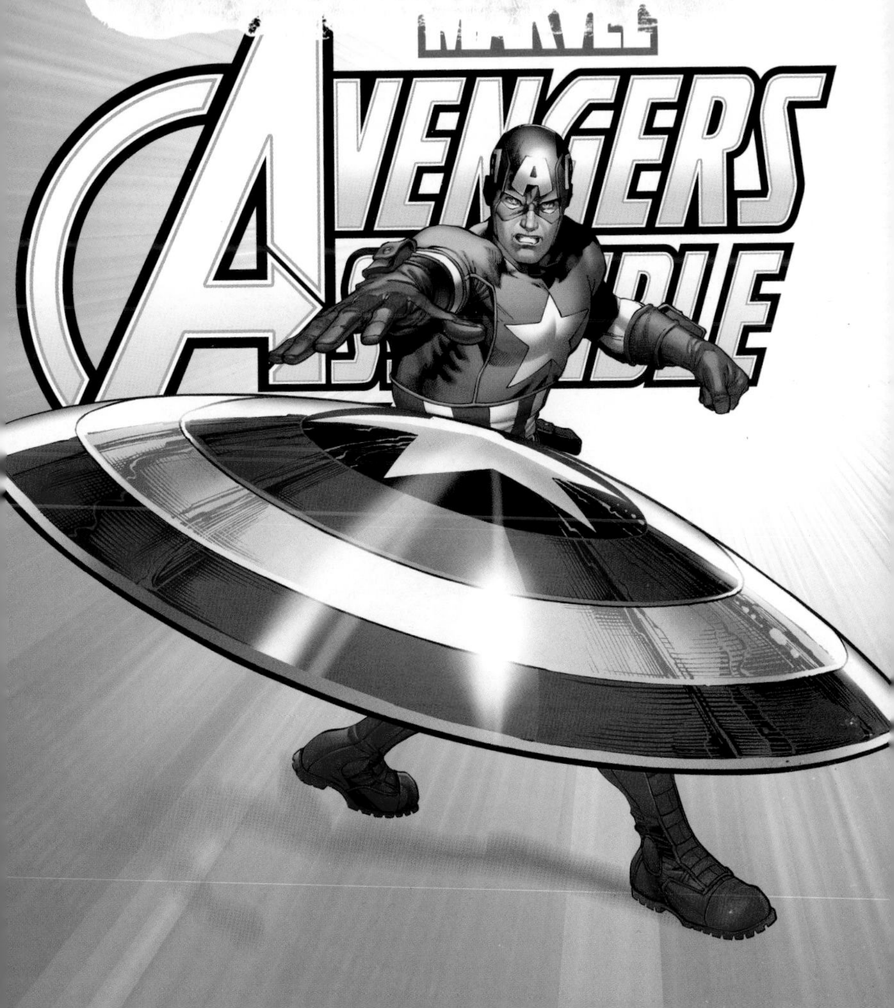
MARVEL
AVENGERS

MARVEL UNIVERSE AVENGERS ASSEMBLE VOL. 1. Contains material originally published in magazine form as MARVEL UNIVERSE AVENGERS ASSEMBLE #1-4 and FREE COMIC BOOK DAY 2013. First printing 2014. ISBN# 978-0-7851-8418-8. Published by MARVEL WORLDWIDE, INC., a subsidiary of MARVEL ENTERTAINMENT, LLC. OFFICE OF PUBLICATION: 135 West 50th Street, New York, NY 10020. Copyright © 2014 Marvel Characters, Inc. All rights reserved. All characters featured in this issue and the distinctive names and likenesses thereof, and all related indicia are trademarks of Marvel Characters, Inc. No similarity between any of the names, characters, persons, and/or institutions in this m ... living or dead person or institution is intended, and any such similarity which may exist is purely coincidental. **Printed in the U.S.A.** ALA ... Inc. and EVP & CMO Marvel Characters B.V.; DAN BUCKLEY, Publisher & President - Print, Animation & Digit ... of Publishing; DAVID BOGART, SVP of Operations & Procurement, Publishing; C.B. CEBULSKI, SV ... & Marketing; JIM O'KEEFE, VP of Operations & Logistics; DAN CARR, Executive ... , Publishing Operations Manager; STAN LEE, Chairman Emeritus. F ... Director of Marvel Partnerships, at ndisla@marvel.com. For Marvel ... **2014 by SHERIDAN BOOKS, INC., CHELSEA, MI, USA.**

10 9 8 7 6 5 4 3 2 1

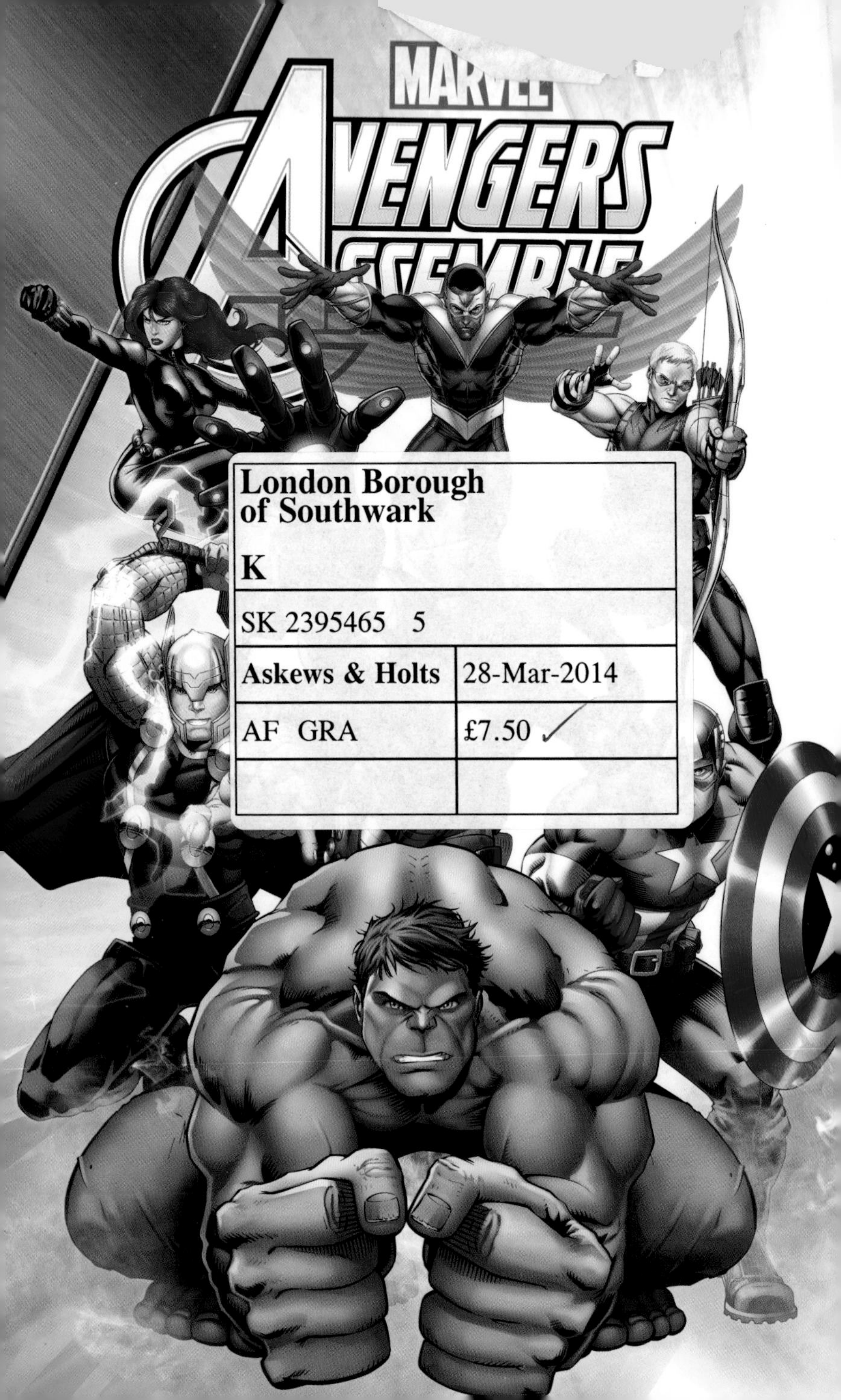
MARVEL
AVENGERS

Based on the TV series episodes by
MAN OF ACTION
& **PAUL GIACOPPO**

Adapted by
JOE CARAMAGNA

Editor
SEBASTIAN GIRNER

Consulting Editor
JON MOISAN

Senior Editor
MARK PANICCIA

Collection Editor
ALEX STARBUCK

Editors, Special Projects
JENNIFER GRÜNWALD
& **MARK D. BEAZLEY**

Senior Editor, Special Projects
JEFF YOUNGQUIST

SVP Print, Sales & Marketing
DAVID GABRIEL

Editor In Chief
AXEL ALONSO

Chief Creative Officer
JOE QUESADA

Publisher
DAN BUCKLEY

Executive Producer
ALAN FINE

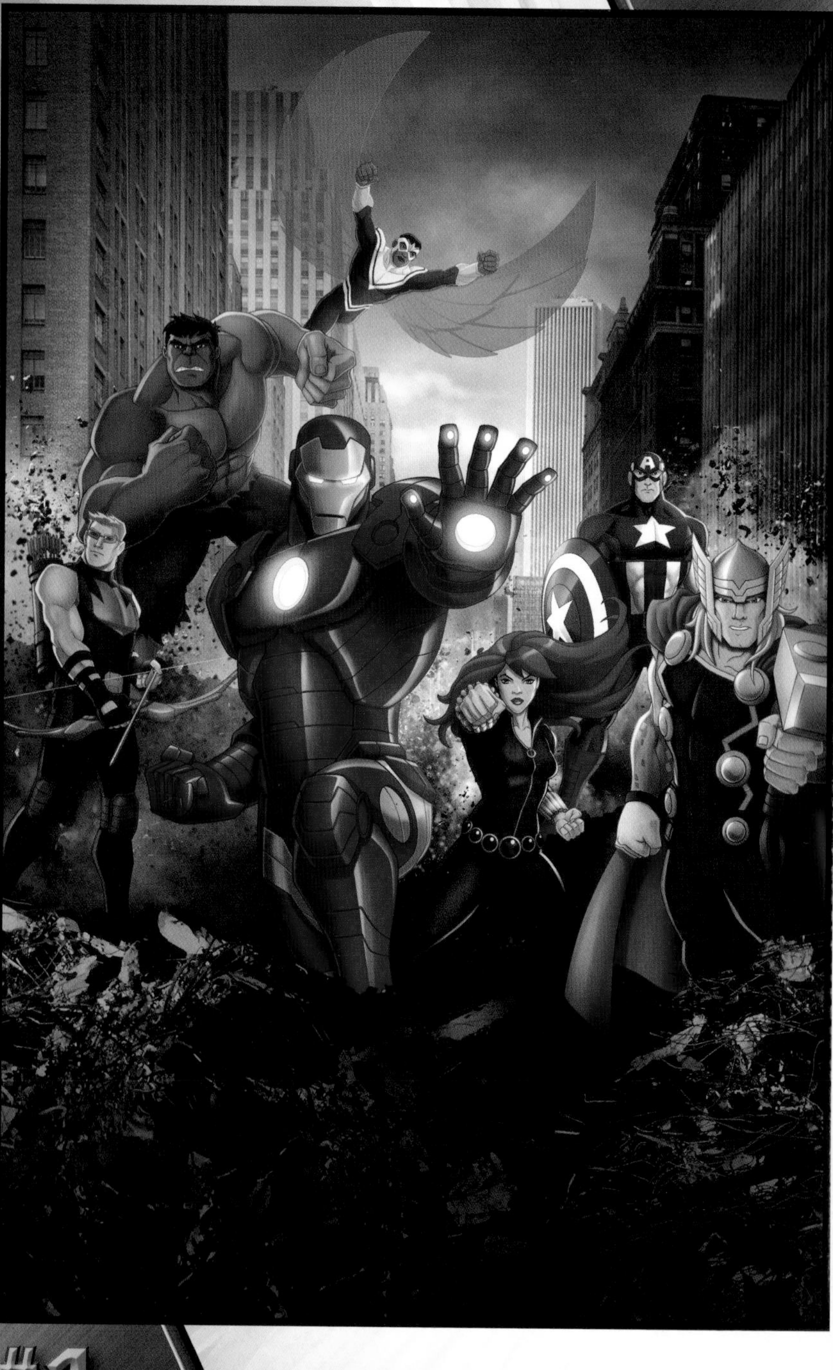

#1 BASED ON "THE AVENGERS PROTOCOL"

MARVEL

AVENGERS ASSEMBLE

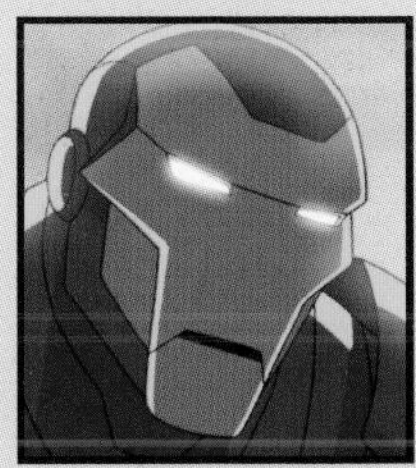

IRON MAN

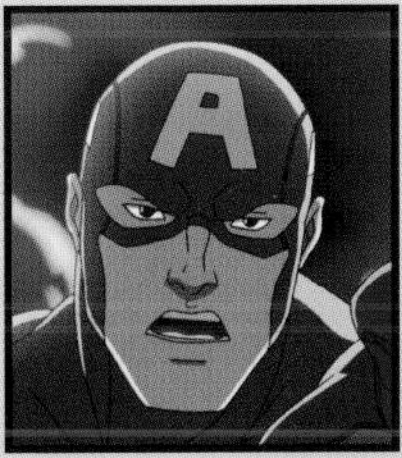

CAPTAIN AMERICA

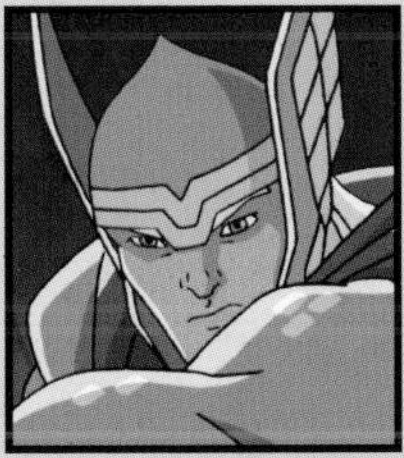

THOR

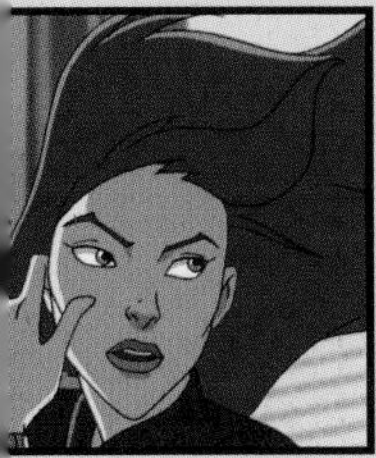

BLACK WIDOW

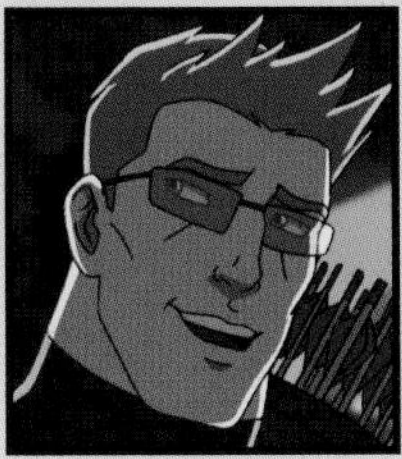

HAWKEYE

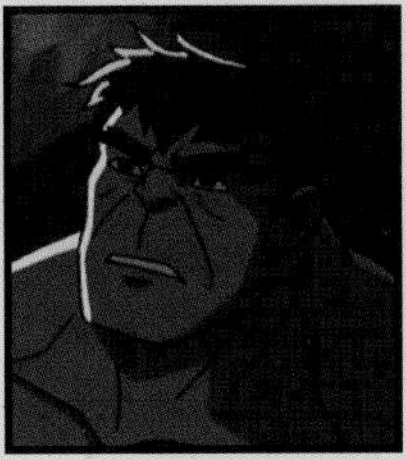

HULK

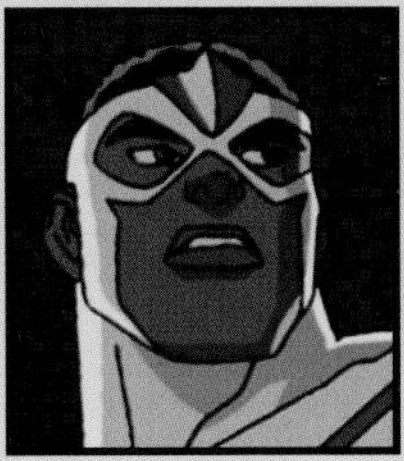

FALCON

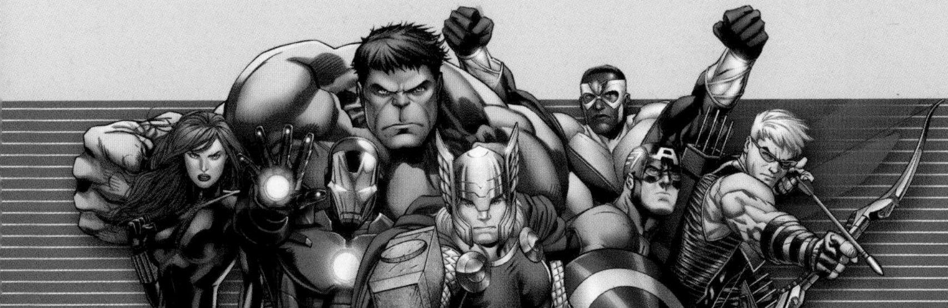

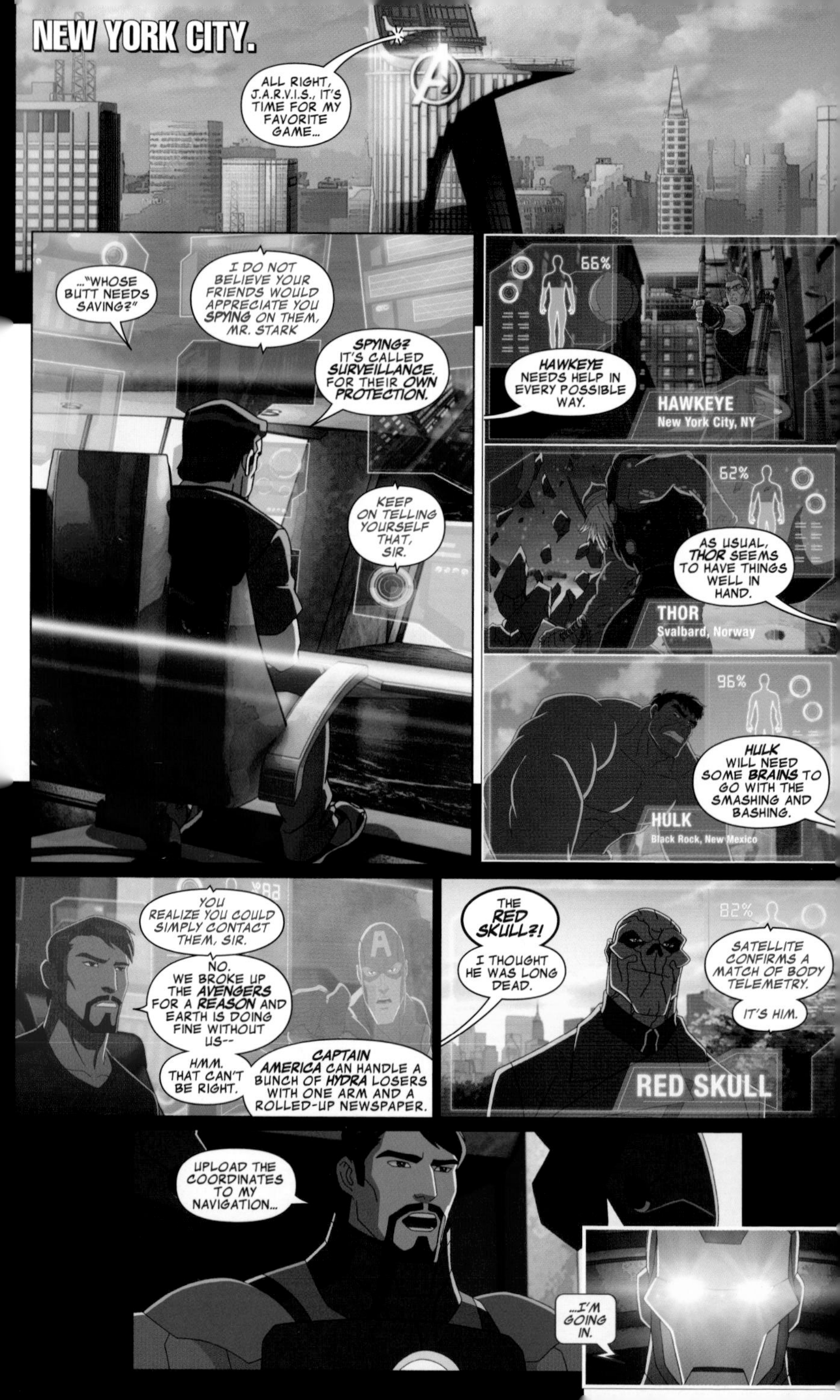
NEW YORK CITY.
ALL RIGHT, J.A.R.V.I.S., IT'S TIME FOR MY FAVORITE GAME...
..."WHOSE BUTT NEEDS SAVING?"
I DO NOT BELIEVE YOUR FRIENDS WOULD APPRECIATE YOU SPYING ON THEM, MR. STARK
SPYING? IT'S CALLED SURVEILLANCE. FOR THEIR OWN PROTECTION.
KEEP ON TELLING YOURSELF THAT, SIR.
66%
HAWKEYE NEEDS HELP IN EVERY POSSIBLE WAY.
HAWKEYE
New York City, NY
62%
AS USUAL, THOR SEEMS TO HAVE THINGS WELL IN HAND.
THOR
Svalbard, Norway
96%
HULK WILL NEED SOME BRAINS TO GO WITH THE SMASHING AND BASHING.
HULK
Black Rock, New Mexico
YOU REALIZE YOU COULD SIMPLY CONTACT THEM, SIR.
NO. WE BROKE UP THE AVENGERS FOR A REASON AND EARTH IS DOING FINE WITHOUT US--
HMM. THAT CAN'T BE RIGHT.
CAPTAIN AMERICA CAN HANDLE A BUNCH OF HYDRA LOSERS WITH ONE ARM AND A ROLLED-UP NEWSPAPER.
THE RED SKULL?!
I THOUGHT HE WAS LONG DEAD.
82%
SATELLITE CONFIRMS A MATCH OF BODY TELEMETRY.
IT'S HIM.
RED SKULL
UPLOAD THE COORDINATES TO MY NAVIGATION...
...I'M GOING IN.

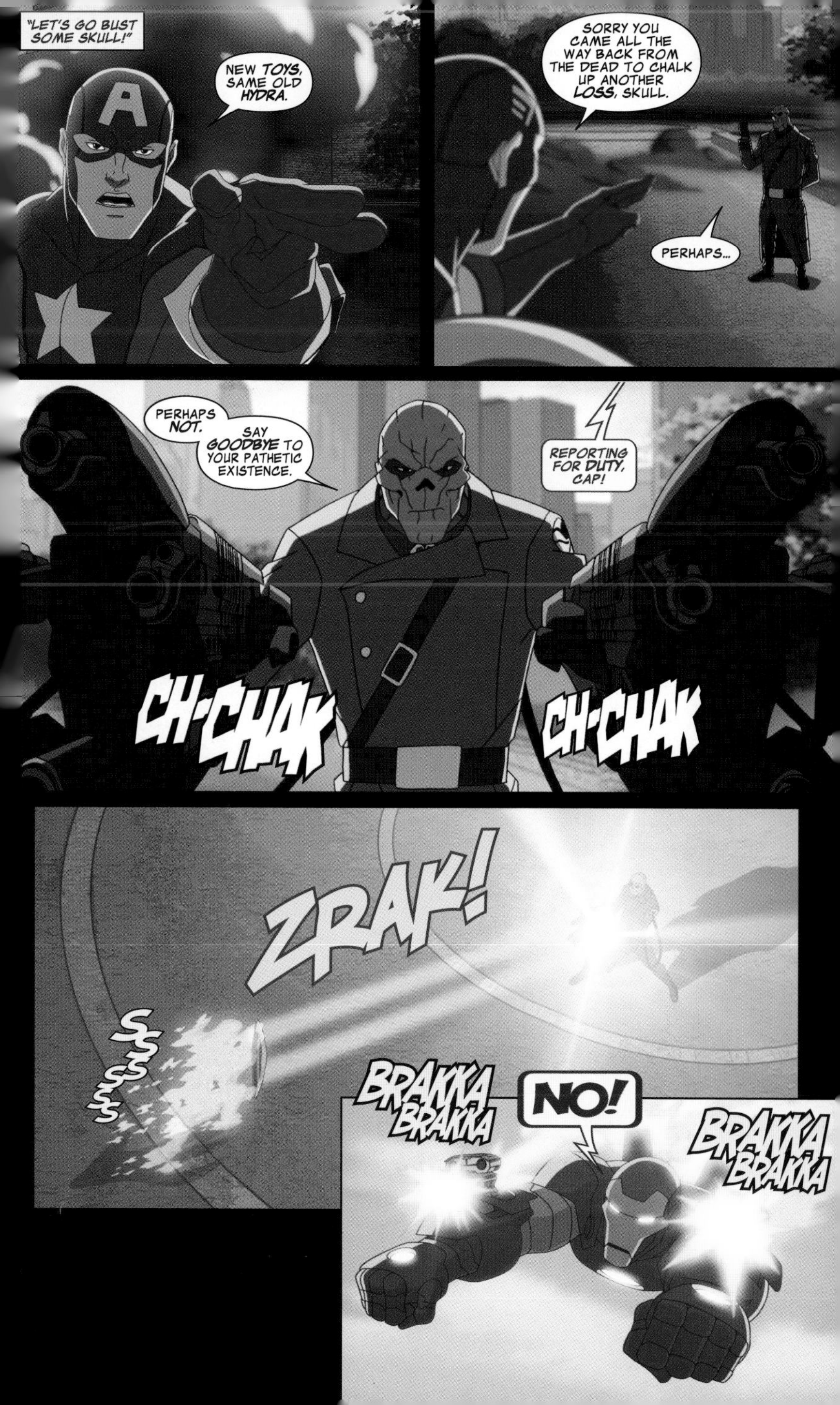
"LET'S GO BUST SOME SKULL!"
NEW TOYS, SAME OLD HYDRA.
SORRY YOU CAME ALL THE WAY BACK FROM THE DEAD TO CHALK UP ANOTHER LOSS, SKULL.
PERHAPS...
PERHAPS NOT.
SAY GOODBYE TO YOUR PATHETIC EXISTENCE.
REPORTING FOR DUTY, CAP!
CH-CHAK
CH-CHAK
ZRAK!
SSSSSS
BRAKKA BRAKKA
NO!
BRAKKA BRAKKA

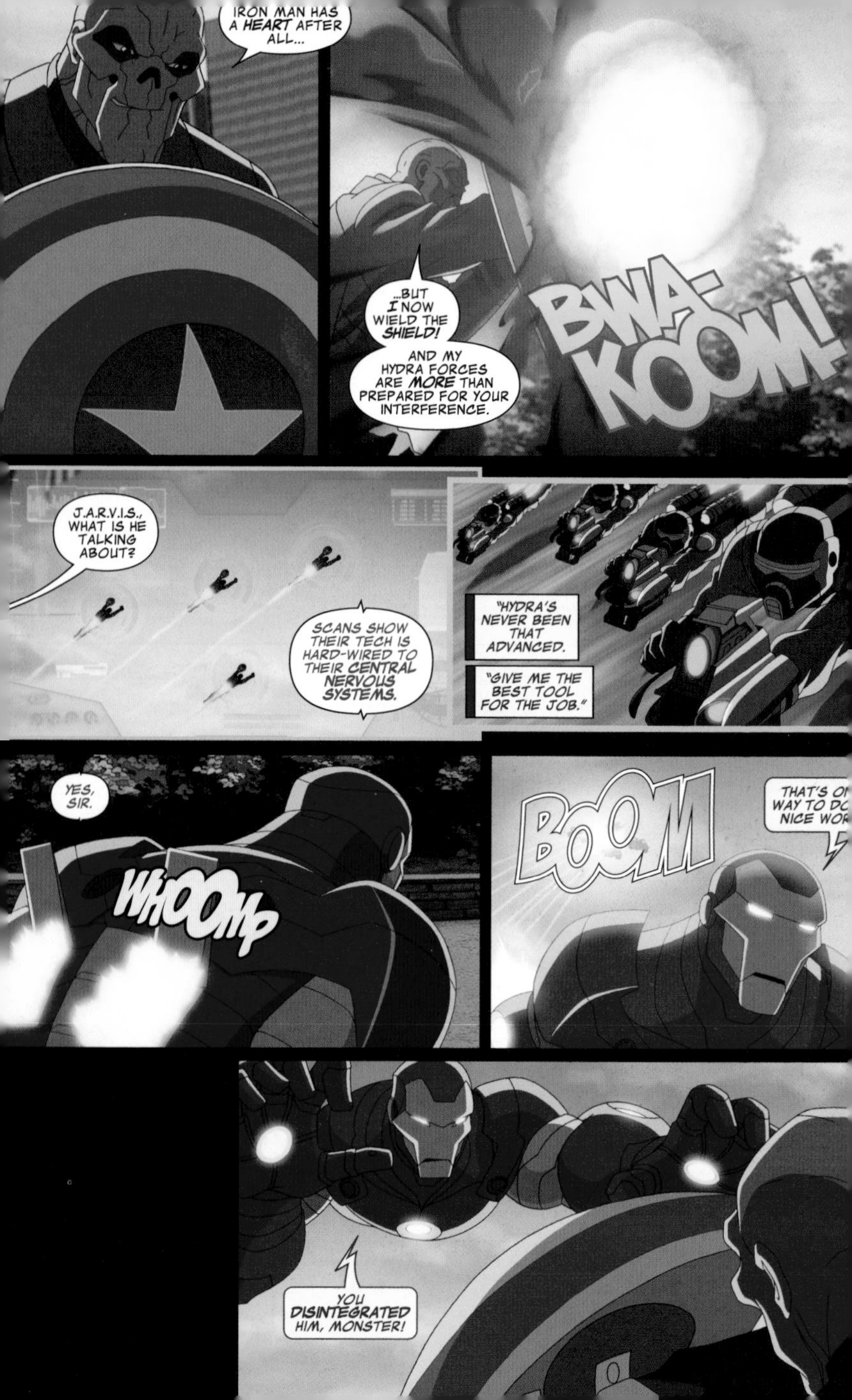

IRON MAN HAS A HEART AFTER ALL...
...BUT I NOW WIELD THE SHIELD!
AND MY HYDRA FORCES ARE MORE THAN PREPARED FOR YOUR INTERFERENCE.
BWA-KOOM!
J.A.R.V.I.S., WHAT IS HE TALKING ABOUT?
SCANS SHOW THEIR TECH IS HARD-WIRED TO THEIR CENTRAL NERVOUS SYSTEMS.
"HYDRA'S NEVER BEEN THAT ADVANCED.
"GIVE ME THE BEST TOOL FOR THE JOB."
YES, SIR.
WHOOMP
BOOM
YOU DISINTEGRATED HIM, MONSTER!

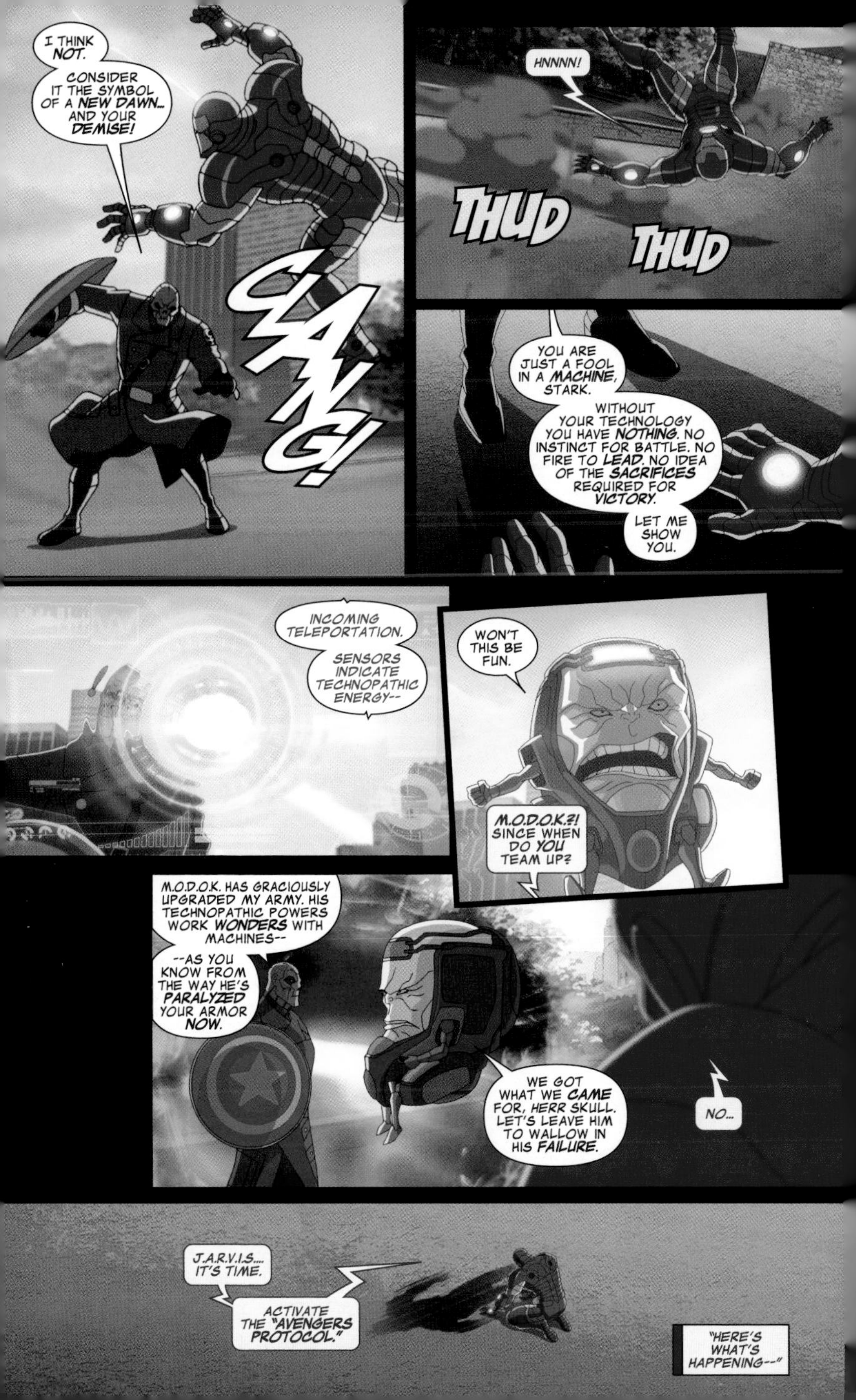
I THINK NOT.
CONSIDER IT THE SYMBOL OF A NEW DAWN... AND YOUR DEMISE!
CLANG!
HNNNN!
THUD
THUD
YOU ARE JUST A FOOL IN A MACHINE, STARK.
WITHOUT YOUR TECHNOLOGY YOU HAVE NOTHING. NO INSTINCT FOR BATTLE. NO FIRE TO LEAD. NO IDEA OF THE SACRIFICES REQUIRED FOR VICTORY.
LET ME SHOW YOU.
INCOMING TELEPORTATION.
SENSORS INDICATE TECHNOPATHIC ENERGY--
WON'T THIS BE FUN.
M.O.D.O.K.?! SINCE WHEN DO YOU TEAM UP?
M.O.D.O.K. HAS GRACIOUSLY UPGRADED MY ARMY. HIS TECHNOPATHIC POWERS WORK WONDERS WITH MACHINES--
--AS YOU KNOW FROM THE WAY HE'S PARALYZED YOUR ARMOR NOW.
WE GOT WHAT WE CAME FOR, HERR SKULL. LET'S LEAVE HIM TO WALLOW IN HIS FAILURE.
NO...
J.A.R.V.I.S.... IT'S TIME.
ACTIVATE THE "AVENGERS PROTOCOL."
"HERE'S WHAT'S HAPPENING--"

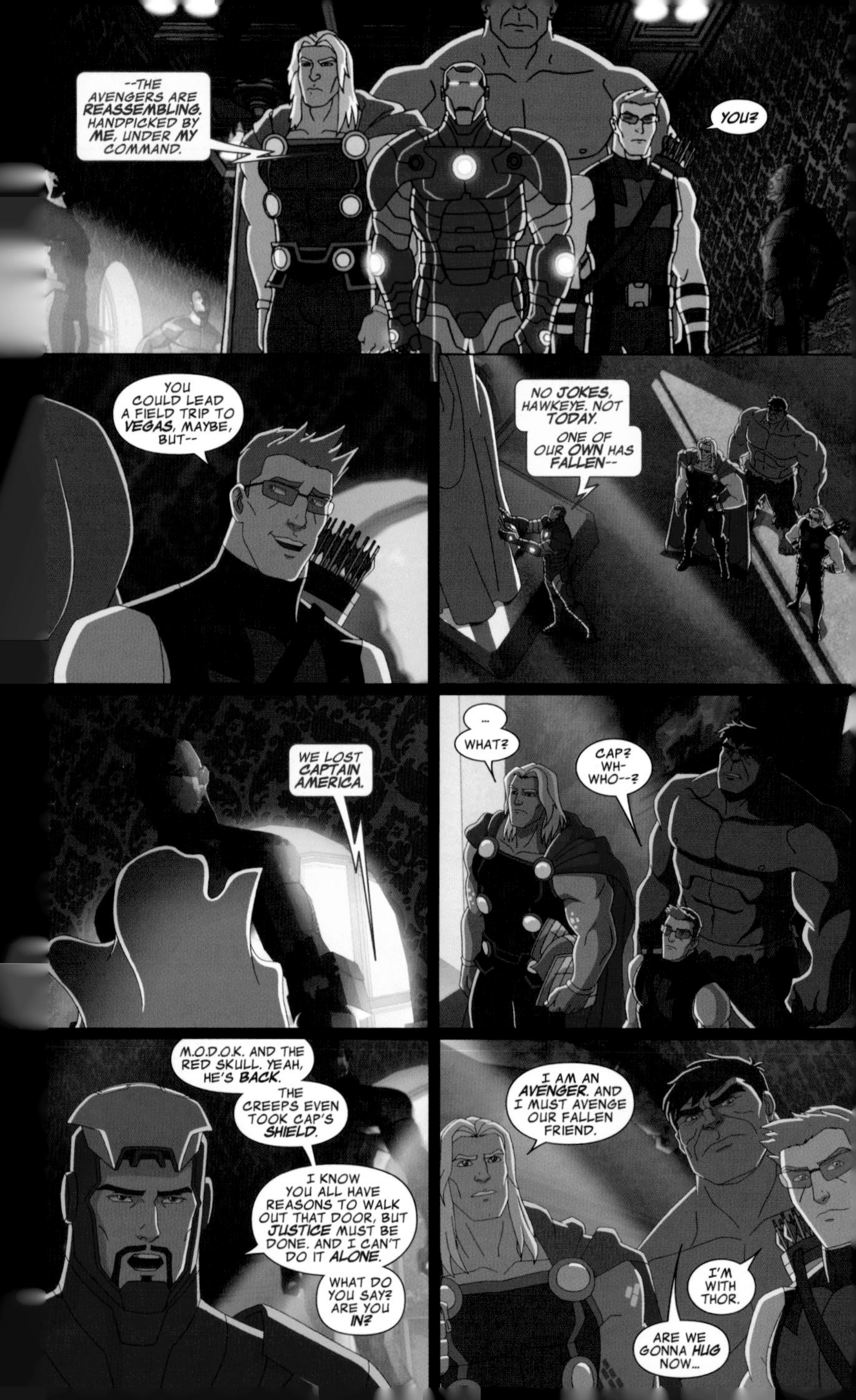
--THE AVENGERS ARE REASSEMBLING. HANDPICKED BY ME, UNDER MY COMMAND.
YOU?
YOU COULD LEAD A FIELD TRIP TO VEGAS, MAYBE, BUT--
NO JOKES, HAWKEYE. NOT TODAY.
ONE OF OUR OWN HAS FALLEN--
WE LOST CAPTAIN AMERICA.
...
WHAT?
CAP? WH-WHO--?
M.O.D.O.K. AND THE RED SKULL. YEAH, HE'S BACK.
THE CREEPS EVEN TOOK CAP'S SHIELD.
I KNOW YOU ALL HAVE REASONS TO WALK OUT THAT DOOR, BUT JUSTICE MUST BE DONE. AND I CAN'T DO IT ALONE.
WHAT DO YOU SAY? ARE YOU IN?
I AM AN AVENGER. AND I MUST AVENGE OUR FALLEN FRIEND.
I'M WITH THOR.
ARE WE GONNA HUG NOW...

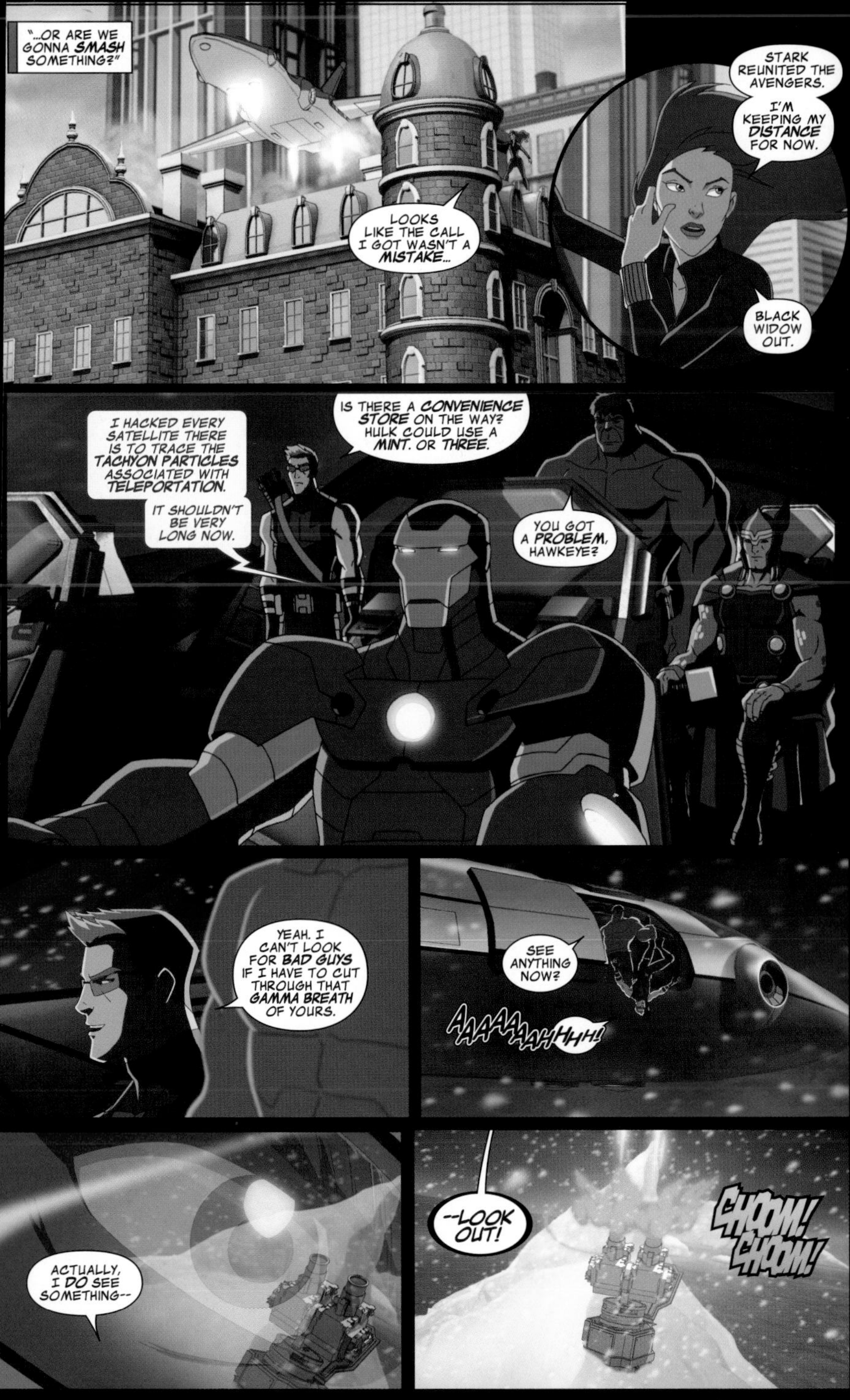
"...OR ARE WE GONNA SMASH SOMETHING?"
LOOKS LIKE THE CALL I GOT WASN'T A MISTAKE...
STARK REUNITED THE AVENGERS.
I'M KEEPING MY DISTANCE FOR NOW.
BLACK WIDOW OUT.
I HACKED EVERY SATELLITE THERE IS TO TRACE THE TACHYON PARTICLES ASSOCIATED WITH TELEPORTATION.
IT SHOULDN'T BE VERY LONG NOW.
IS THERE A CONVENIENCE STORE ON THE WAY? HULK COULD USE A MINT. OR THREE.
YOU GOT A PROBLEM, HAWKEYE?
YEAH. I CAN'T LOOK FOR BAD GUYS IF I HAVE TO CUT THROUGH THAT GAMMA BREATH OF YOURS.
SEE ANYTHING NOW?
AAAAAAHHHH!
ACTUALLY, I DO SEE SOMETHING--
--LOOK OUT!
CHOOM! CHOOM!

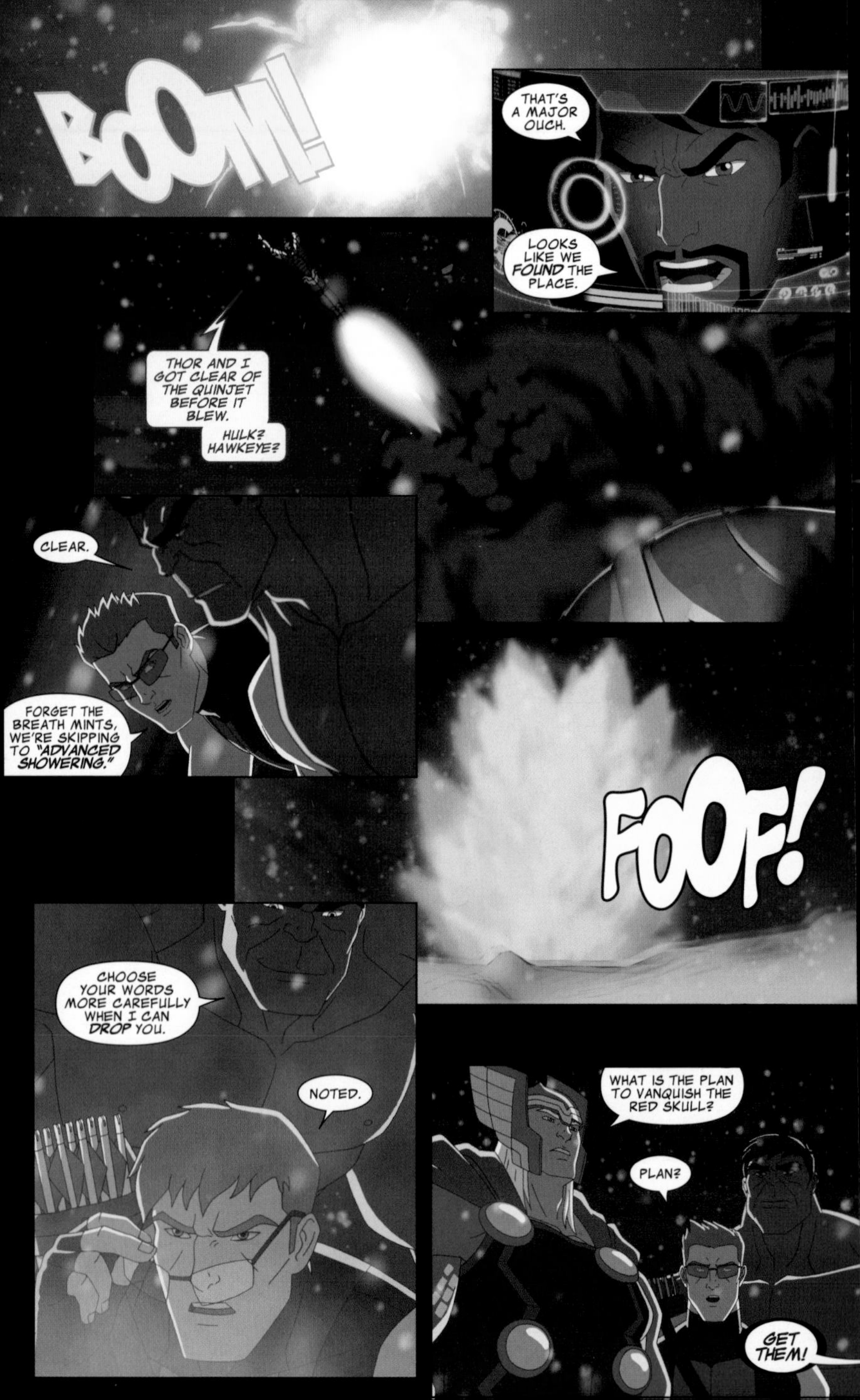
BOOM!
THAT'S A MAJOR OUCH.
LOOKS LIKE WE FOUND THE PLACE.
THOR AND I GOT CLEAR OF THE QUINJET BEFORE IT BLEW.
HULK? HAWKEYE?
CLEAR.
FORGET THE BREATH MINTS, WE'RE SKIPPING TO "ADVANCED SHOWERING."
FOOF!
CHOOSE YOUR WORDS MORE CAREFULLY WHEN I CAN DROP YOU.
NOTED.
WHAT IS THE PLAN TO VANQUISH THE RED SKULL?
PLAN?
GET THEM!

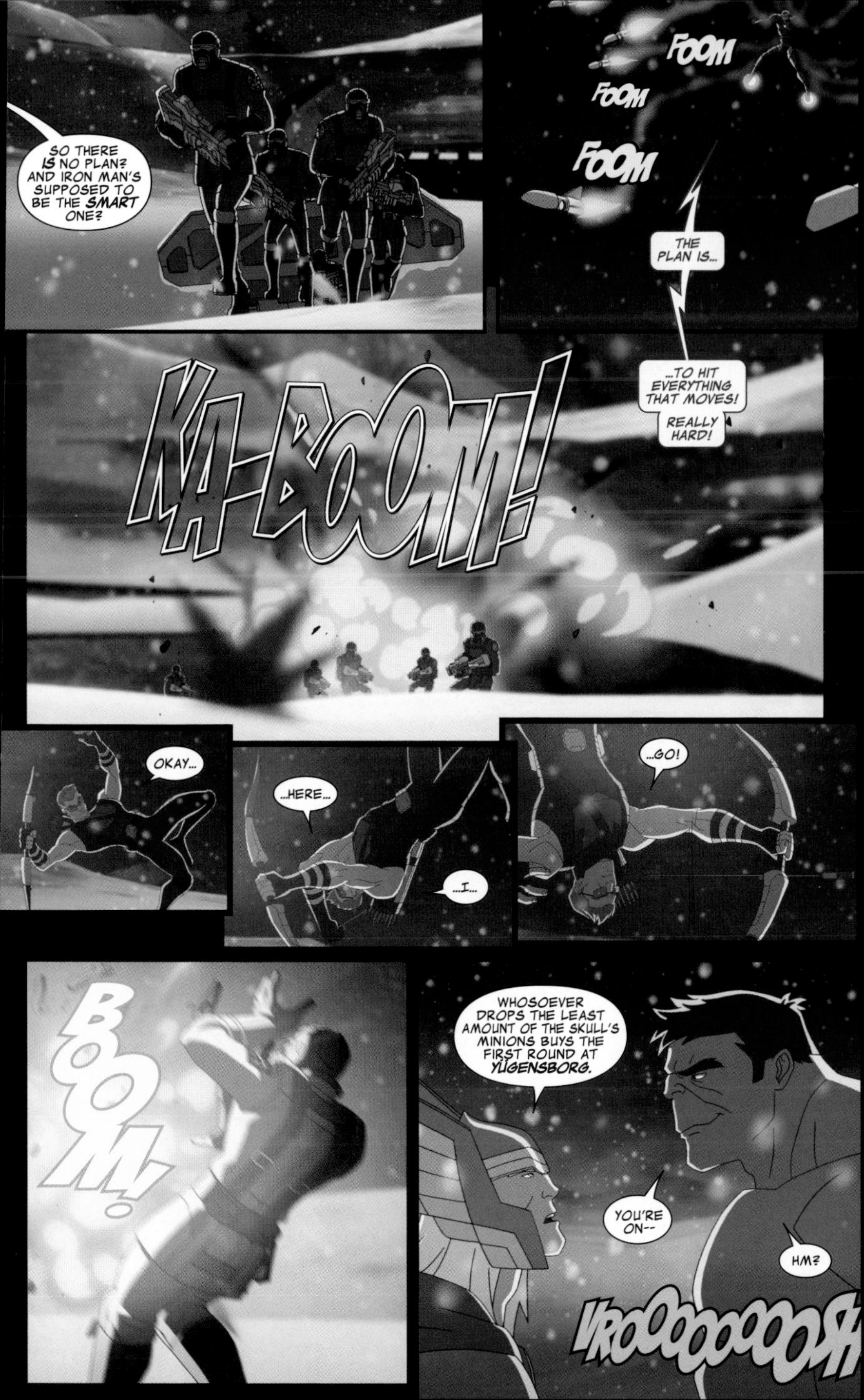
SO THERE IS NO PLAN? AND IRON MAN'S SUPPOSED TO BE THE SMART ONE?
FOOM
FOOM
FOOM
THE PLAN IS...
...TO HIT EVERYTHING THAT MOVES!
REALLY HARD!
KA-BOOM!
OKAY...
...HERE...
...I...
...GO!
BOOM!
WHOSOEVER DROPS THE LEAST AMOUNT OF THE SKULL'S MINIONS BUYS THE FIRST ROUND AT YÜGENSBORG.
YOU'RE ON--
HM?
VROOOOOOOOSH

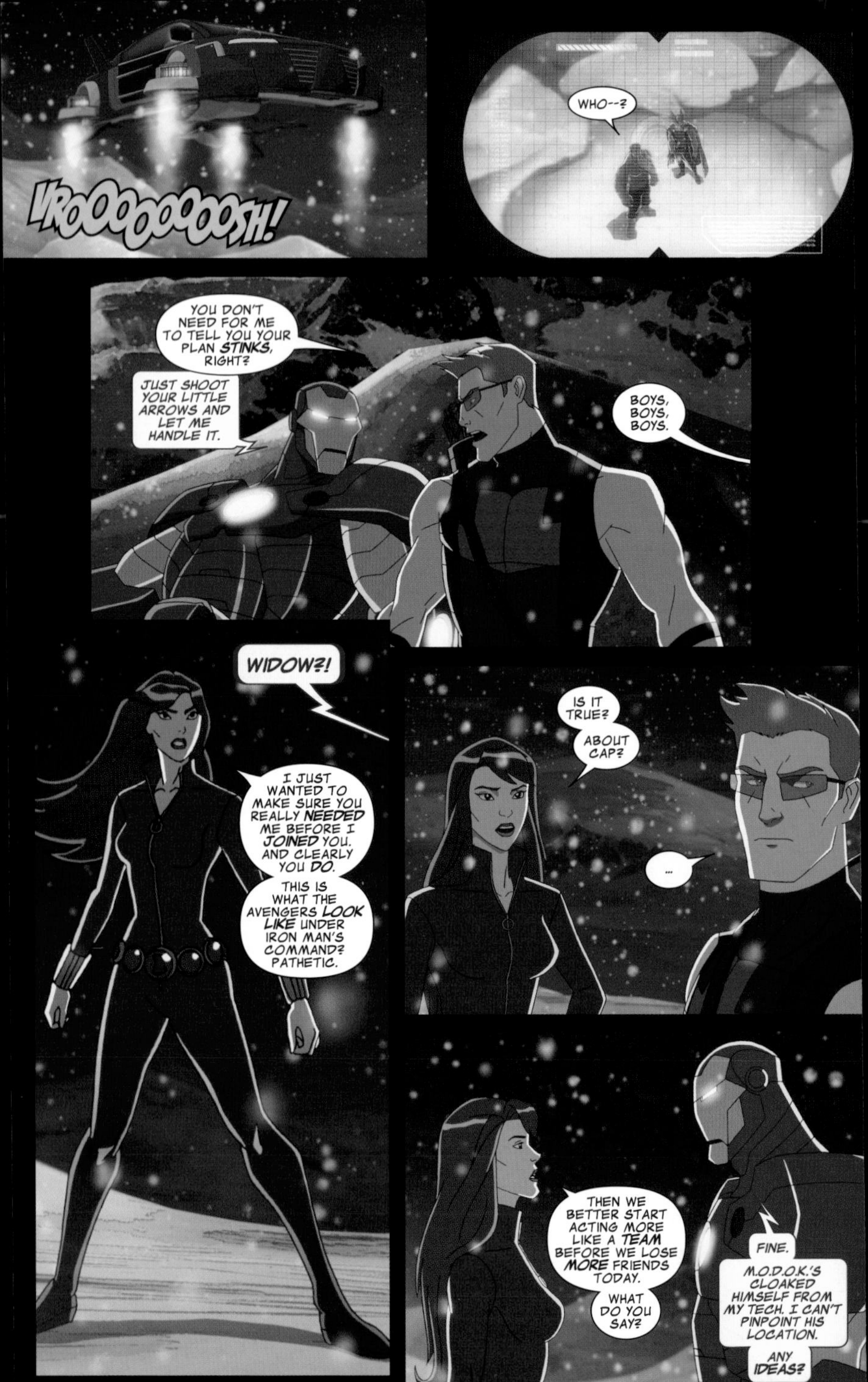
VROOOOOOOOOSH!
WHO--?
YOU DON'T NEED FOR ME TO TELL YOU YOUR PLAN STINKS, RIGHT?
JUST SHOOT YOUR LITTLE ARROWS AND LET ME HANDLE IT.
BOYS, BOYS, BOYS.
WIDOW?!
I JUST WANTED TO MAKE SURE YOU REALLY NEEDED ME BEFORE I JOINED YOU. AND CLEARLY YOU DO.
THIS IS WHAT THE AVENGERS LOOK LIKE UNDER IRON MAN'S COMMAND? PATHETIC.
IS IT TRUE?
ABOUT CAP?
...
THEN WE BETTER START ACTING MORE LIKE A TEAM BEFORE WE LOSE MORE FRIENDS TODAY.
WHAT DO YOU SAY?
FINE.
M.O.D.O.K.'S CLOAKED HIMSELF FROM MY TECH. I CAN'T PINPOINT HIS LOCATION.
ANY IDEAS?

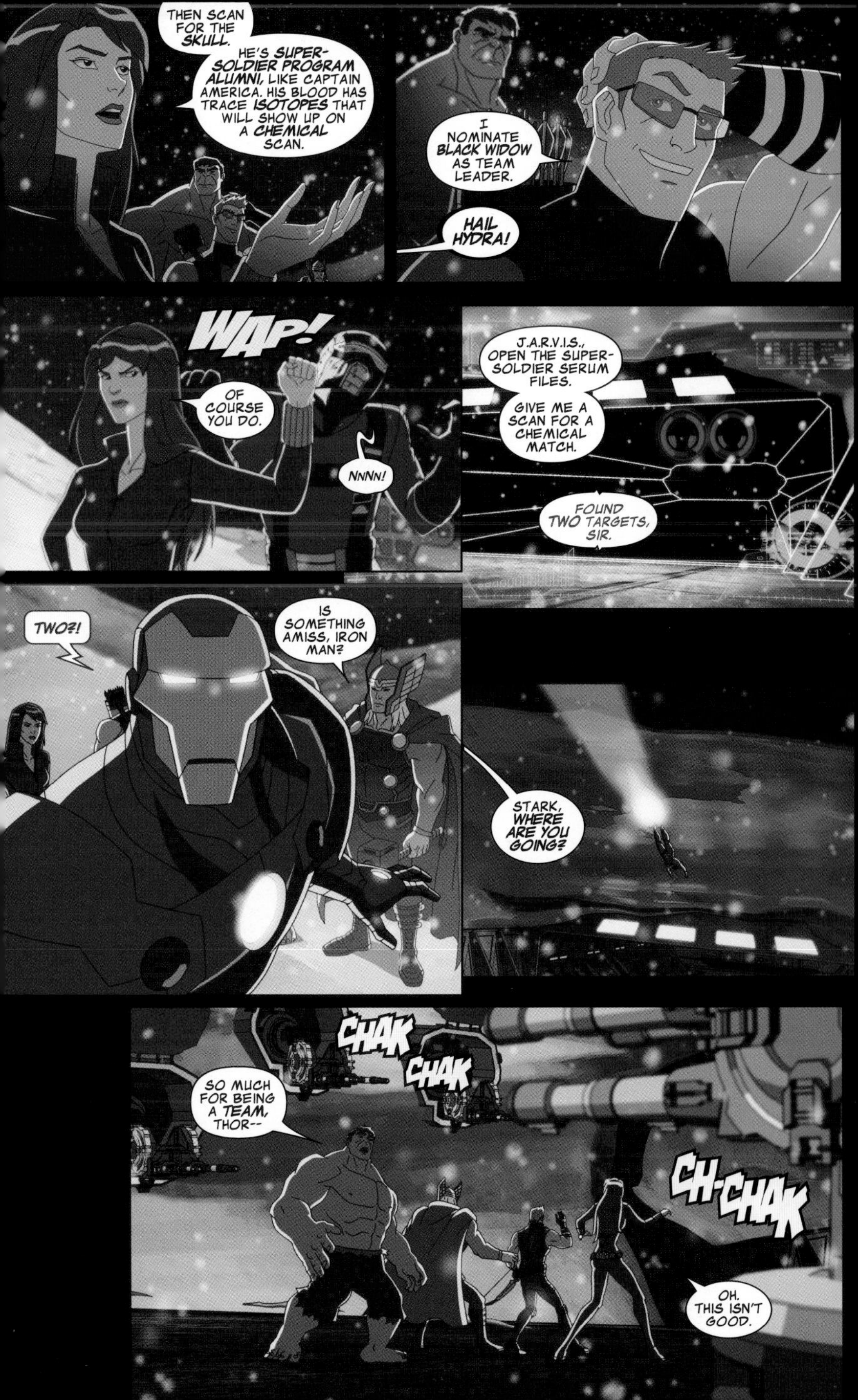
THEN SCAN FOR THE SKULL.
HE'S SUPER-SOLDIER PROGRAM ALUMNI, LIKE CAPTAIN AMERICA. HIS BLOOD HAS TRACE ISOTOPES THAT WILL SHOW UP ON A CHEMICAL SCAN.
I NOMINATE BLACK WIDOW AS TEAM LEADER.
HAIL HYDRA!
WAP!
OF COURSE YOU DO.
NNNN!
J.A.R.V.I.S., OPEN THE SUPER-SOLDIER SERUM FILES.
GIVE ME A SCAN FOR A CHEMICAL MATCH.
FOUND TWO TARGETS, SIR.
TWO?!
IS SOMETHING AMISS, IRON MAN?
STARK, WHERE ARE YOU GOING?
CHAK
CHAK
SO MUCH FOR BEING A TEAM, THOR--
CH-CHAK
OH. THIS ISN'T GOOD.

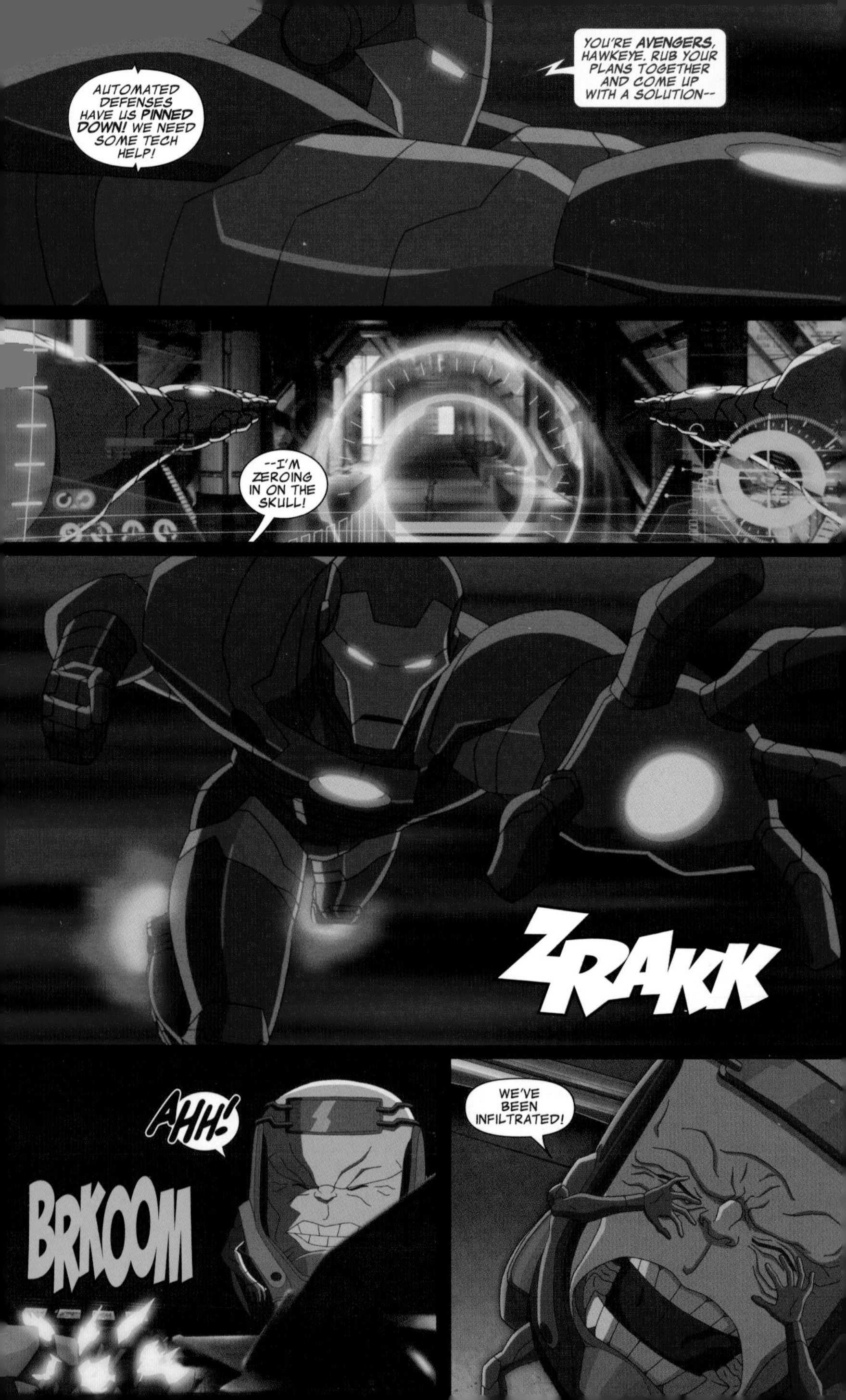
AUTOMATED DEFENSES HAVE US PINNED DOWN! WE NEED SOME TECH HELP!
YOU'RE AVENGERS, HAWKEYE. RUB YOUR PLANS TOGETHER AND COME UP WITH A SOLUTION--
--I'M ZEROING IN ON THE SKULL!
ZRAKK
AHH!
BRKOOM
WE'VE BEEN INFILTRATED!

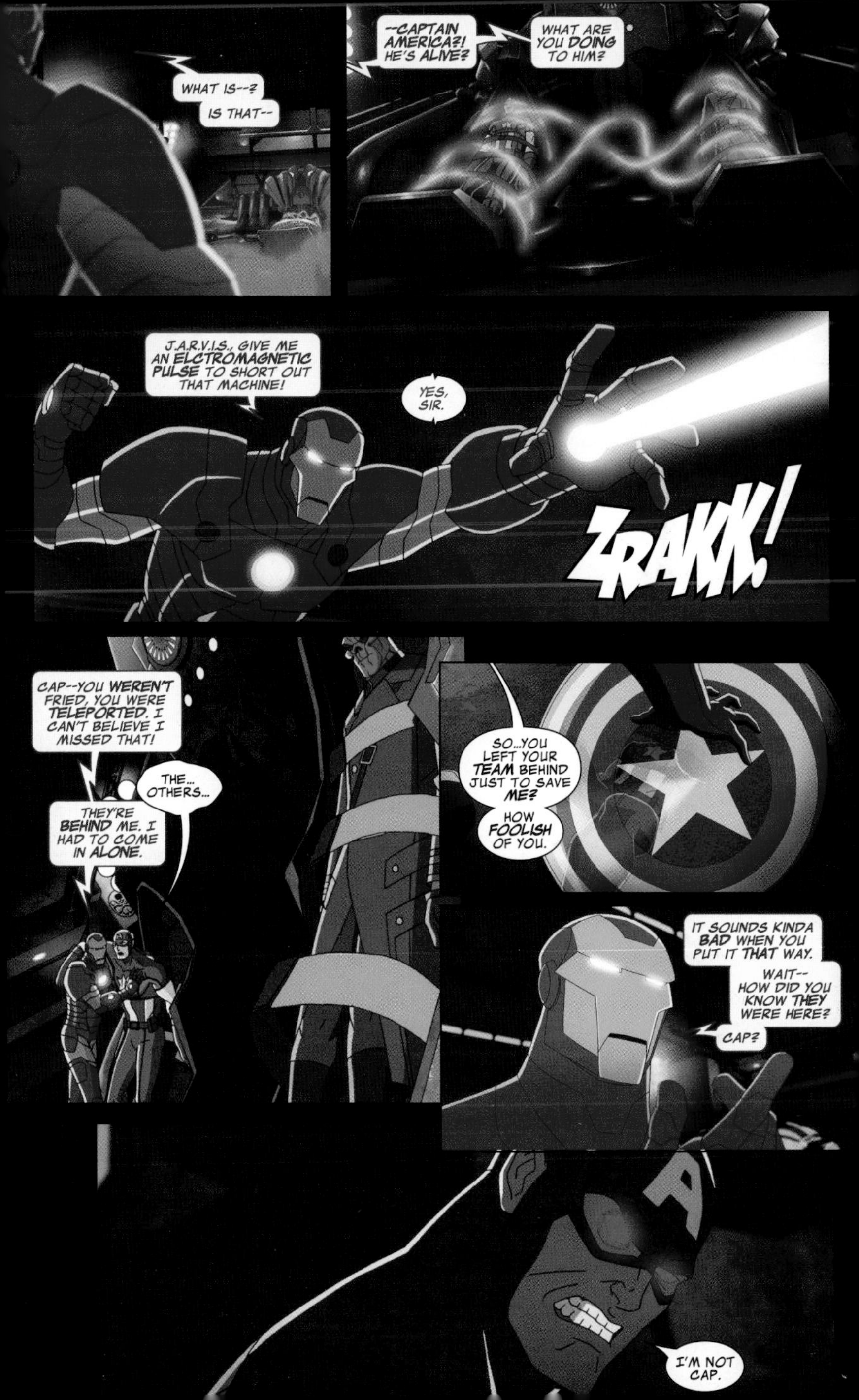
WHAT IS--?
IS THAT--
--CAPTAIN AMERICA?! HE'S ALIVE?
WHAT ARE YOU DOING TO HIM?
J.A.R.V.I.S., GIVE ME AN ELCTROMAGNETIC PULSE TO SHORT OUT THAT MACHINE!
YES, SIR.
ZRAKK!
CAP--YOU WEREN'T FRIED, YOU WERE TELEPORTED. I CAN'T BELIEVE I MISSED THAT!
THE... OTHERS...
THEY'RE BEHIND ME. I HAD TO COME IN ALONE.
SO...YOU LEFT YOUR TEAM BEHIND JUST TO SAVE ME?
HOW FOOLISH OF YOU.
IT SOUNDS KINDA BAD WHEN YOU PUT IT THAT WAY.
WAIT-- HOW DID YOU KNOW THEY WERE HERE?
CAP?
I'M NOT CAP.

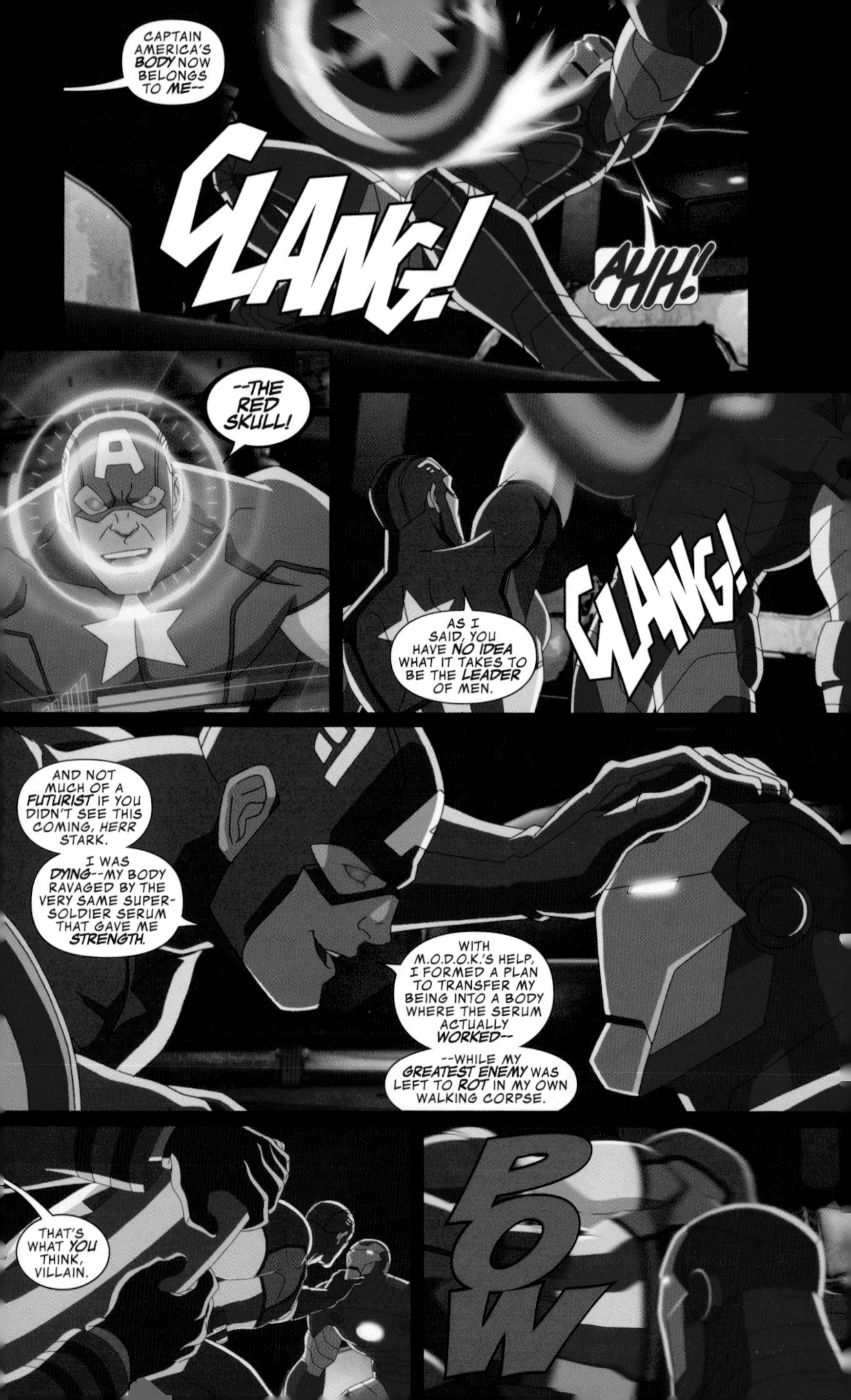
CAPTAIN AMERICA'S BODY NOW BELONGS TO ME--
CLANG!
AHH!
--THE RED SKULL!
AS I SAID, YOU HAVE NO IDEA WHAT IT TAKES TO BE THE LEADER OF MEN.
CLANG!
AND NOT MUCH OF A FUTURIST IF YOU DIDN'T SEE THIS COMING, HERR STARK.
I WAS DYING--MY BODY RAVAGED BY THE VERY SAME SUPER-SOLDIER SERUM THAT GAVE ME STRENGTH.
WITH M.O.D.O.K.'S HELP, I FORMED A PLAN TO TRANSFER MY BEING INTO A BODY WHERE THE SERUM ACTUALLY WORKED--
--WHILE MY GREATEST ENEMY WAS LEFT TO ROT IN MY OWN WALKING CORPSE.
THAT'S WHAT YOU THINK, VILLAIN.
POW

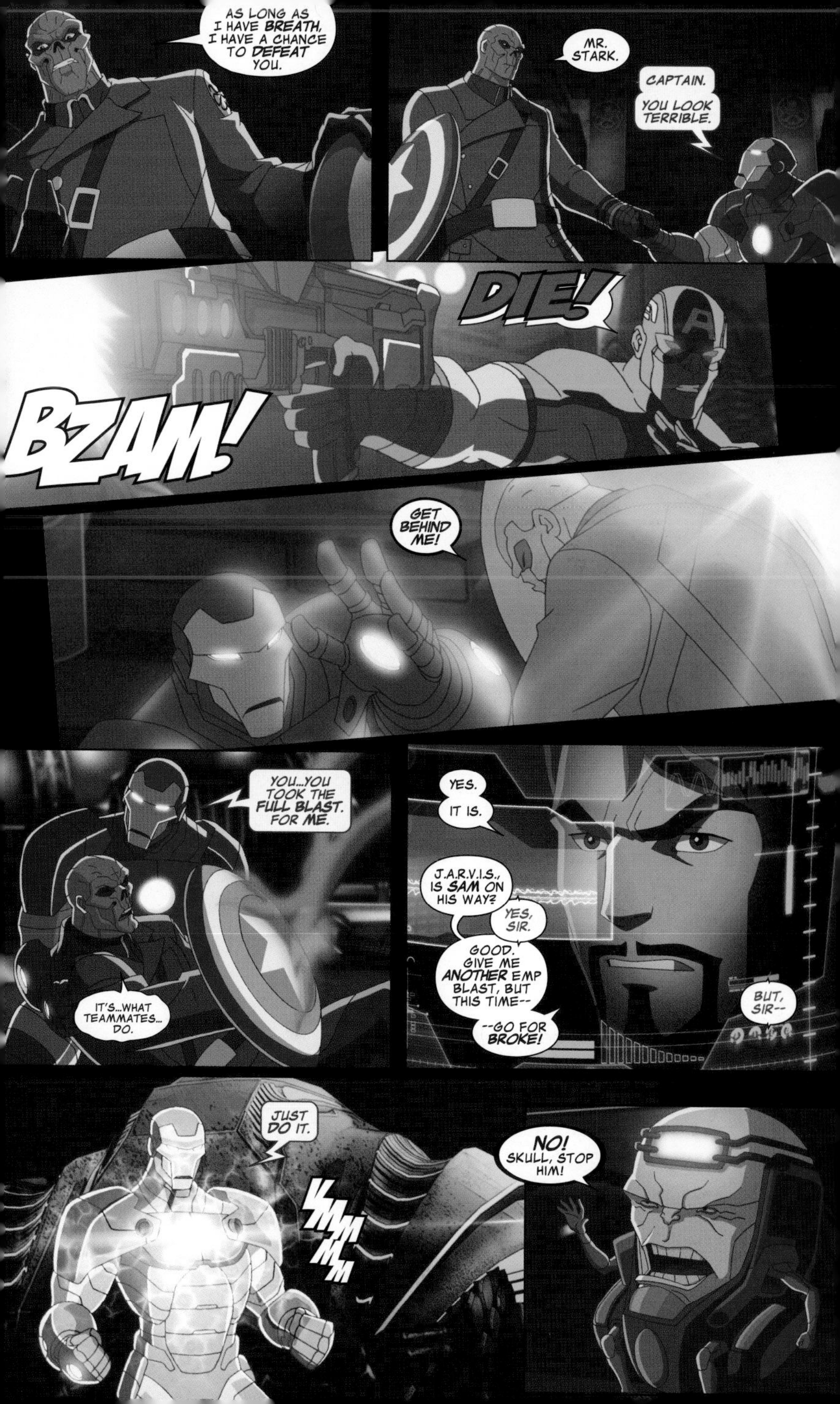
AS LONG AS I HAVE BREATH, I HAVE A CHANCE TO DEFEAT YOU.
MR. STARK.
CAPTAIN.
YOU LOOK TERRIBLE.
DIE!
BZAM!
GET BEHIND ME!
YOU...YOU TOOK THE FULL BLAST. FOR ME.
IT'S...WHAT TEAMMATES... DO.
YES.
IT IS.
J.A.R.V.I.S., IS SAM ON HIS WAY?
YES, SIR.
GOOD. GIVE ME ANOTHER EMP BLAST, BUT THIS TIME--
--GO FOR BROKE!
BUT, SIR--
JUST DO IT.
VMMMMM
NO! SKULL, STOP HIM!

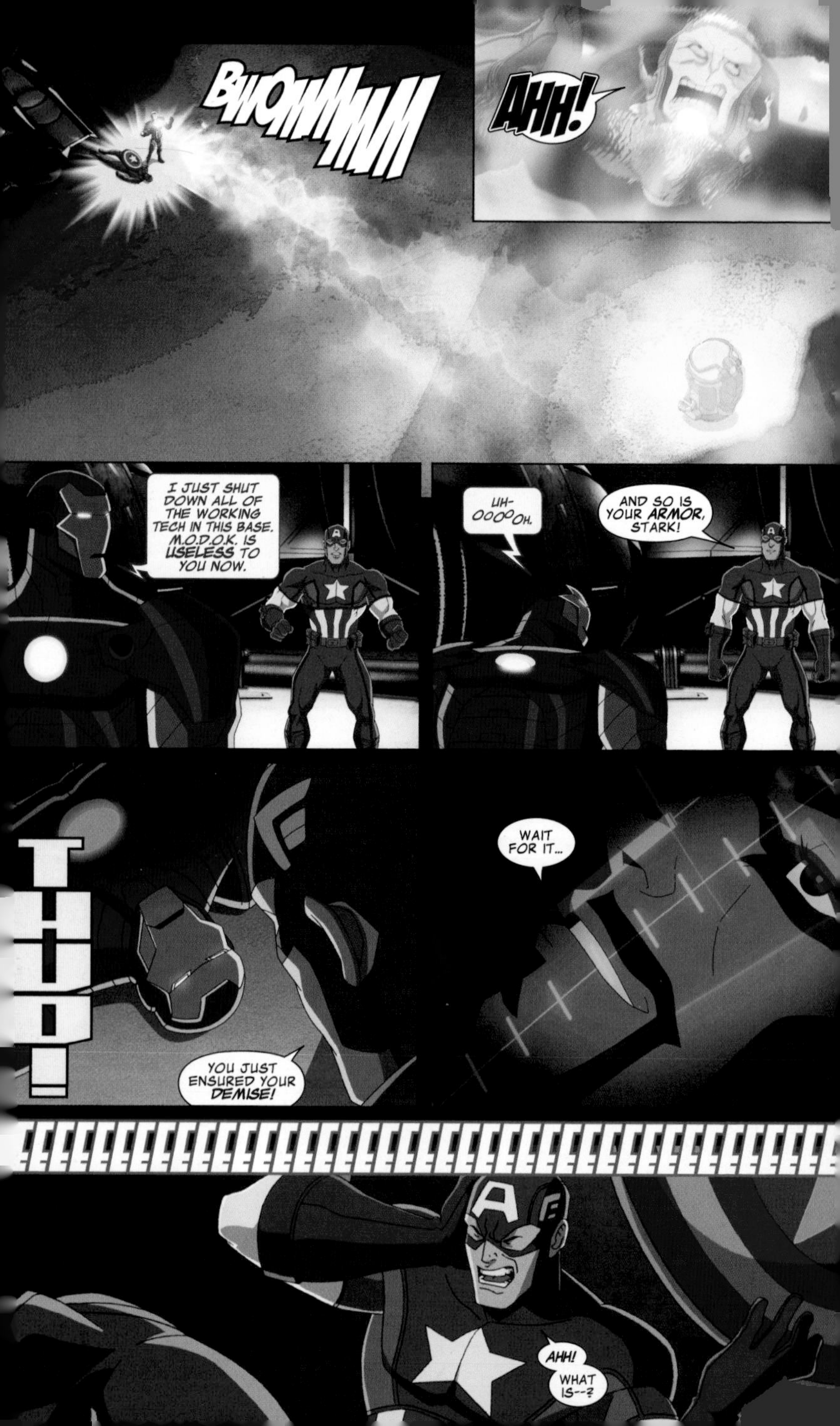
BWOMMMM
AHH!
I JUST SHUT DOWN ALL OF THE WORKING TECH IN THIS BASE. M.O.D.O.K. IS USELESS TO YOU NOW.
UH-OOOOOH.
AND SO IS YOUR ARMOR, STARK!
THUD!
WAIT FOR IT...
YOU JUST ENSURED YOUR DEMISE!
EEEEEEEEEEEEEEEEEEEEEEEEEEEEEEEEEEEEEEEEEE
AHH! WHAT IS--?

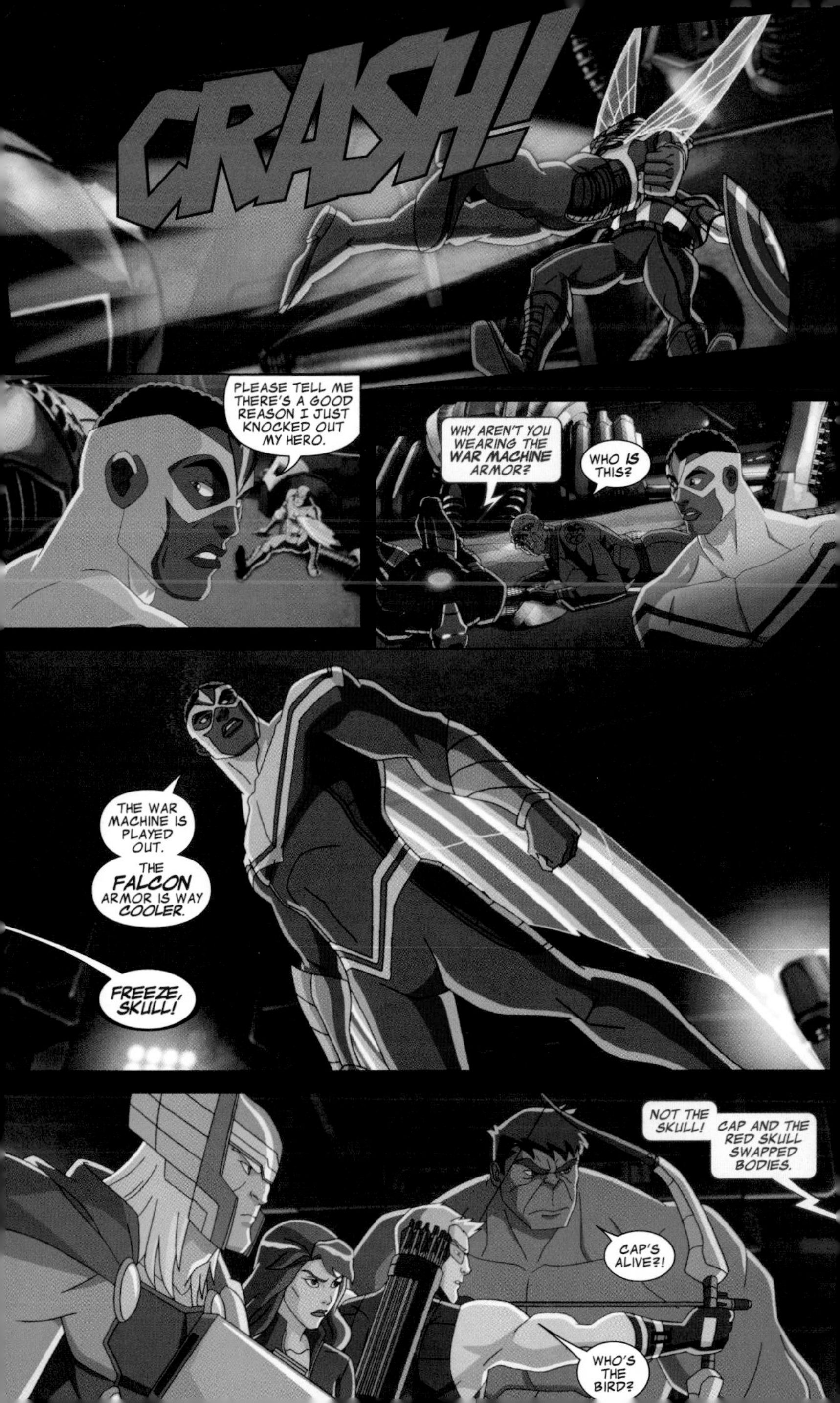
CRASH!
PLEASE TELL ME THERE'S A GOOD REASON I JUST KNOCKED OUT MY HERO.
WHY AREN'T YOU WEARING THE WAR MACHINE ARMOR?
WHO IS THIS?
THE WAR MACHINE IS PLAYED OUT.
THE FALCON ARMOR IS WAY COOLER.
FREEZE, SKULL!
NOT THE SKULL!
CAP AND THE RED SKULL SWAPPED BODIES.
CAP'S ALIVE?!
WHO'S THE BIRD?

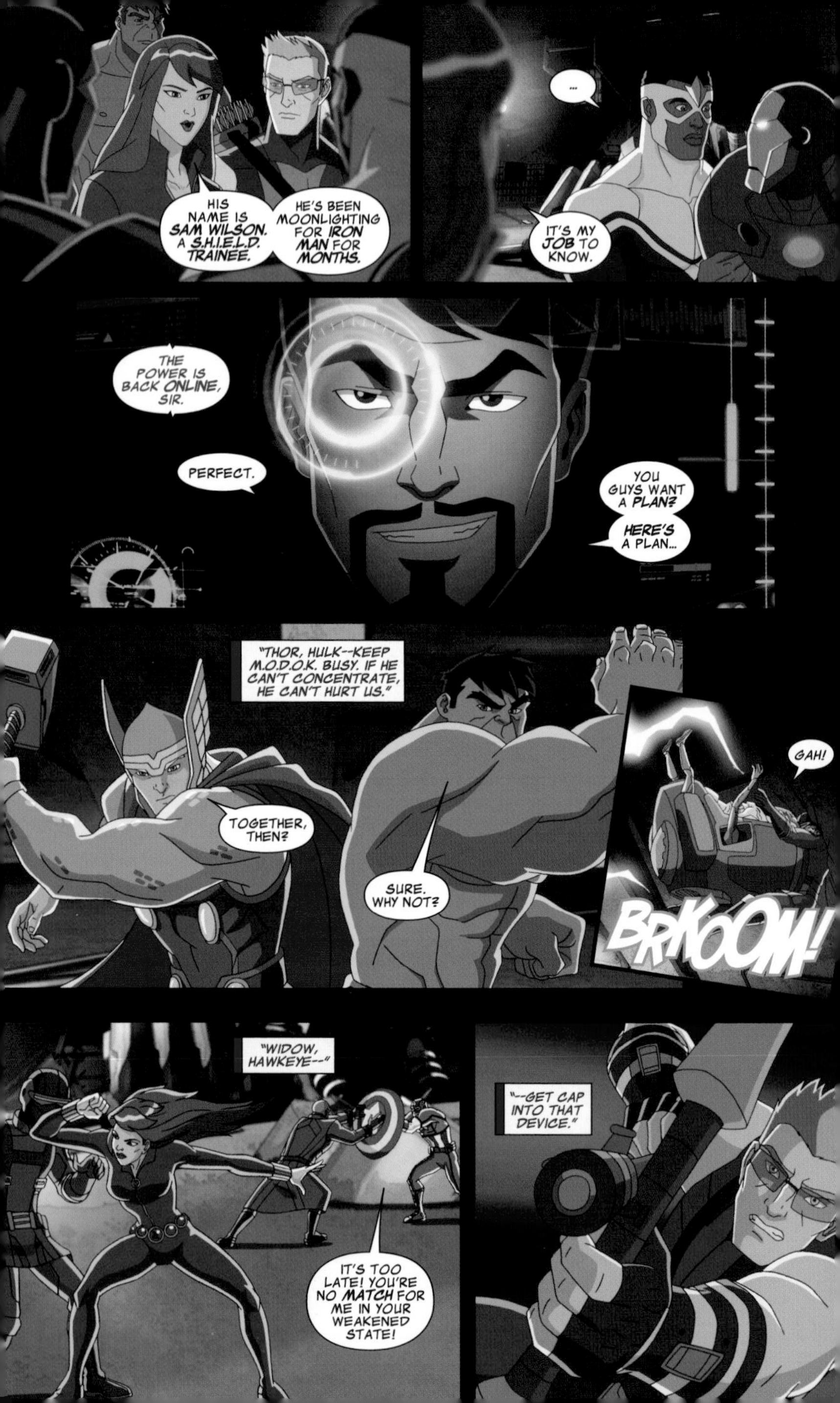
HIS NAME IS SAM WILSON. A S.H.I.E.L.D. TRAINEE.
HE'S BEEN MOONLIGHTING FOR IRON MAN FOR MONTHS.
...
IT'S MY JOB TO KNOW.
THE POWER IS BACK ONLINE, SIR.
PERFECT.
YOU GUYS WANT A PLAN?
HERE'S A PLAN...
"THOR, HULK--KEEP M.O.D.O.K. BUSY. IF HE CAN'T CONCENTRATE, HE CAN'T HURT US."
TOGETHER, THEN?
SURE. WHY NOT?
GAH!
BRKOOM!
"WIDOW, HAWKEYE--"
IT'S TOO LATE! YOU'RE NO MATCH FOR ME IN YOUR WEAKENED STATE!
"--GET CAP INTO THAT DEVICE."

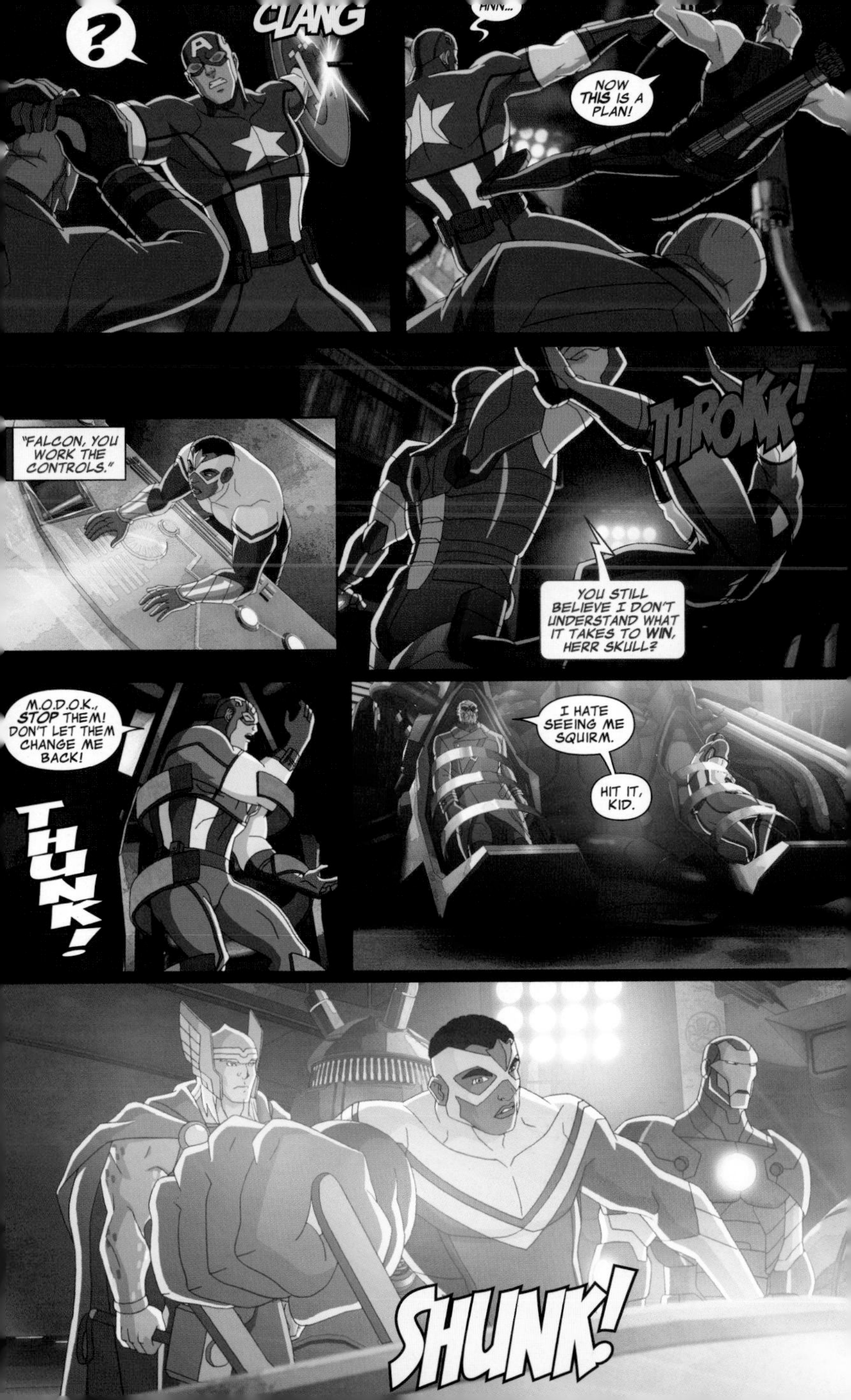
?
CLANG
HNN...
NOW THIS IS A PLAN!
"FALCON, YOU WORK THE CONTROLS."
THROKK!
YOU STILL BELIEVE I DON'T UNDERSTAND WHAT IT TAKES TO WIN, HERR SKULL?
M.O.D.O.K., STOP THEM! DON'T LET THEM CHANGE ME BACK!
THUNK!
I HATE SEEING ME SQUIRM.
HIT IT, KID.
SHUNK!

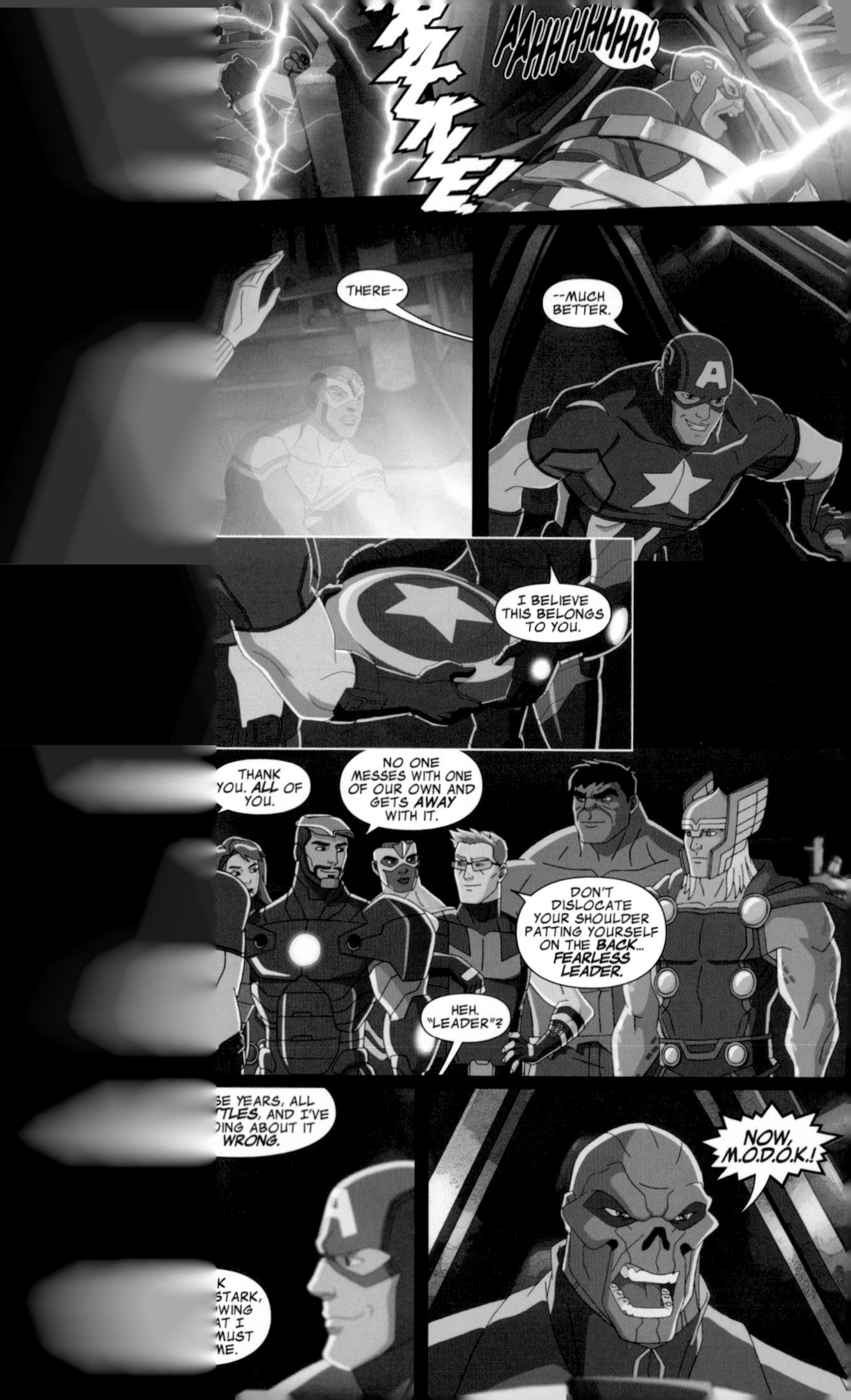
THERE--
--MUCH BETTER.
I BELIEVE THIS BELONGS TO YOU.
THANK YOU. ALL OF YOU.
NO ONE MESSES WITH ONE OF OUR OWN AND GETS AWAY WITH IT.
DON'T DISLOCATE YOUR SHOULDER PATTING YOURSELF ON THE BACK... FEARLESS LEADER.
HEH. "LEADER"?
NOW, M.O.D.O.K.!

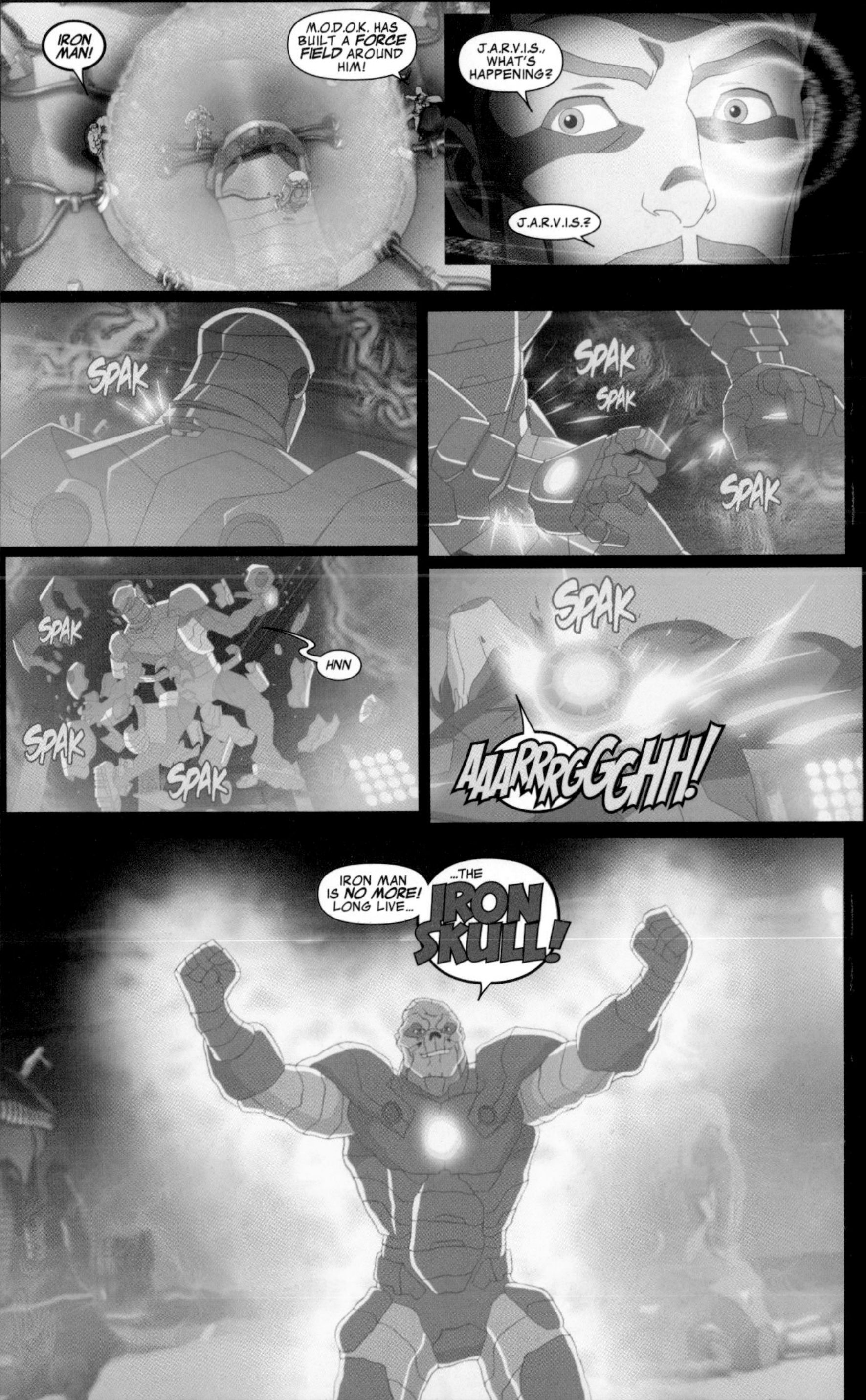

IRON MAN!
M.O.D.O.K. HAS BUILT A FORCE FIELD AROUND HIM!
J.A.R.V.I.S., WHAT'S HAPPENING?
J.A.R.V.I.S.?
SPAK
SPAK
SPAK
SPAK
SPAK
HNN
SPAK
SPAK
SPAK
AAARRRGGGHH!
IRON MAN IS NO MORE! LONG LIVE...
...THE IRON SKULL!

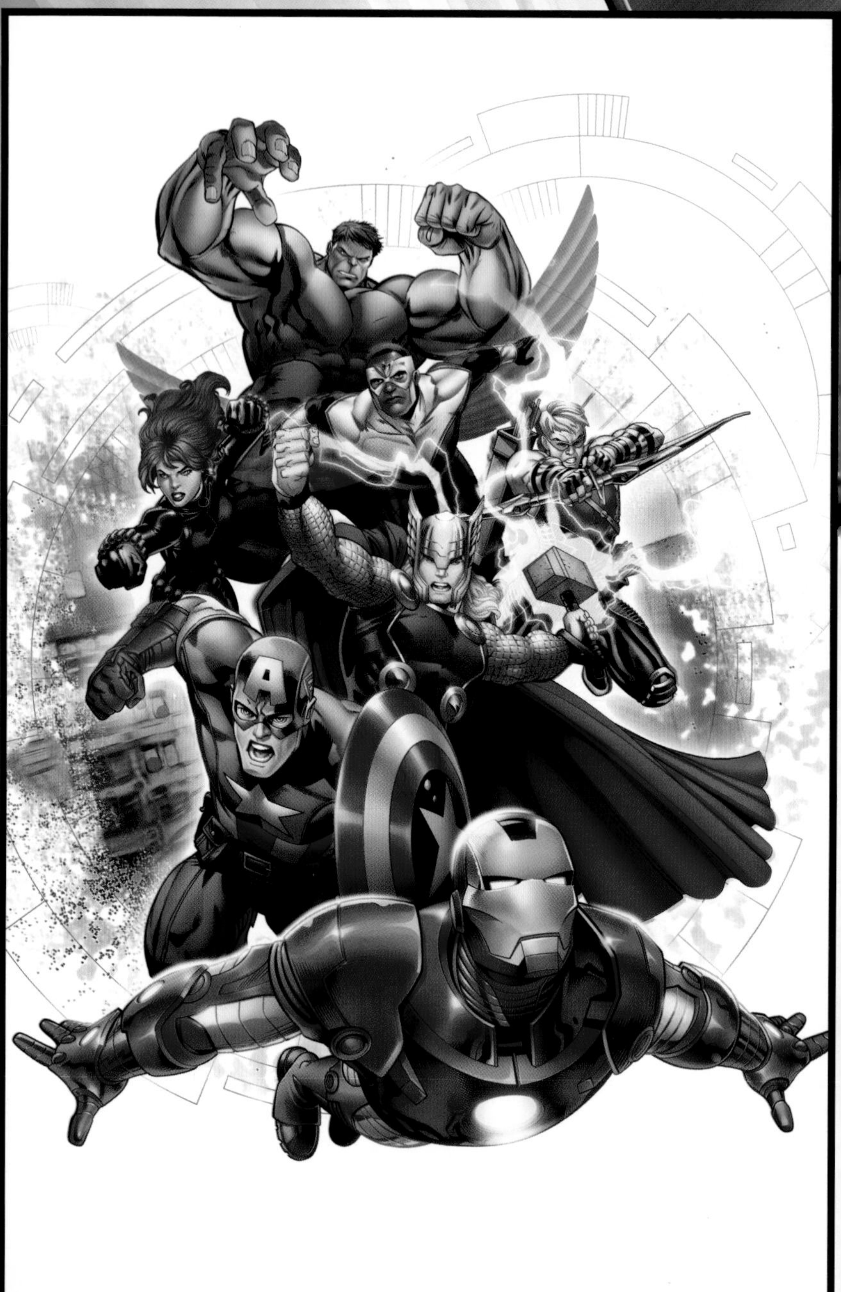

#2 BASED ON "THE AVENGERS PROTOCOL"

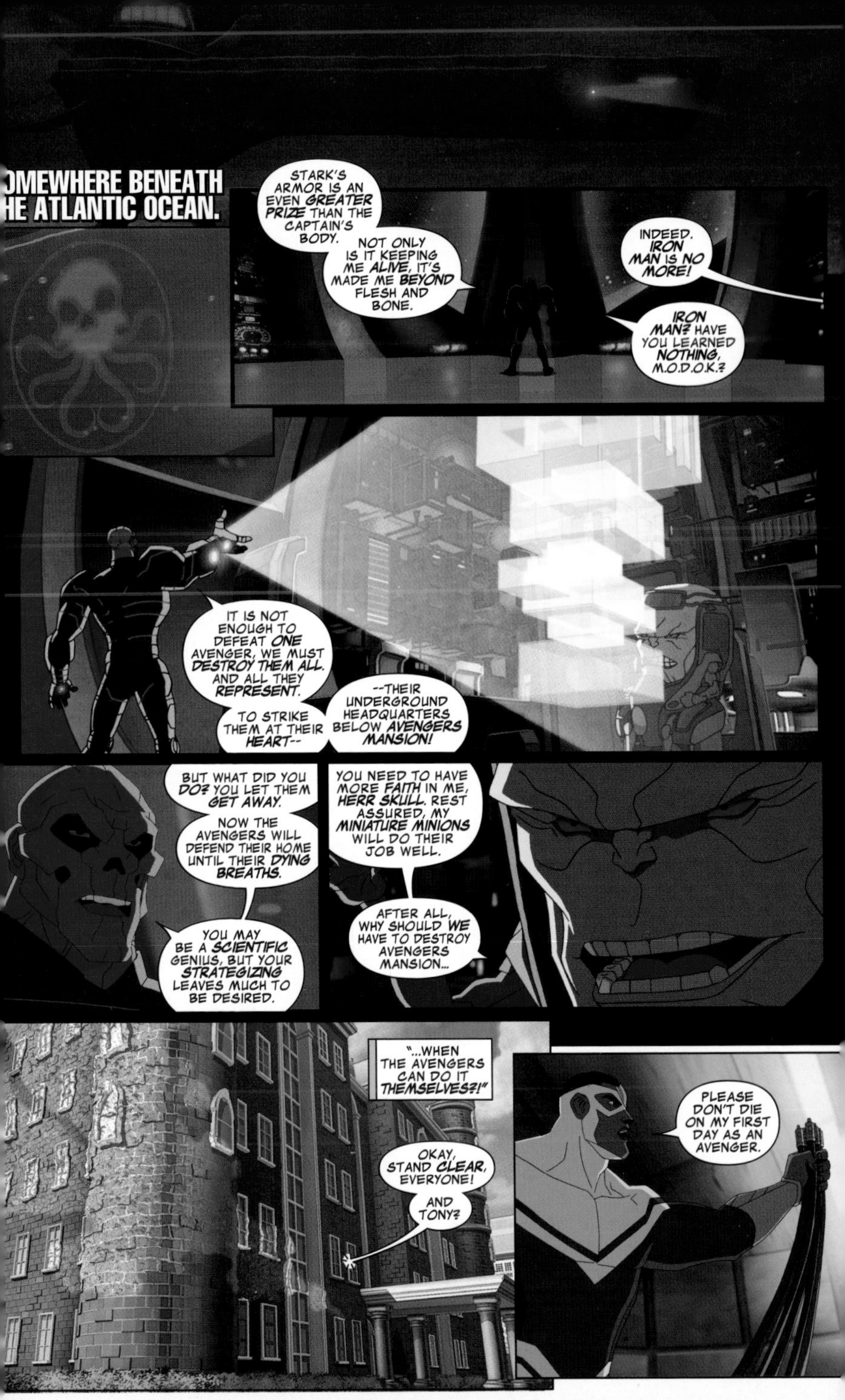
OMEWHERE BENEATH HE ATLANTIC OCEAN.
STARK'S ARMOR IS AN EVEN GREATER PRIZE THAN THE CAPTAIN'S BODY.
NOT ONLY IS IT KEEPING ME ALIVE, IT'S MADE ME BEYOND FLESH AND BONE.
INDEED. IRON MAN IS NO MORE!
IRON MAN? HAVE YOU LEARNED NOTHING, M.O.D.O.K.?
IT IS NOT ENOUGH TO DEFEAT ONE AVENGER, WE MUST DESTROY THEM ALL. AND ALL THEY REPRESENT.
TO STRIKE THEM AT THEIR HEART--
--THEIR UNDERGROUND HEADQUARTERS BELOW AVENGERS MANSION!
BUT WHAT DID YOU DO? YOU LET THEM GET AWAY.
NOW THE AVENGERS WILL DEFEND THEIR HOME UNTIL THEIR DYING BREATHS.
YOU MAY BE A SCIENTIFIC GENIUS, BUT YOUR STRATEGIZING LEAVES MUCH TO BE DESIRED.
YOU NEED TO HAVE MORE FAITH IN ME, HERR SKULL. REST ASSURED, MY MINIATURE MINIONS WILL DO THEIR JOB WELL.
AFTER ALL, WHY SHOULD WE HAVE TO DESTROY AVENGERS MANSION...
"...WHEN THE AVENGERS CAN DO IT THEMSELVES?!"
OKAY, STAND CLEAR, EVERYONE!
AND TONY?
PLEASE DON'T DIE ON MY FIRST DAY AS AN AVENGER.

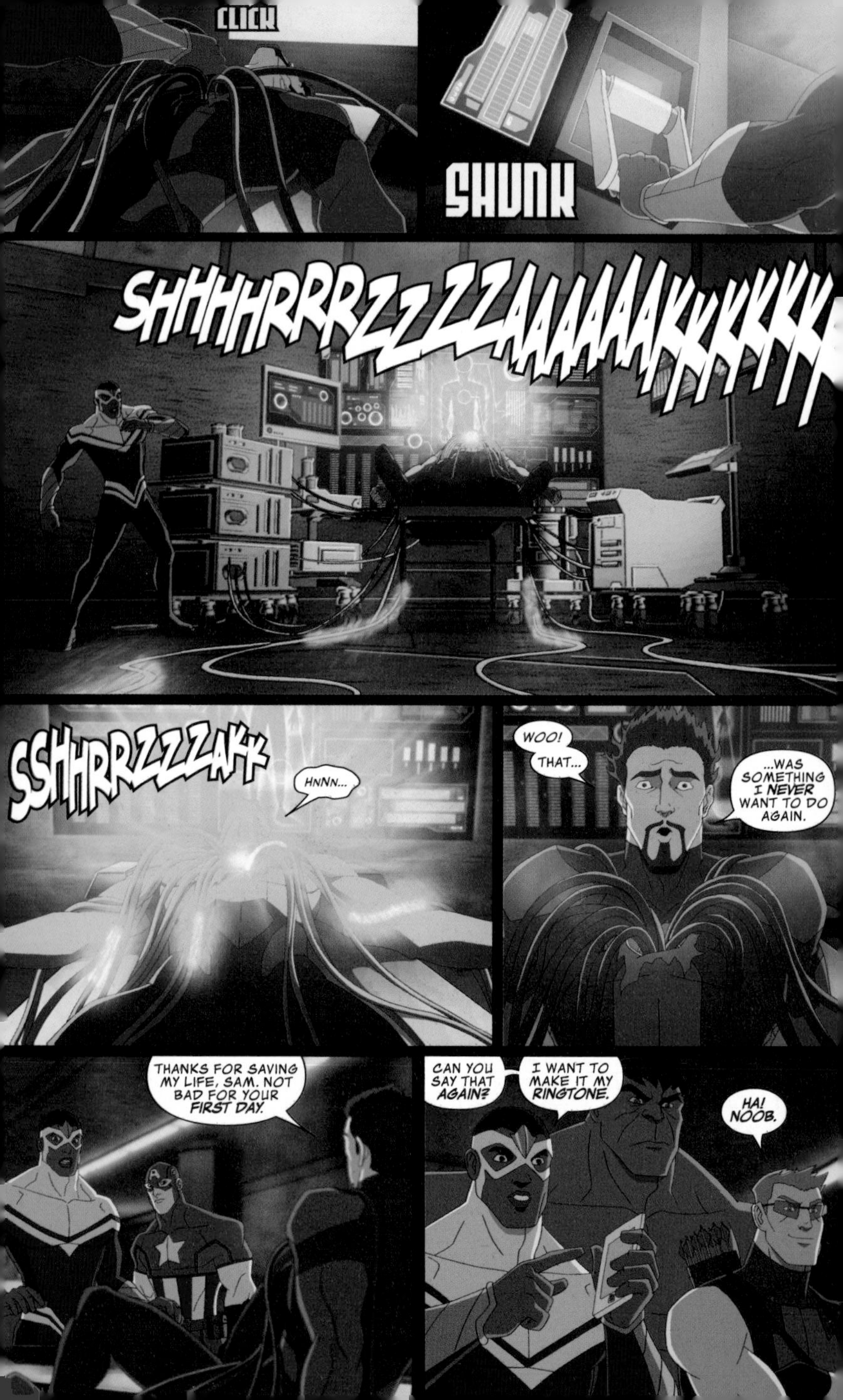

CLICK
SHUNK
SHHHHRRRZZZZAAAAAAKKKKKK
SSHHRRZZZAKK
HNNN...
WOO! THAT...
...WAS SOMETHING I NEVER WANT TO DO AGAIN.
THANKS FOR SAVING MY LIFE, SAM. NOT BAD FOR YOUR FIRST DAY.
CAN YOU SAY THAT AGAIN?
I WANT TO MAKE IT MY RINGTONE.
HA! NOOB.

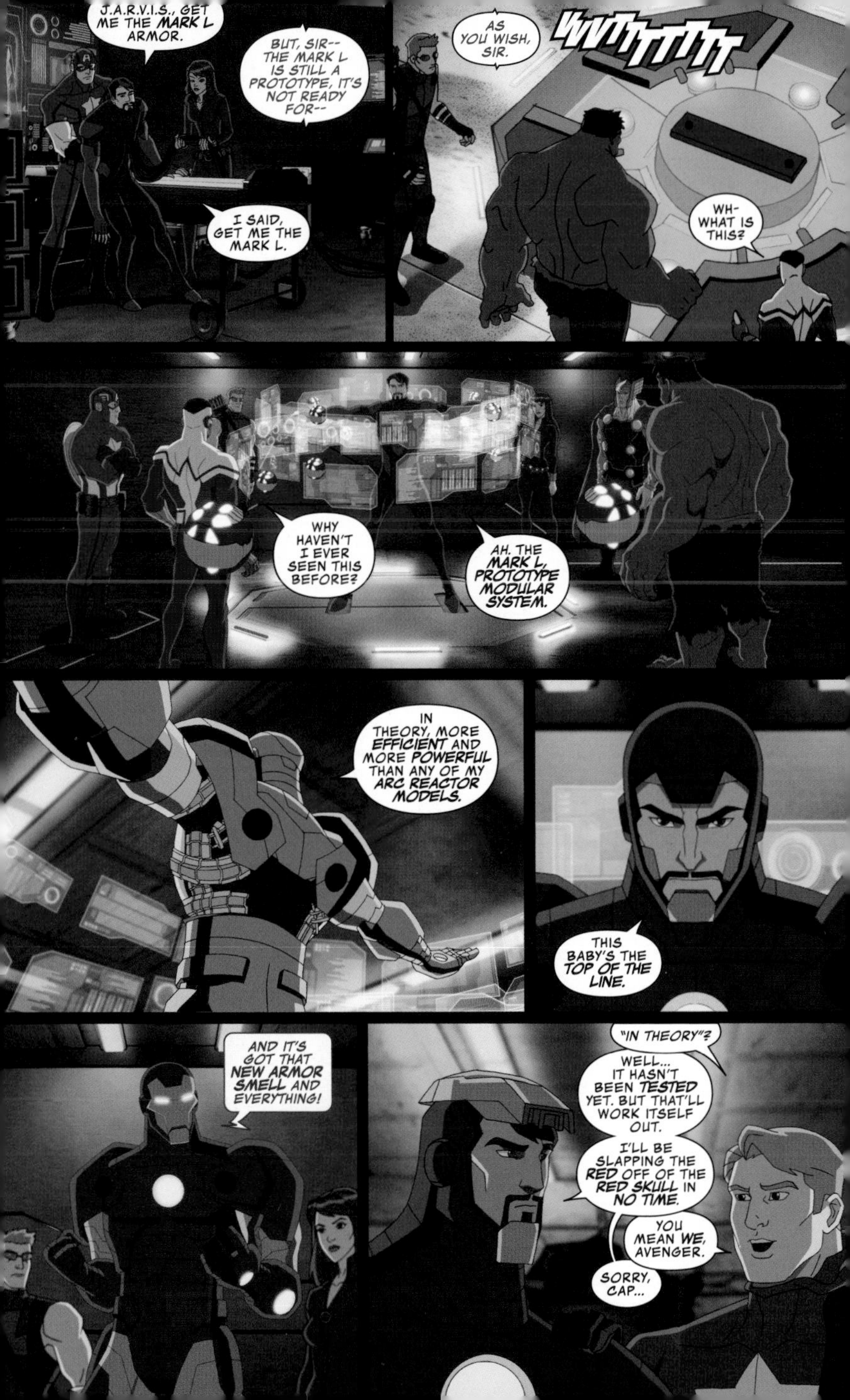
J.A.R.V.I.S., GET ME THE MARK L ARMOR.
BUT, SIR-- THE MARK L IS STILL A PROTOTYPE, IT'S NOT READY FOR--
I SAID, GET ME THE MARK L.
AS YOU WISH, SIR.
VVVTTTTTT
WH-WHAT IS THIS?
WHY HAVEN'T I EVER SEEN THIS BEFORE?
AH. THE MARK L, PROTOTYPE MODULAR SYSTEM.
IN THEORY, MORE EFFICIENT AND MORE POWERFUL THAN ANY OF MY ARC REACTOR MODELS.
THIS BABY'S THE TOP OF THE LINE.
AND IT'S GOT THAT NEW ARMOR SMELL AND EVERYTHING!
"IN THEORY"?
WELL... IT HASN'T BEEN TESTED YET. BUT THAT'LL WORK ITSELF OUT.
I'LL BE SLAPPING THE RED OFF OF THE RED SKULL IN NO TIME.
YOU MEAN WE, AVENGER.
SORRY, CAP...

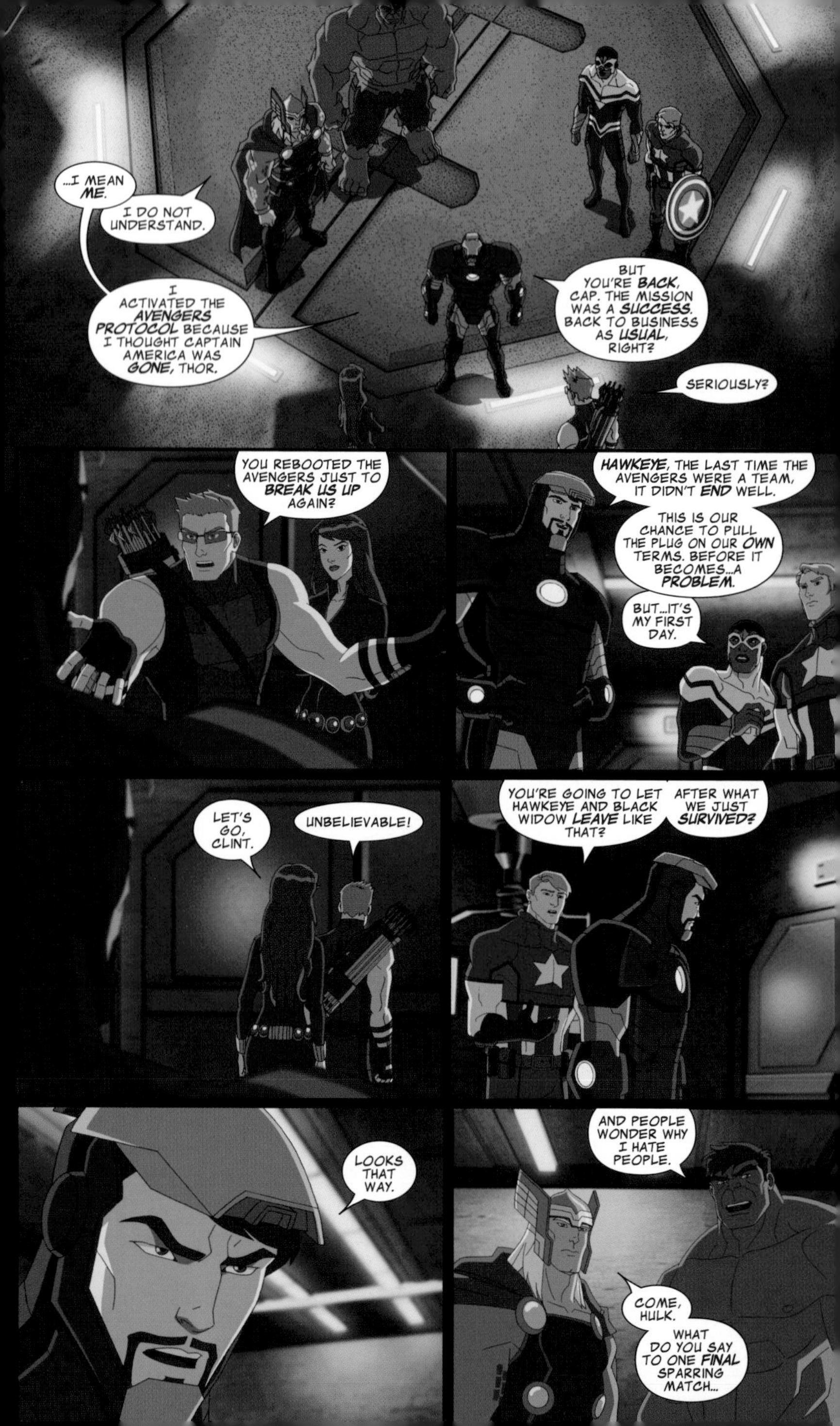
...I MEAN ME.
I DO NOT UNDERSTAND.
I ACTIVATED THE AVENGERS PROTOCOL BECAUSE I THOUGHT CAPTAIN AMERICA WAS GONE, THOR.
BUT YOU'RE BACK, CAP. THE MISSION WAS A SUCCESS. BACK TO BUSINESS AS USUAL, RIGHT?
SERIOUSLY?
YOU REBOOTED THE AVENGERS JUST TO BREAK US UP AGAIN?
HAWKEYE, THE LAST TIME THE AVENGERS WERE A TEAM, IT DIDN'T END WELL.
THIS IS OUR CHANCE TO PULL THE PLUG ON OUR OWN TERMS. BEFORE IT BECOMES...A PROBLEM.
BUT...IT'S MY FIRST DAY.
LET'S GO, CLINT.
UNBELIEVABLE!
YOU'RE GOING TO LET HAWKEYE AND BLACK WIDOW LEAVE LIKE THAT?
AFTER WHAT WE JUST SURVIVED?
LOOKS THAT WAY.
AND PEOPLE WONDER WHY I HATE PEOPLE.
COME, HULK.
WHAT DO YOU SAY TO ONE FINAL SPARRING MATCH...

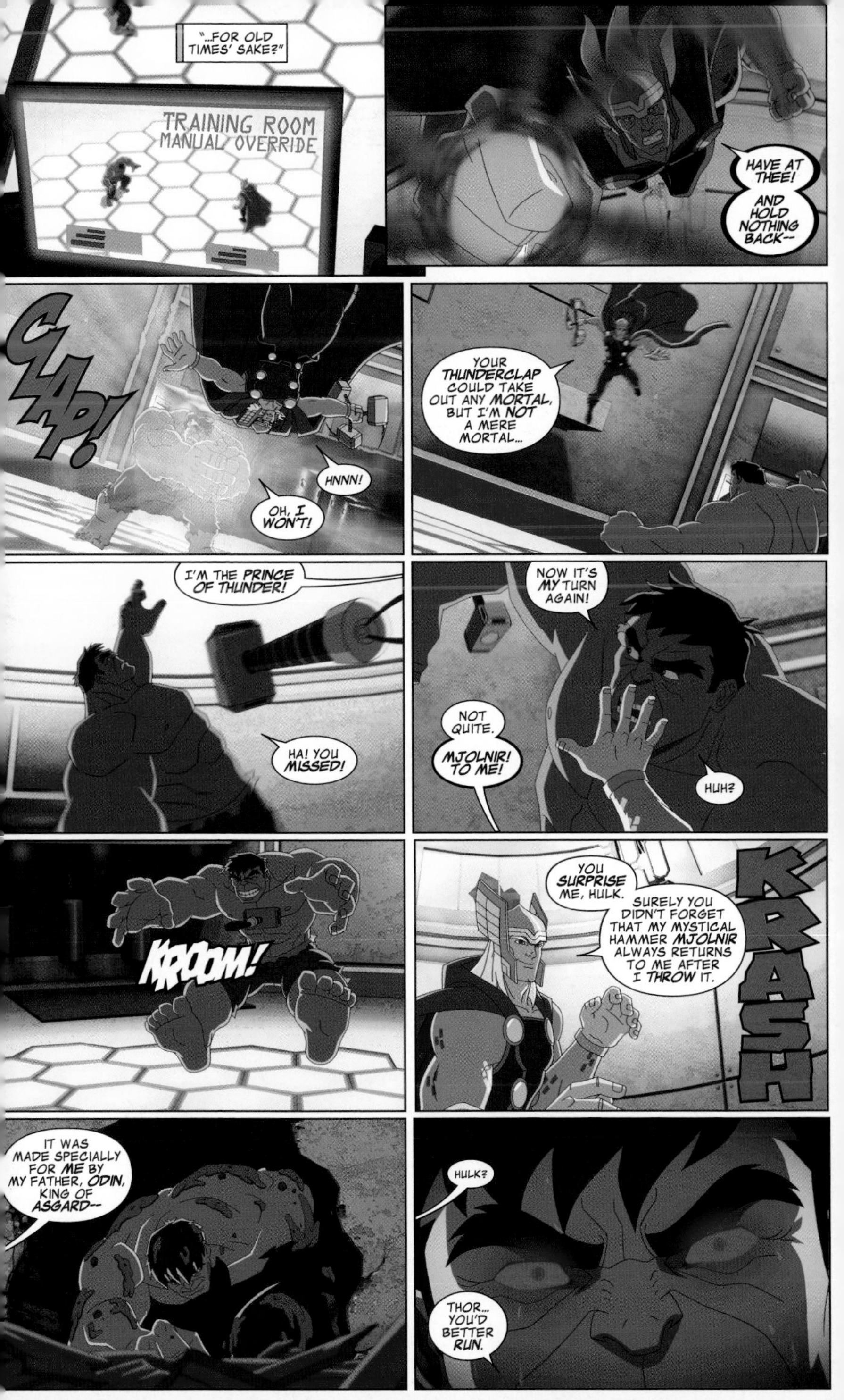
"...FOR OLD TIMES' SAKE?"
TRAINING ROOM MANUAL OVERRIDE
HAVE AT THEE!
AND HOLD NOTHING BACK--
CLAP!
HNNN!
OH, I WON'T!
YOUR THUNDERCLAP COULD TAKE OUT ANY MORTAL, BUT I'M NOT A MERE MORTAL...
I'M THE PRINCE OF THUNDER!
HA! YOU MISSED!
NOW IT'S MY TURN AGAIN!
NOT QUITE.
MJOLNIR! TO ME!
HUH?
KROOM!
YOU SURPRISE ME, HULK.
SURELY YOU DIDN'T FORGET THAT MY MYSTICAL HAMMER MJOLNIR ALWAYS RETURNS TO ME AFTER I THROW IT.
KRASH
IT WAS MADE SPECIALLY FOR ME BY MY FATHER, ODIN, KING OF ASGARD--
HULK?
THOR... YOU'D BETTER RUN.

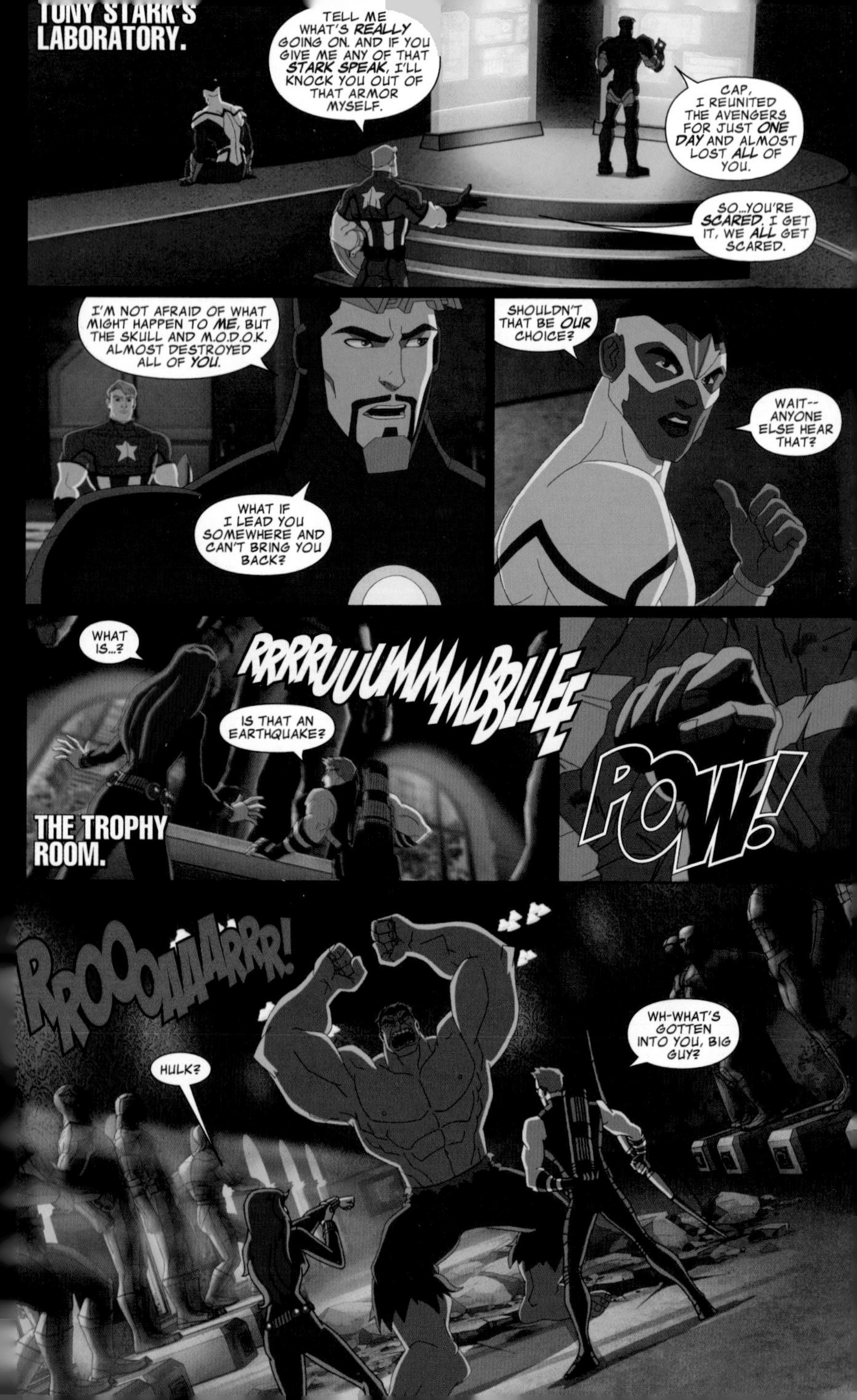
TONY STARK'S LABORATORY.
TELL ME WHAT'S REALLY GOING ON. AND IF YOU GIVE ME ANY OF THAT STARK SPEAK, I'LL KNOCK YOU OUT OF THAT ARMOR MYSELF.
CAP, I REUNITED THE AVENGERS FOR JUST ONE DAY AND ALMOST LOST ALL OF YOU.
SO...YOU'RE SCARED. I GET IT, WE ALL GET SCARED.
I'M NOT AFRAID OF WHAT MIGHT HAPPEN TO ME, BUT THE SKULL AND M.O.D.O.K. ALMOST DESTROYED ALL OF YOU.
WHAT IF I LEAD YOU SOMEWHERE AND CAN'T BRING YOU BACK?
SHOULDN'T THAT BE OUR CHOICE?
WAIT-- ANYONE ELSE HEAR THAT?
WHAT IS...?
RRRRUUUMMMBBLLEE
IS THAT AN EARTHQUAKE?
THE TROPHY ROOM.
POW!
RROOOAARRR!
HULK?
WH-WHAT'S GOTTEN INTO YOU, BIG GUY?

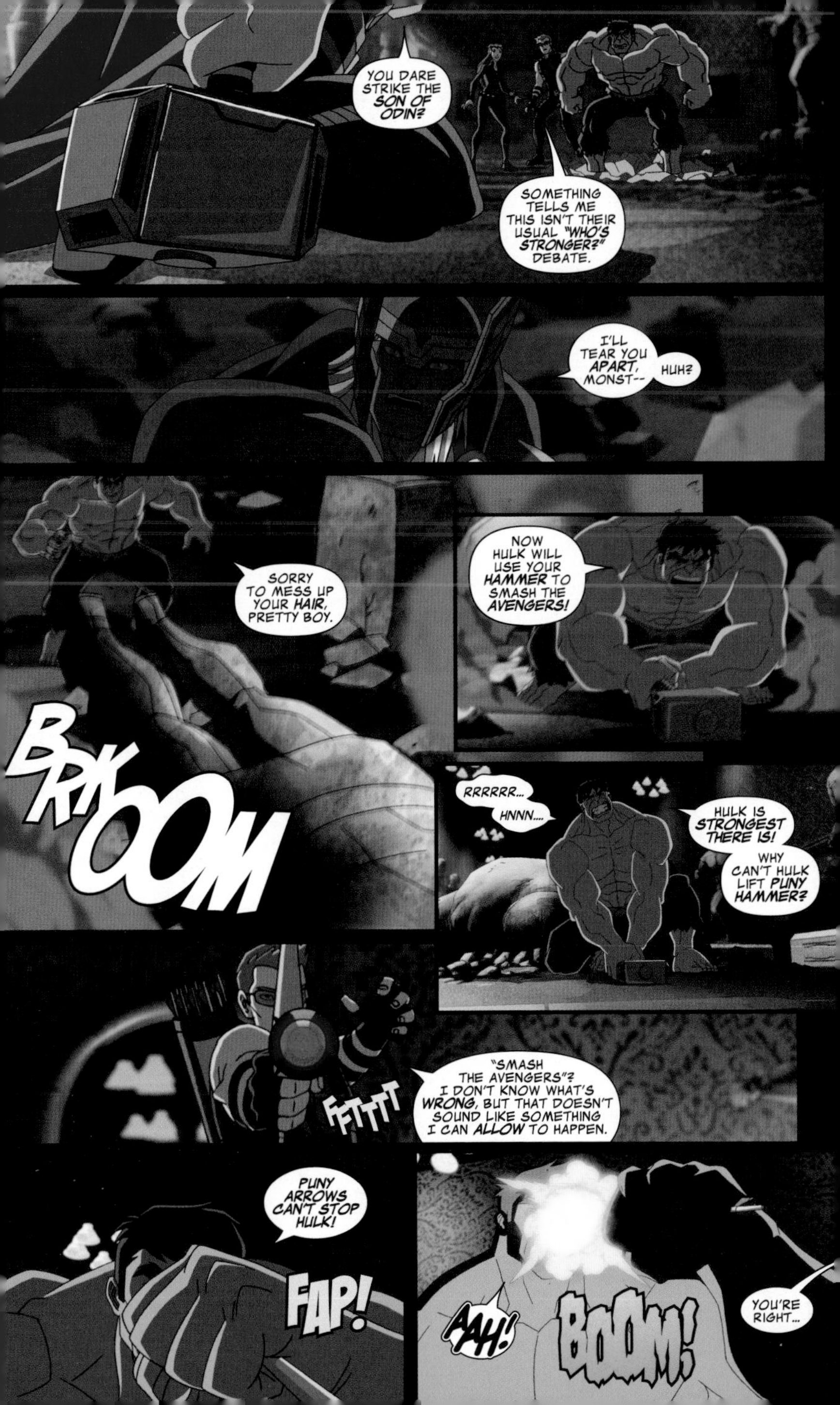
YOU DARE STRIKE THE SON OF ODIN?
SOMETHING TELLS ME THIS ISN'T THEIR USUAL "WHO'S STRONGER?" DEBATE.
I'LL TEAR YOU APART, MONST--
HUH?
SORRY TO MESS UP YOUR HAIR, PRETTY BOY.
BRRKOOM
NOW HULK WILL USE YOUR HAMMER TO SMASH THE AVENGERS!
RRRRRR...
HNNN....
HULK IS STRONGEST THERE IS!
WHY CAN'T HULK LIFT PUNY HAMMER?
FFTTTT
"SMASH THE AVENGERS"? I DON'T KNOW WHAT'S WRONG, BUT THAT DOESN'T SOUND LIKE SOMETHING I CAN ALLOW TO HAPPEN.
PUNY ARROWS CAN'T STOP HULK!
FAP!
AAH!
BOOM!
YOU'RE RIGHT...

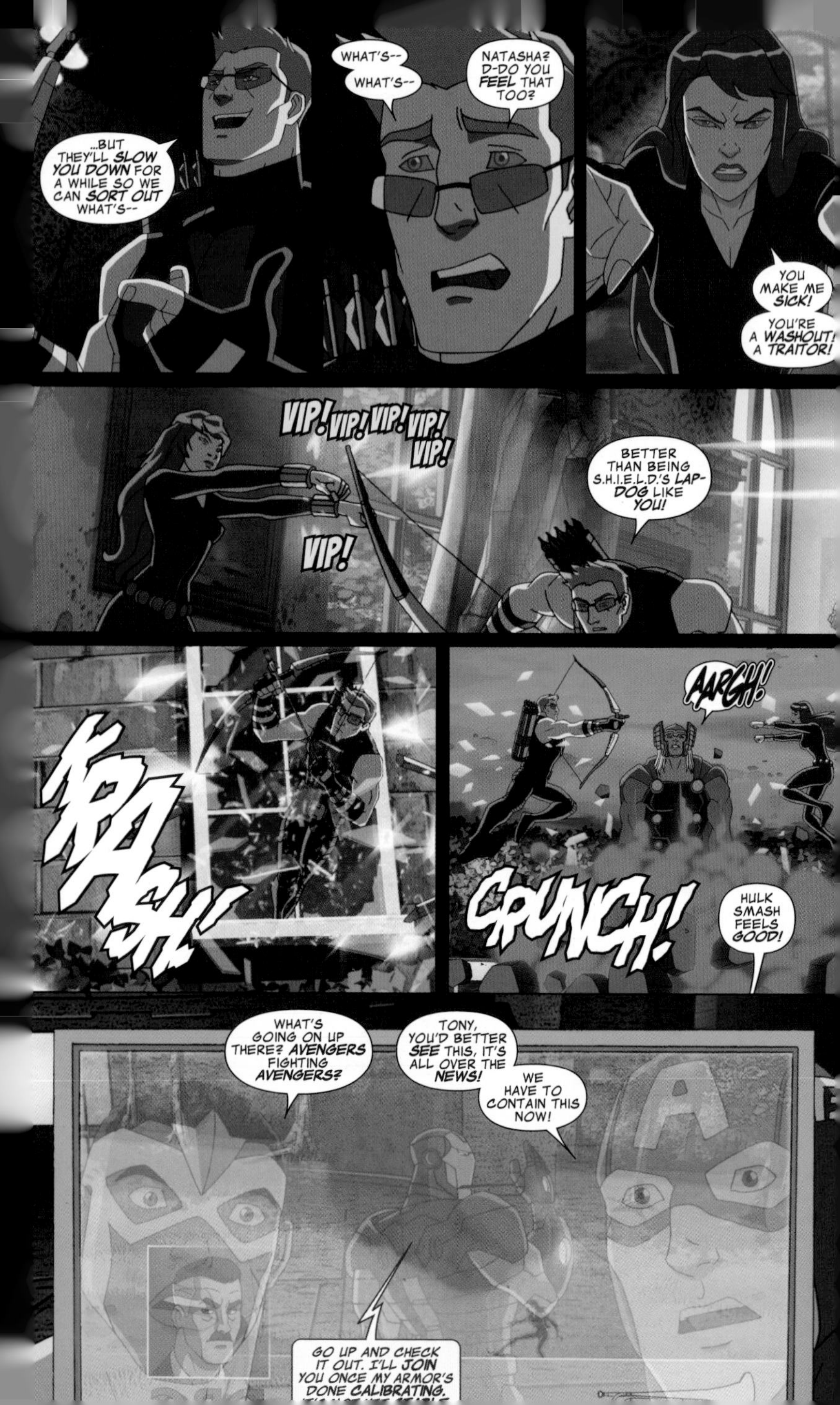
...BUT THEY'LL SLOW YOU DOWN FOR A WHILE SO WE CAN SORT OUT WHAT'S--
WHAT'S--
WHAT'S--
NATASHA? D-DO YOU FEEL THAT TOO?
YOU MAKE ME SICK!
YOU'RE A WASHOUT! A TRAITOR!
VIP! VIP! VIP! VIP! VIP!
VIP!
BETTER THAN BEING S.H.I.E.L.D.'S LAP-DOG LIKE YOU!
KRASH!
AARGH!
CRUNCH!
HULK SMASH FEELS GOOD!
WHAT'S GOING ON UP THERE? AVENGERS FIGHTING AVENGERS?
TONY, YOU'D BETTER SEE THIS, IT'S ALL OVER THE NEWS!
WE HAVE TO CONTAIN THIS NOW!
GO UP AND CHECK IT OUT. I'LL JOIN YOU ONCE MY ARMOR'S DONE CALIBRATING.

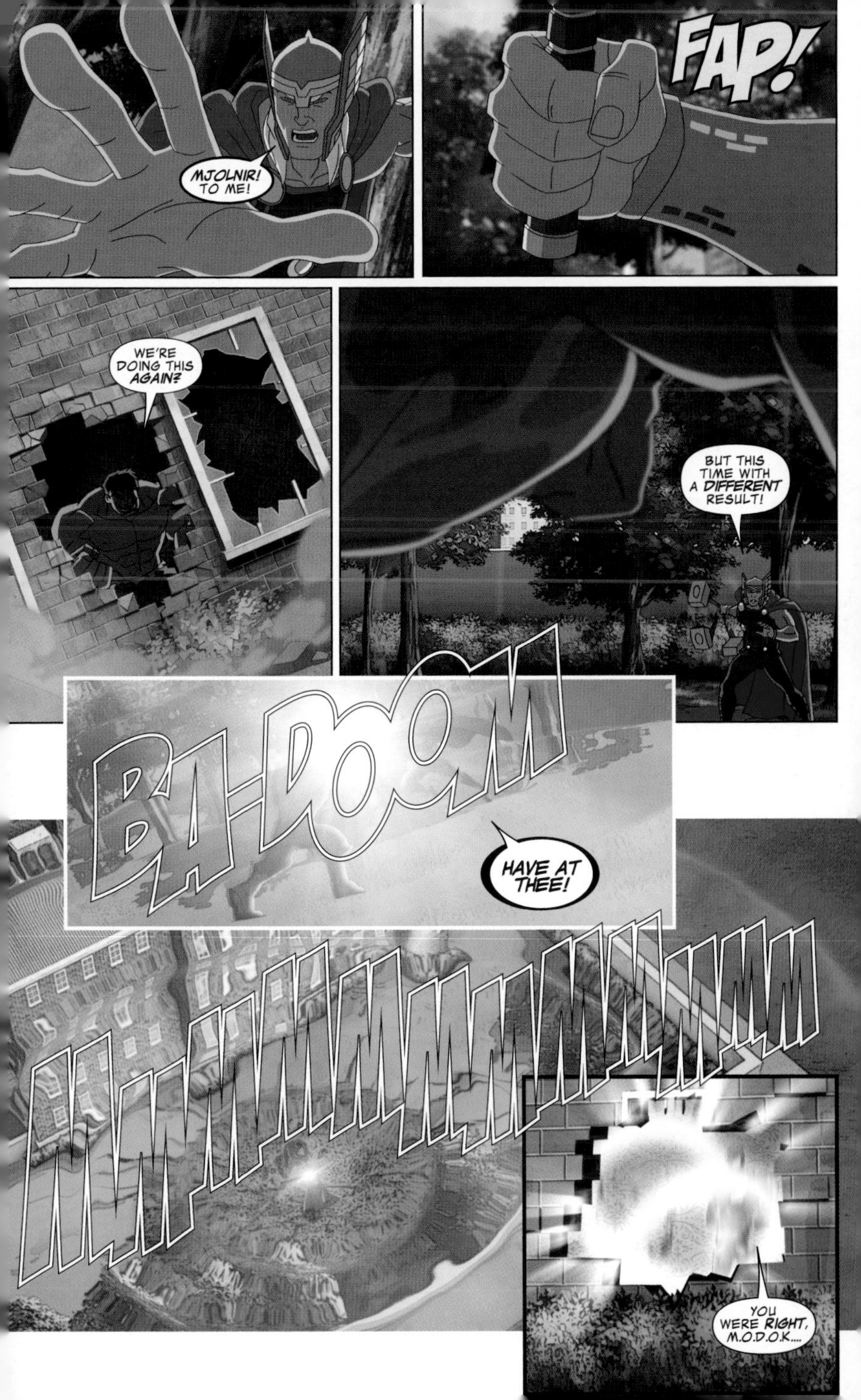
MJOLNIR! TO ME!
FAP!
WE'RE DOING THIS AGAIN?
BUT THIS TIME WITH A DIFFERENT RESULT!
BA-DOOM
HAVE AT THEE!
MMMMMMMMMMMMMMMMM
YOU WERE RIGHT, M.O.D.O.K....

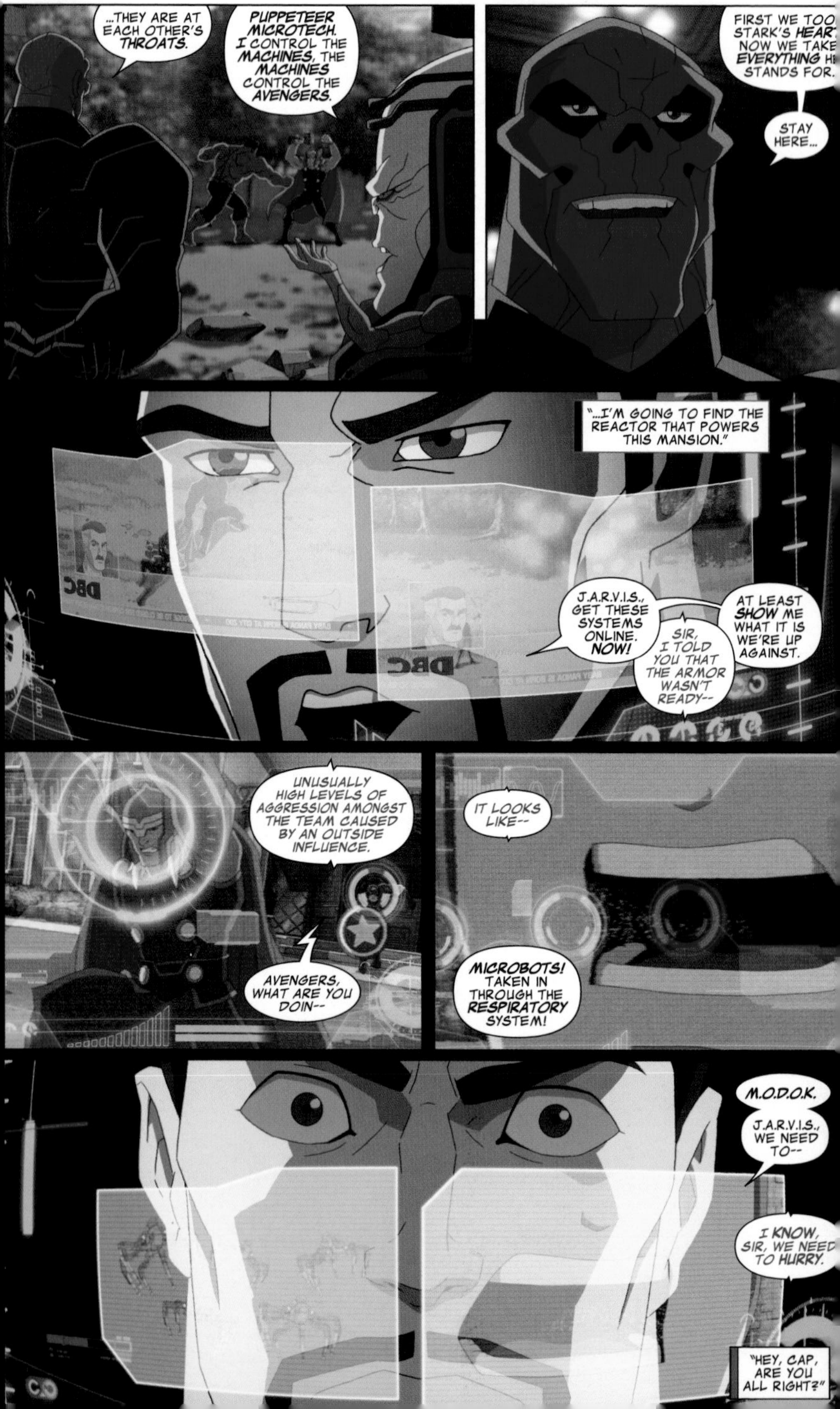
...THEY ARE AT EACH OTHER'S THROATS.
PUPPETEER MICROTECH. I CONTROL THE MACHINES, THE MACHINES CONTROL THE AVENGERS.
FIRST WE TOO STARK'S HEAR NOW WE TAKE EVERYTHING H STANDS FOR.
STAY HERE...
"...I'M GOING TO FIND THE REACTOR THAT POWERS THIS MANSION."
J.A.R.V.I.S., GET THESE SYSTEMS ONLINE. NOW!
SIR, I TOLD YOU THAT THE ARMOR WASN'T READY--
AT LEAST SHOW ME WHAT IT IS WE'RE UP AGAINST.
UNUSUALLY HIGH LEVELS OF AGGRESSION AMONGST THE TEAM CAUSED BY AN OUTSIDE INFLUENCE.
AVENGERS, WHAT ARE YOU DOIN--
IT LOOKS LIKE--
MICROBOTS! TAKEN IN THROUGH THE RESPIRATORY SYSTEM!
M.O.D.O.K.
J.A.R.V.I.S., WE NEED TO--
I KNOW, SIR, WE NEED TO HURRY.
"HEY, CAP, ARE YOU ALL RIGHT?"

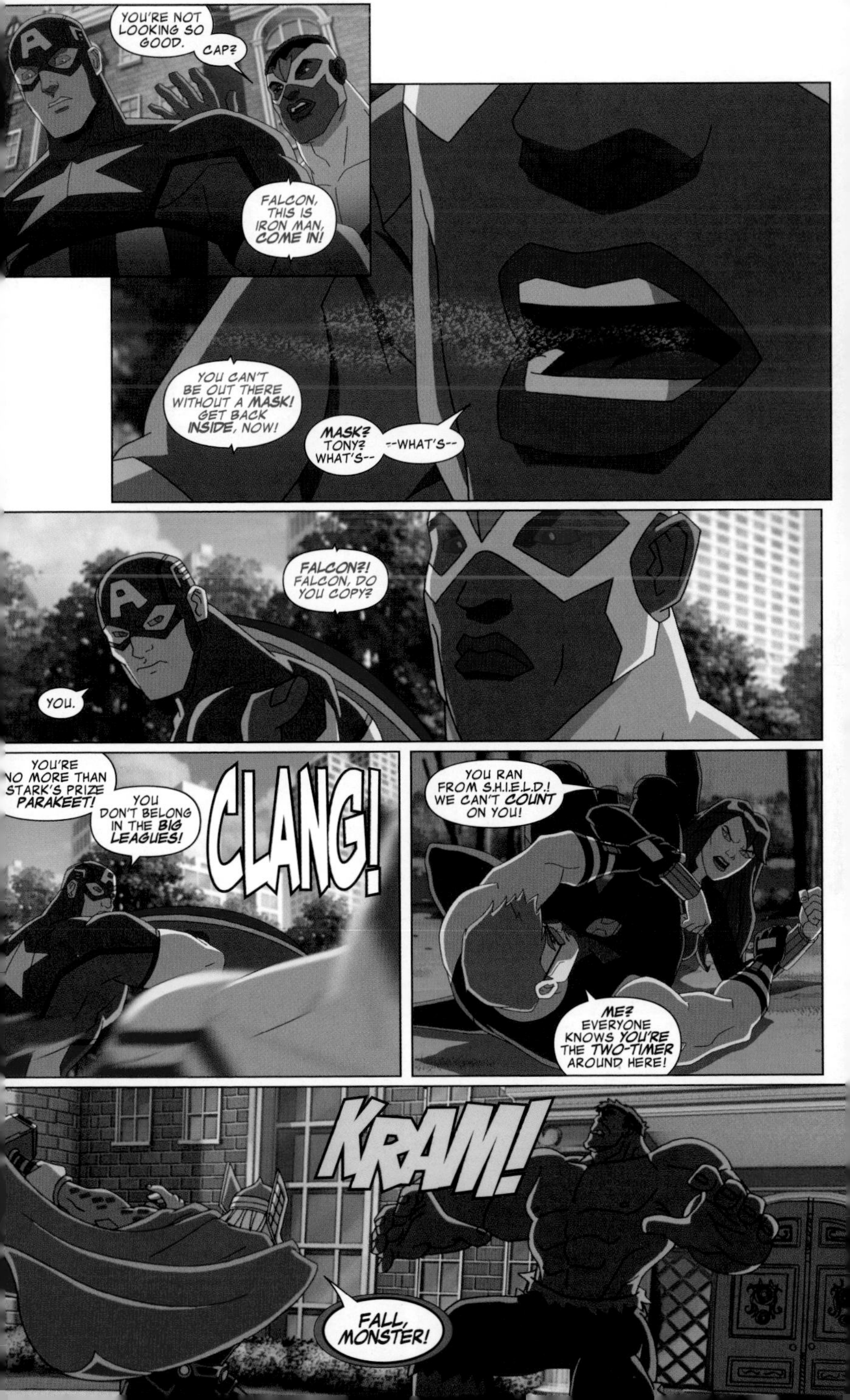

YOU'RE NOT LOOKING SO GOOD.
CAP?
FALCON, THIS IS IRON MAN, COME IN!
YOU CAN'T BE OUT THERE WITHOUT A MASK! GET BACK INSIDE, NOW!
MASK? TONY? WHAT'S--
--WHAT'S--
FALCON?! FALCON, DO YOU COPY?
YOU.
YOU'RE NO MORE THAN STARK'S PRIZE PARAKEET!
YOU DON'T BELONG IN THE BIG LEAGUES!
CLANG!
YOU RAN FROM S.H.I.E.L.D.! WE CAN'T COUNT ON YOU!
ME? EVERYONE KNOWS YOU'RE THE TWO-TIMER AROUND HERE!
KRAM!
FALL, MONSTER!

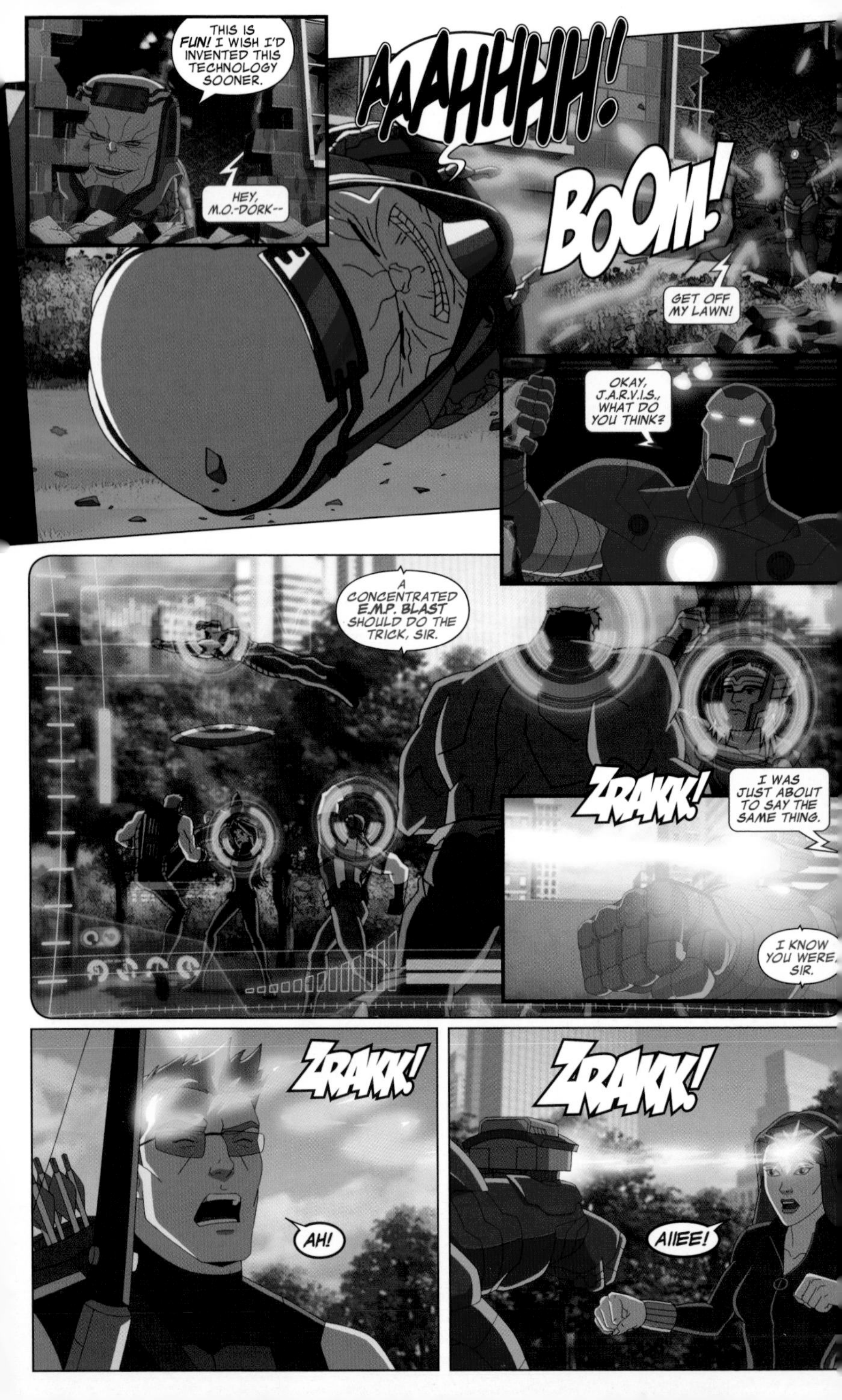
THIS IS FUN! I WISH I'D INVENTED THIS TECHNOLOGY SOONER.
HEY, M.O.-DORK--
AAAHHHH!
BOOM!
GET OFF MY LAWN!
OKAY, J.A.R.V.I.S., WHAT DO YOU THINK?
A CONCENTRATED E.M.P. BLAST SHOULD DO THE TRICK, SIR.
ZRAKK!
I WAS JUST ABOUT TO SAY THE SAME THING.
I KNOW YOU WERE, SIR.
ZRAKK!
AH!
ZRAKK!
AIIEE!

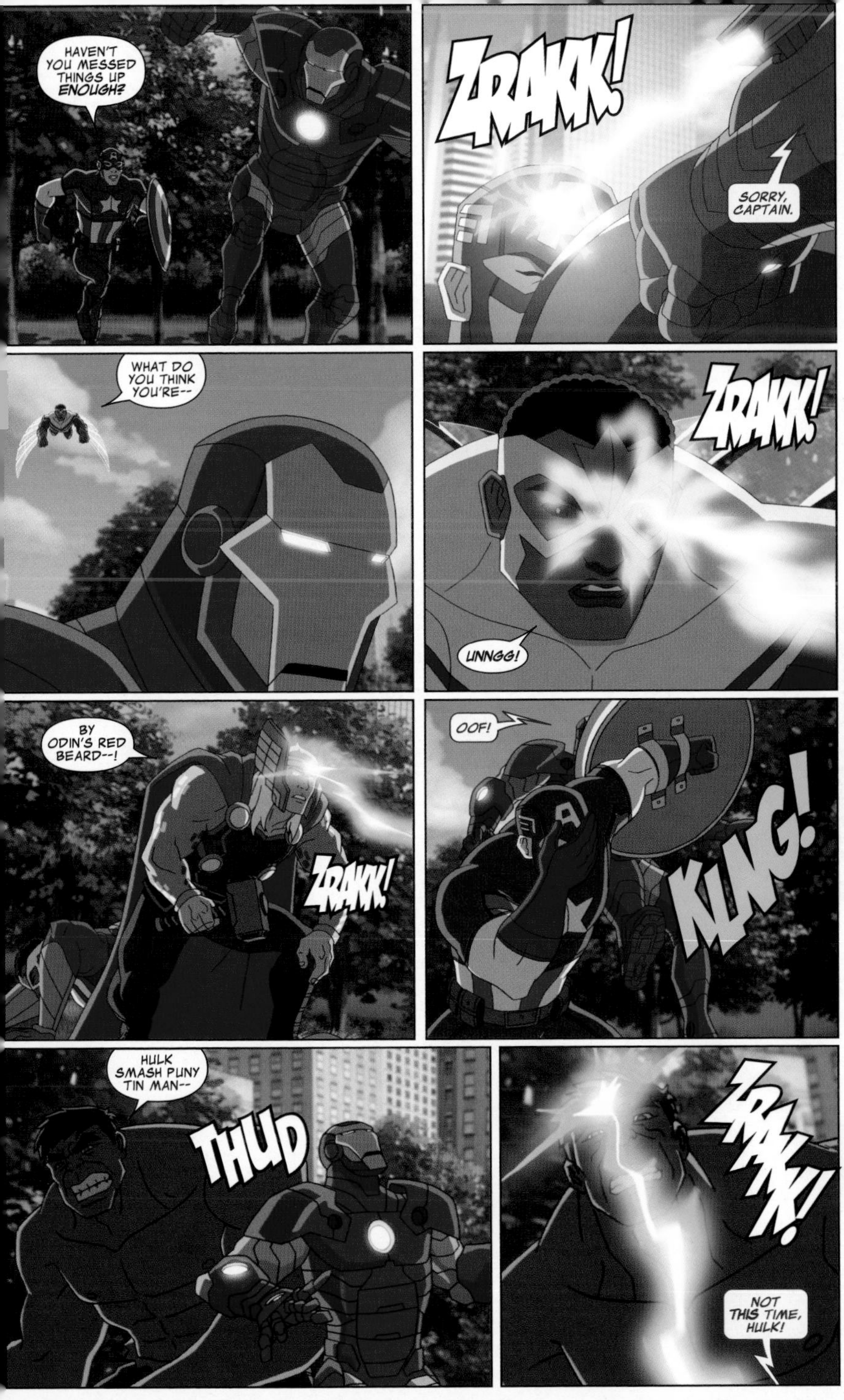
HAVEN'T YOU MESSED THINGS UP ENOUGH?
ZRAKK!
SORRY, CAPTAIN.
WHAT DO YOU THINK YOU'RE--
ZRAKK!
UNNGG!
BY ODIN'S RED BEARD--!
ZRAKK!
OOF!
KLANG!
HULK SMASH PUNY TIN MAN--
THUD
ZRAKK!
NOT THIS TIME, HULK!

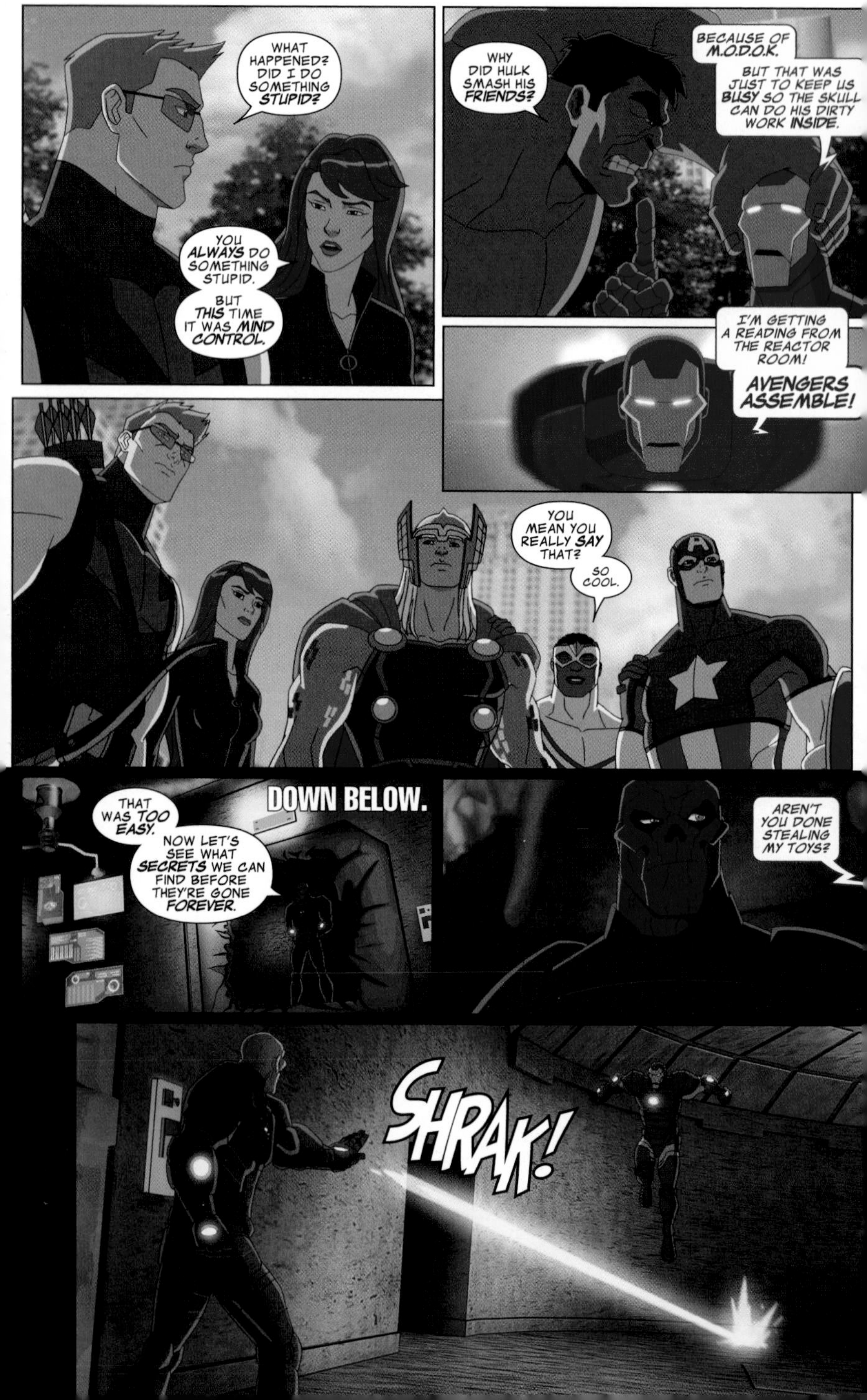
WHAT HAPPENED? DID I DO SOMETHING STUPID?
YOU ALWAYS DO SOMETHING STUPID.
BUT THIS TIME IT WAS MIND CONTROL.
WHY DID HULK SMASH HIS FRIENDS?
BECAUSE OF M.O.D.O.K.
BUT THAT WAS JUST TO KEEP US BUSY SO THE SKULL CAN DO HIS DIRTY WORK INSIDE.
I'M GETTING A READING FROM THE REACTOR ROOM!
AVENGERS ASSEMBLE!
YOU MEAN YOU REALLY SAY THAT?
SO COOL.
DOWN BELOW.
THAT WAS TOO EASY.
NOW LET'S SEE WHAT SECRETS WE CAN FIND BEFORE THEY'RE GONE FOREVER.
AREN'T YOU DONE STEALING MY TOYS?
SHRAK!

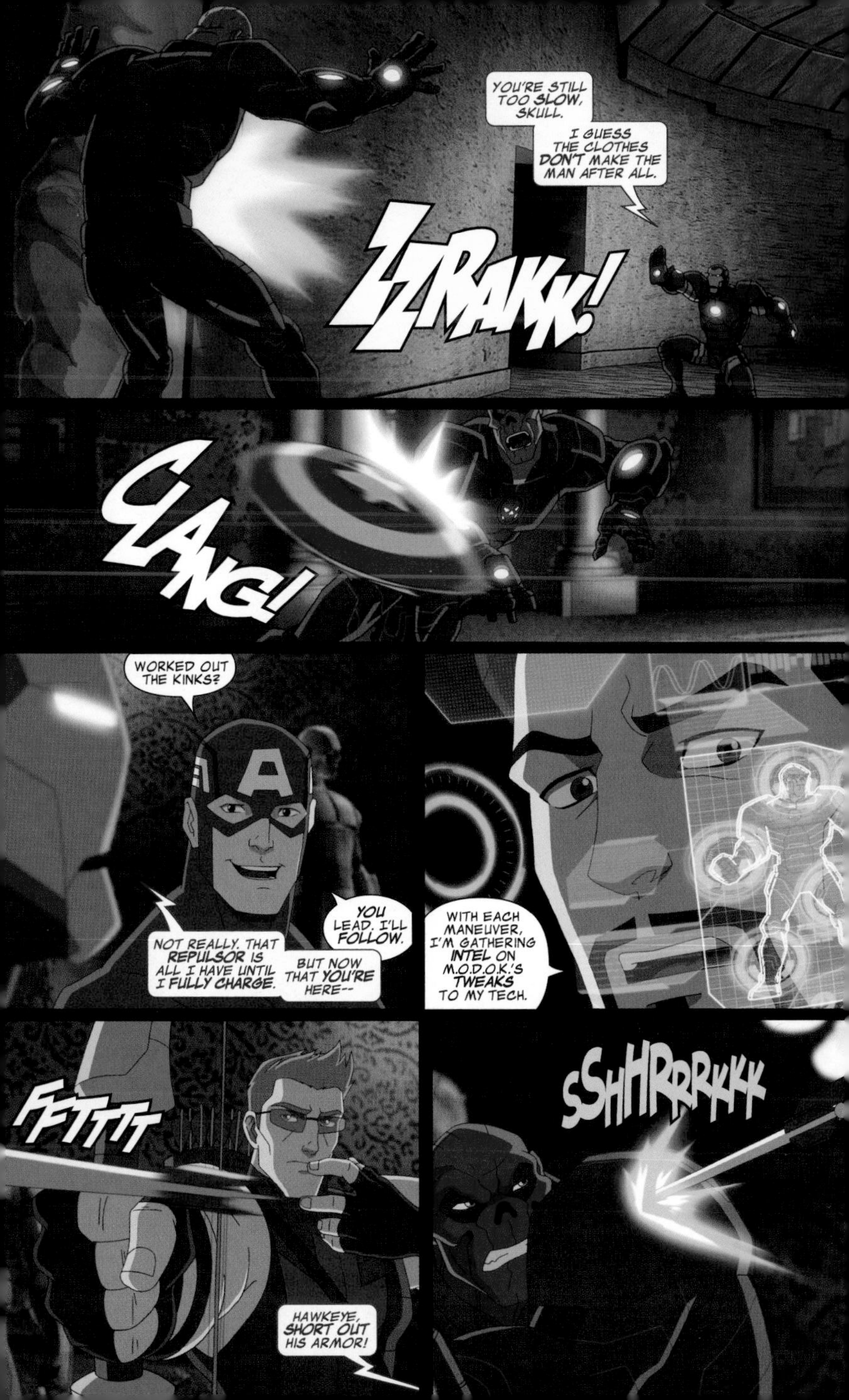
YOU'RE STILL TOO SLOW, SKULL.
I GUESS THE CLOTHES DON'T MAKE THE MAN AFTER ALL.
ZZRAKK!
CLANG!
WORKED OUT THE KINKS?
NOT REALLY. THAT REPULSOR IS ALL I HAVE UNTIL I FULLY CHARGE.
BUT NOW THAT YOU'RE HERE--
YOU LEAD. I'LL FOLLOW.
WITH EACH MANEUVER, I'M GATHERING INTEL ON M.O.D.O.K.'S TWEAKS TO MY TECH.
FFTTTT
HAWKEYE, SHORT OUT HIS ARMOR!
SSHRRRKKK

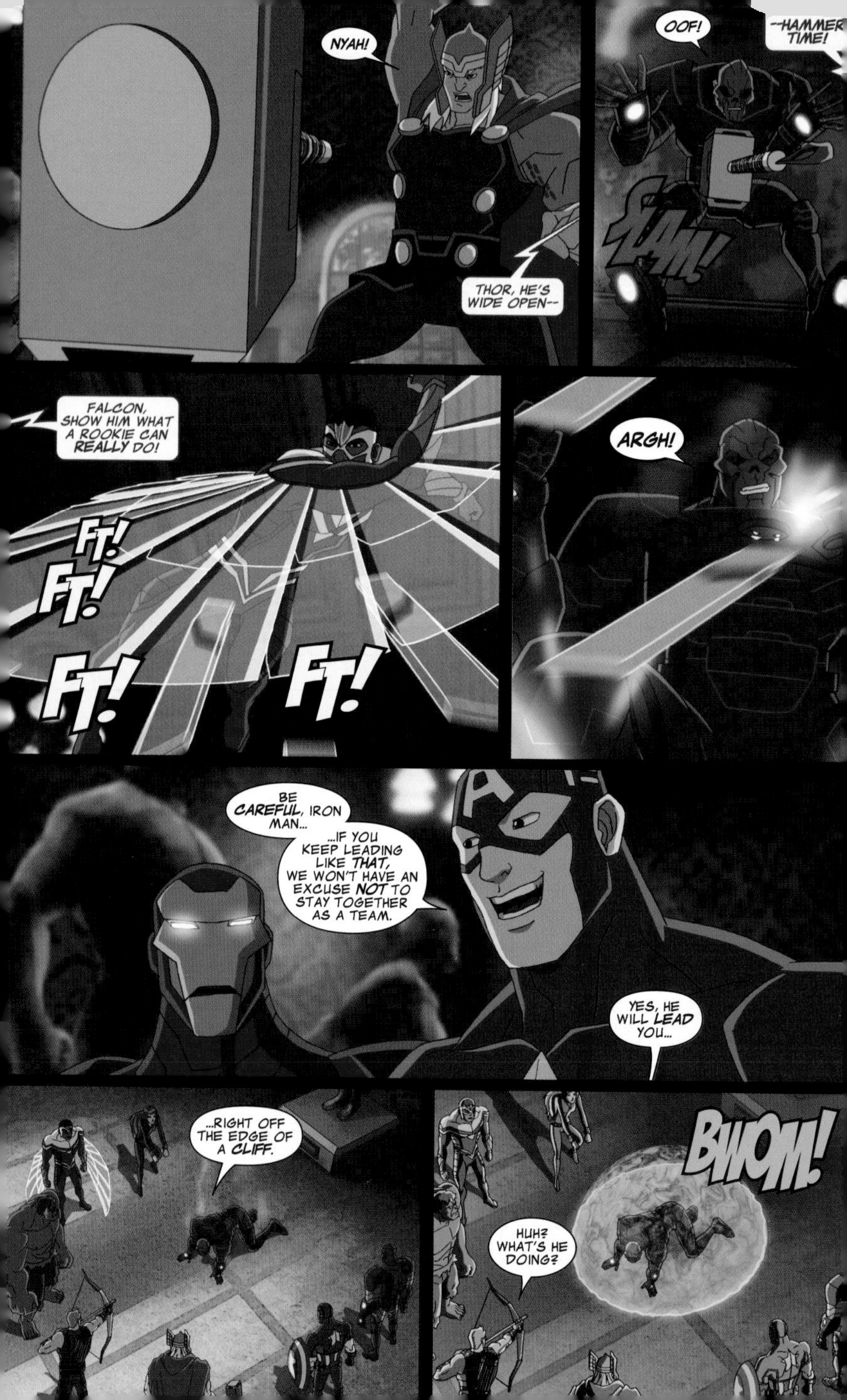
NYAH!
THOR, HE'S WIDE OPEN--
OOF!
--HAMMER TIME!
ZAM!
FALCON, SHOW HIM WHAT A ROOKIE CAN REALLY DO!
FT! FT!
FT!
FT!
ARGH!
BE CAREFUL, IRON MAN...
...IF YOU KEEP LEADING LIKE THAT, WE WON'T HAVE AN EXCUSE NOT TO STAY TOGETHER AS A TEAM.
YES, HE WILL LEAD YOU...
...RIGHT OFF THE EDGE OF A CLIFF.
BWOM!
HUH? WHAT'S HE DOING?

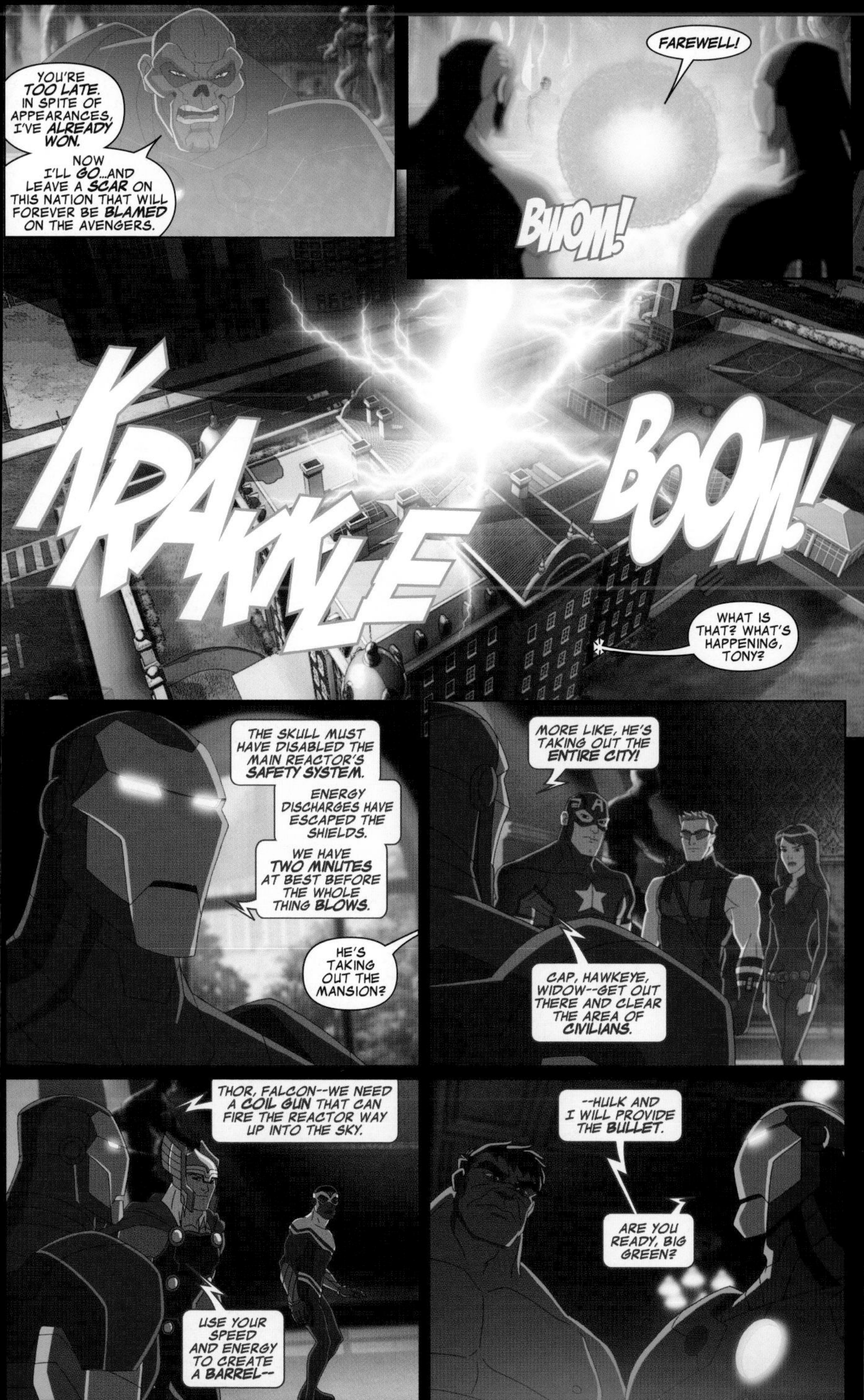
YOU'RE TOO LATE. IN SPITE OF APPEARANCES, I'VE ALREADY WON.
NOW I'LL GO...AND LEAVE A SCAR ON THIS NATION THAT WILL FOREVER BE BLAMED ON THE AVENGERS.
FAREWELL!
BWOM!
KRAKKLE
BOOM!
WHAT IS THAT? WHAT'S HAPPENING, TONY?
THE SKULL MUST HAVE DISABLED THE MAIN REACTOR'S SAFETY SYSTEM.
ENERGY DISCHARGES HAVE ESCAPED THE SHIELDS.
WE HAVE TWO MINUTES AT BEST BEFORE THE WHOLE THING BLOWS.
HE'S TAKING OUT THE MANSION?
MORE LIKE, HE'S TAKING OUT THE ENTIRE CITY!
CAP, HAWKEYE, WIDOW--GET OUT THERE AND CLEAR THE AREA OF CIVILIANS.
THOR, FALCON--WE NEED A COIL GUN THAT CAN FIRE THE REACTOR WAY UP INTO THE SKY.
USE YOUR SPEED AND ENERGY TO CREATE A BARREL--
--HULK AND I WILL PROVIDE THE BULLET.
ARE YOU READY, BIG GREEN?

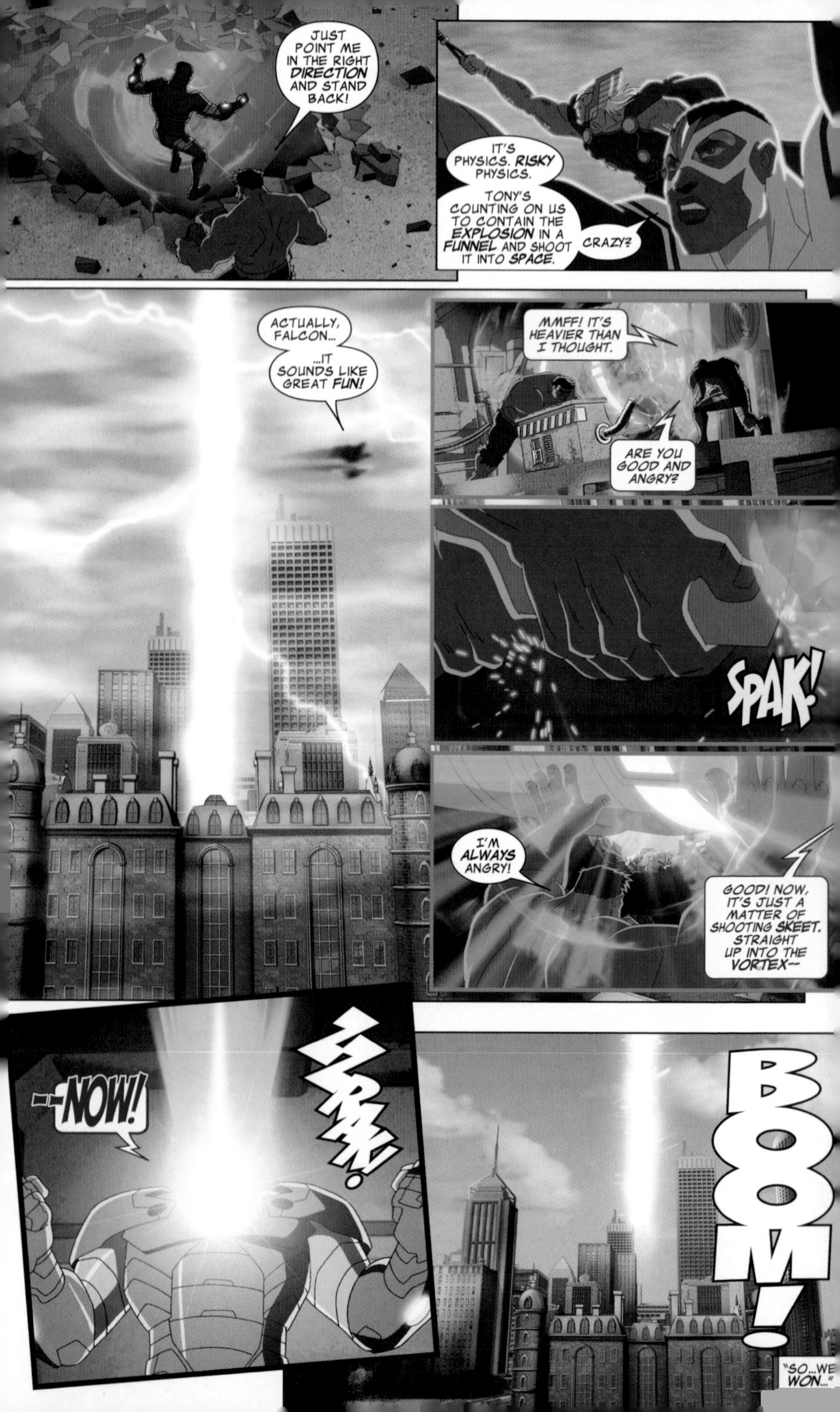

JUST POINT ME IN THE RIGHT DIRECTION AND STAND BACK!
IT'S PHYSICS. RISKY PHYSICS.
TONY'S COUNTING ON US TO CONTAIN THE EXPLOSION IN A FUNNEL AND SHOOT IT INTO SPACE.
CRAZY?
ACTUALLY, FALCON...
...IT SOUNDS LIKE GREAT FUN!
MMFF! IT'S HEAVIER THAN I THOUGHT.
ARE YOU GOOD AND ANGRY?
SPAK!
I'M ALWAYS ANGRY!
GOOD! NOW, IT'S JUST A MATTER OF SHOOTING SKEET. STRAIGHT UP INTO THE VORTEX--
--NOW!
ZZRAK!
BOOM!
"SO...WE WON..."

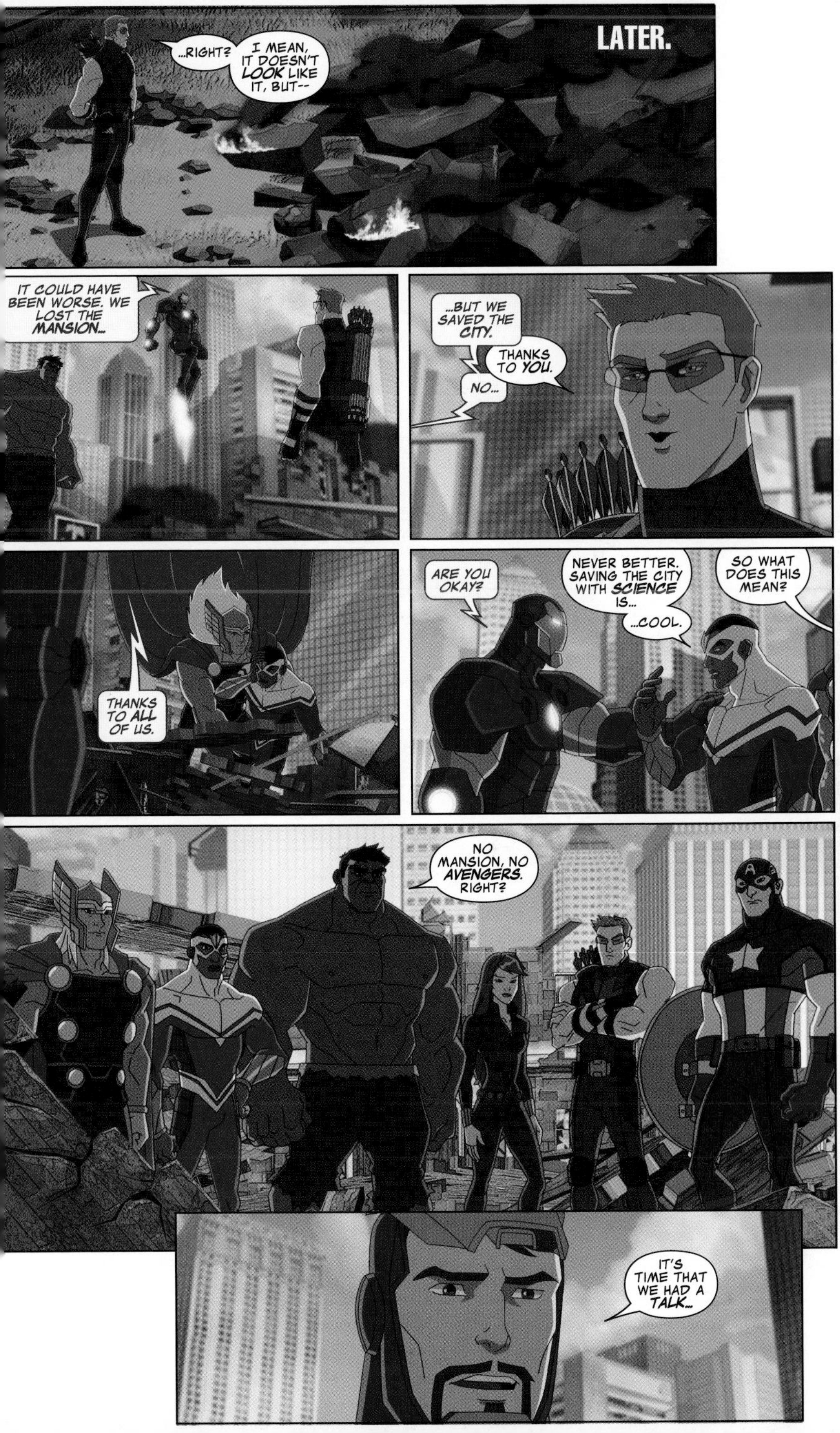
LATER.
...RIGHT?
I MEAN, IT DOESN'T LOOK LIKE IT, BUT--
IT COULD HAVE BEEN WORSE. WE LOST THE MANSION...
...BUT WE SAVED THE CITY.
THANKS TO YOU.
NO...
THANKS TO ALL OF US.
ARE YOU OKAY?
NEVER BETTER. SAVING THE CITY WITH SCIENCE IS...
...COOL.
SO WHAT DOES THIS MEAN?
NO MANSION, NO AVENGERS. RIGHT?
IT'S TIME THAT WE HAD A TALK...

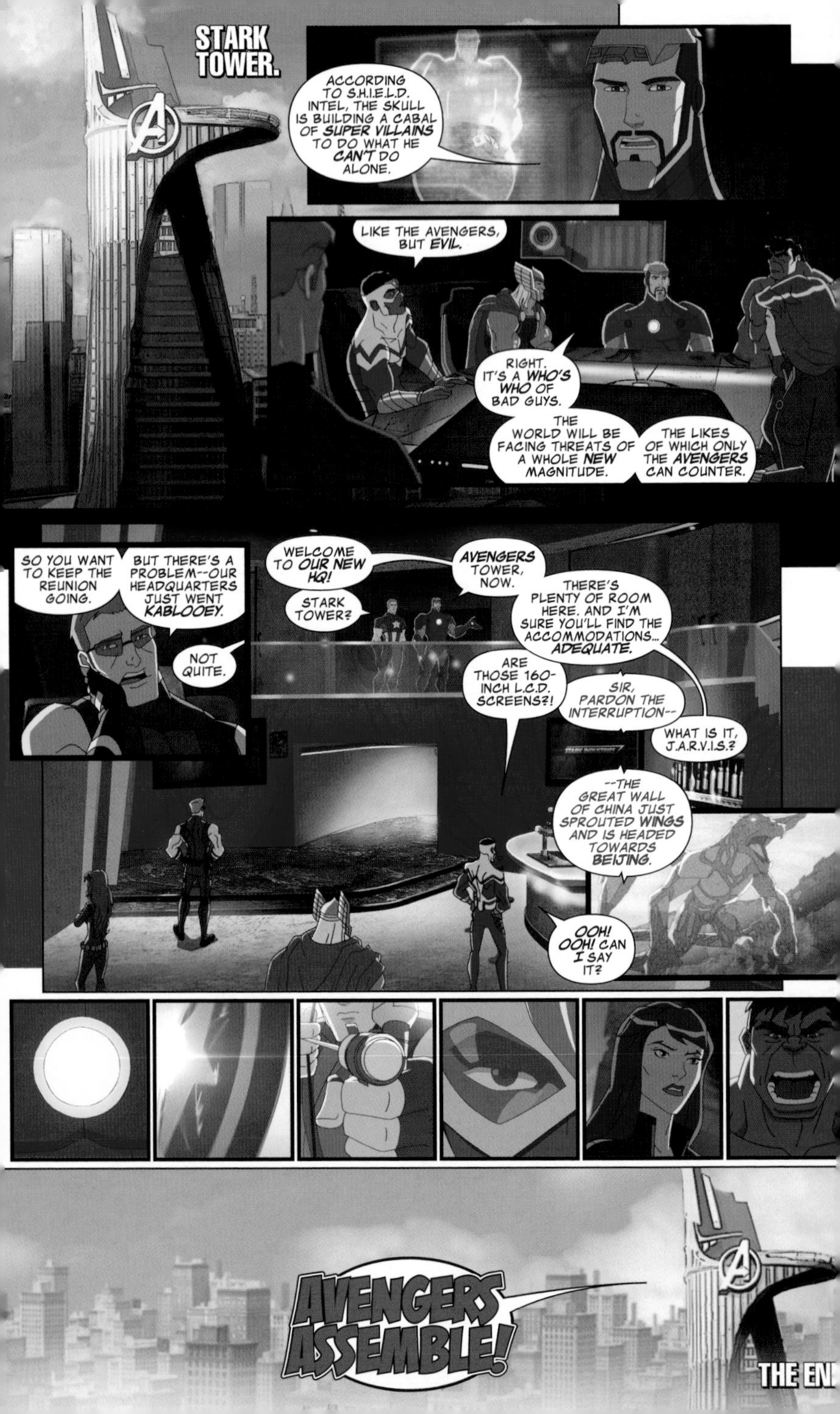
STARK TOWER.
ACCORDING TO S.H.I.E.L.D. INTEL, THE SKULL IS BUILDING A CABAL OF SUPER VILLAINS TO DO WHAT HE CAN'T DO ALONE.
LIKE THE AVENGERS, BUT EVIL.
RIGHT. IT'S A WHO'S WHO OF BAD GUYS.
THE WORLD WILL BE FACING THREATS OF A WHOLE NEW MAGNITUDE.
THE LIKES OF WHICH ONLY THE AVENGERS CAN COUNTER.
SO YOU WANT TO KEEP THE REUNION GOING.
BUT THERE'S A PROBLEM--OUR HEADQUARTERS JUST WENT KABLOOEY.
NOT QUITE.
WELCOME TO OUR NEW HQ!
STARK TOWER?
AVENGERS TOWER, NOW.
THERE'S PLENTY OF ROOM HERE. AND I'M SURE YOU'LL FIND THE ACCOMMODATIONS... ADEQUATE.
ARE THOSE 160-INCH L.C.D. SCREENS?!
SIR, PARDON THE INTERRUPTION--
WHAT IS IT, J.A.R.V.I.S.?
--THE GREAT WALL OF CHINA JUST SPROUTED WINGS AND IS HEADED TOWARDS BEIJING.
OOH! OOH! CAN I SAY IT?
AVENGERS ASSEMBLE!
THE EN

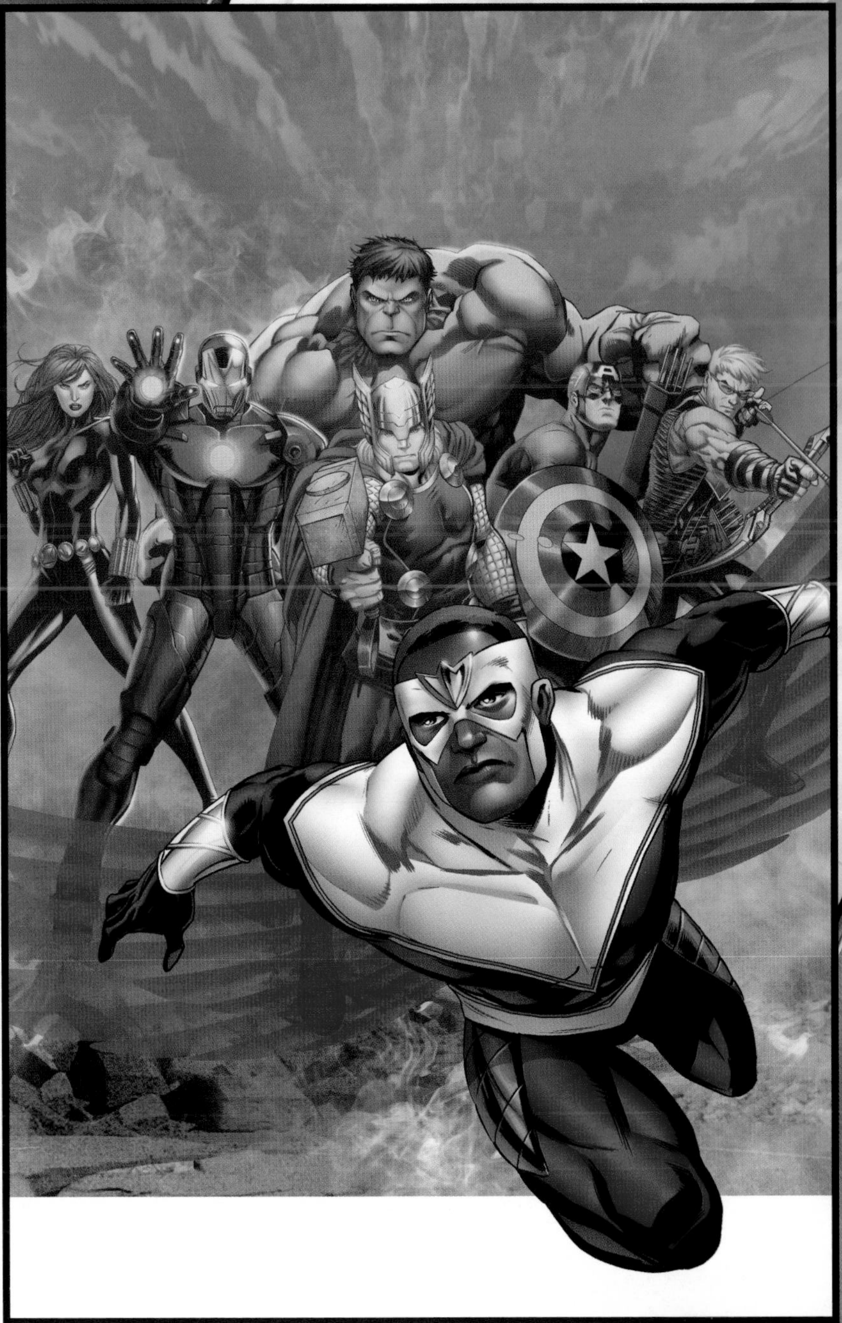

BASED ON "GHOST OF A CHANCE" #3

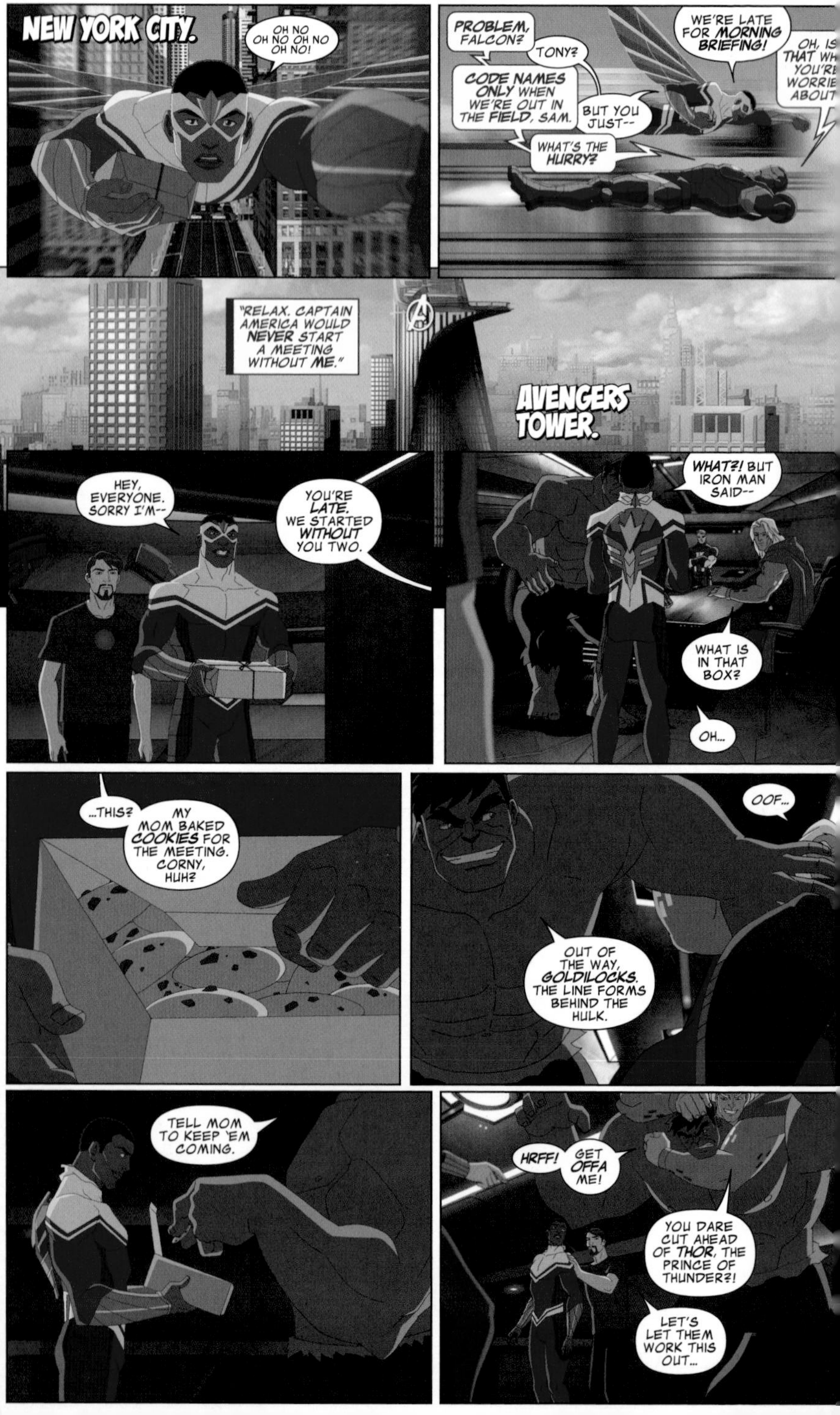

NEW YORK CITY.
OH NO OH NO OH NO OH NO!
PROBLEM, FALCON?
TONY?
CODE NAMES ONLY WHEN WE'RE OUT IN THE FIELD, SAM.
BUT YOU JUST--
WHAT'S THE HURRY?
WE'RE LATE FOR MORNING BRIEFING!
OH, IS THAT WH YOU'R WORRIE ABOUT
"RELAX. CAPTAIN AMERICA WOULD NEVER START A MEETING WITHOUT ME."
AVENGERS TOWER.
HEY, EVERYONE. SORRY I'M--
YOU'RE LATE. WE STARTED WITHOUT YOU TWO.
WHAT?! BUT IRON MAN SAID--
WHAT IS IN THAT BOX?
OH...
...THIS?
MY MOM BAKED COOKIES FOR THE MEETING. CORNY, HUH?
OOF...
OUT OF THE WAY, GOLDILOCKS. THE LINE FORMS BEHIND THE HULK.
TELL MOM TO KEEP 'EM COMING.
HRFF!
GET OFFA ME!
YOU DARE CUT AHEAD OF THOR, THE PRINCE OF THUNDER?!
LET'S LET THEM WORK THIS OUT...

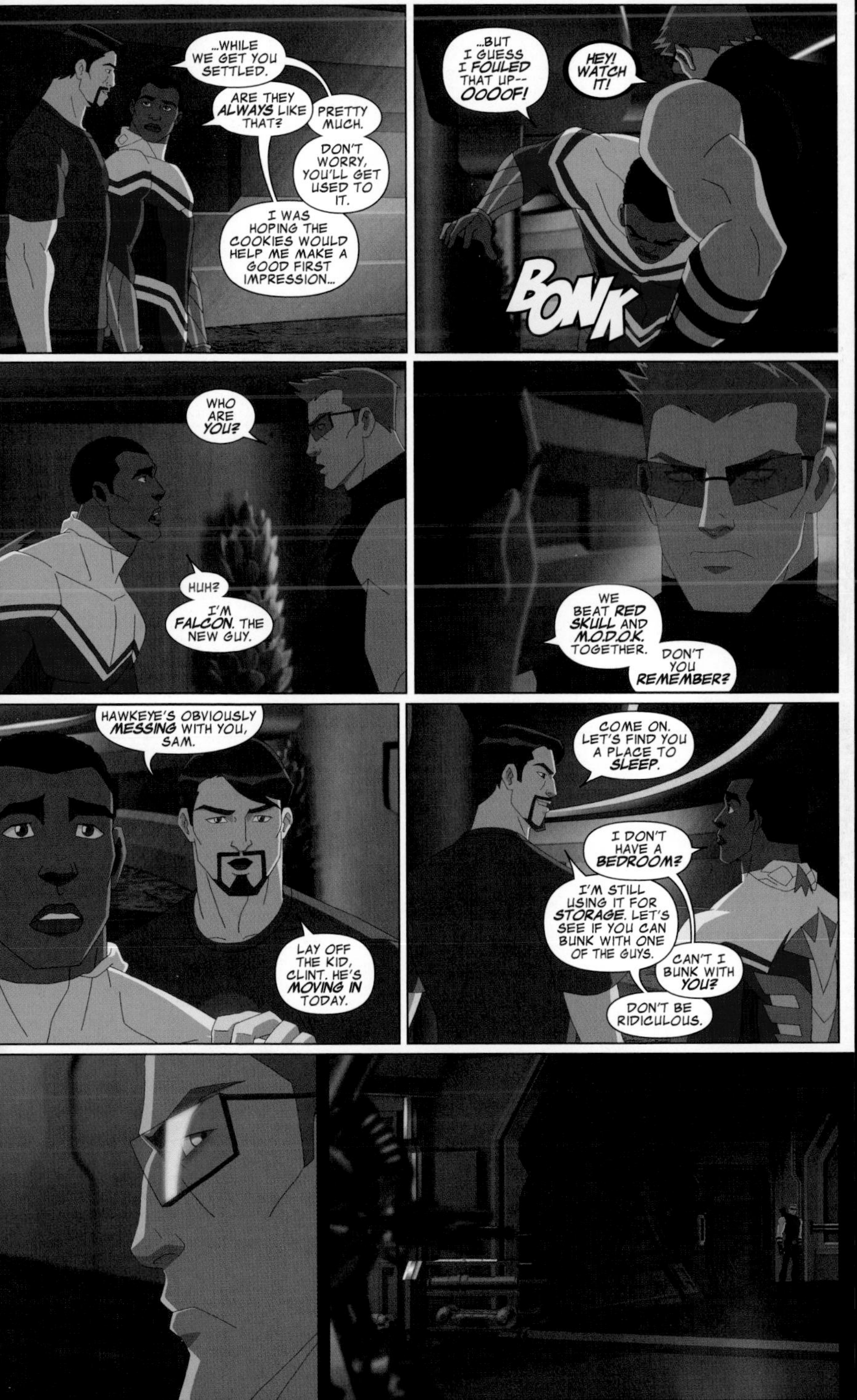
...WHILE WE GET YOU SETTLED.
ARE THEY ALWAYS LIKE THAT?
PRETTY MUCH.
DON'T WORRY, YOU'LL GET USED TO IT.
I WAS HOPING THE COOKIES WOULD HELP ME MAKE A GOOD FIRST IMPRESSION...
...BUT I GUESS I FOULED THAT UP-- OOOOF!
HEY! WATCH IT!
BONK
WHO ARE YOU?
HUH?
I'M FALCON. THE NEW GUY.
WE BEAT RED SKULL AND M.O.D.O.K. TOGETHER.
DON'T YOU REMEMBER?
HAWKEYE'S OBVIOUSLY MESSING WITH YOU, SAM.
LAY OFF THE KID, CLINT. HE'S MOVING IN TODAY.
COME ON. LET'S FIND YOU A PLACE TO SLEEP.
I DON'T HAVE A BEDROOM?
I'M STILL USING IT FOR STORAGE. LET'S SEE IF YOU CAN BUNK WITH ONE OF THE GUYS.
CAN'T I BUNK WITH YOU?
DON'T BE RIDICULOUS.

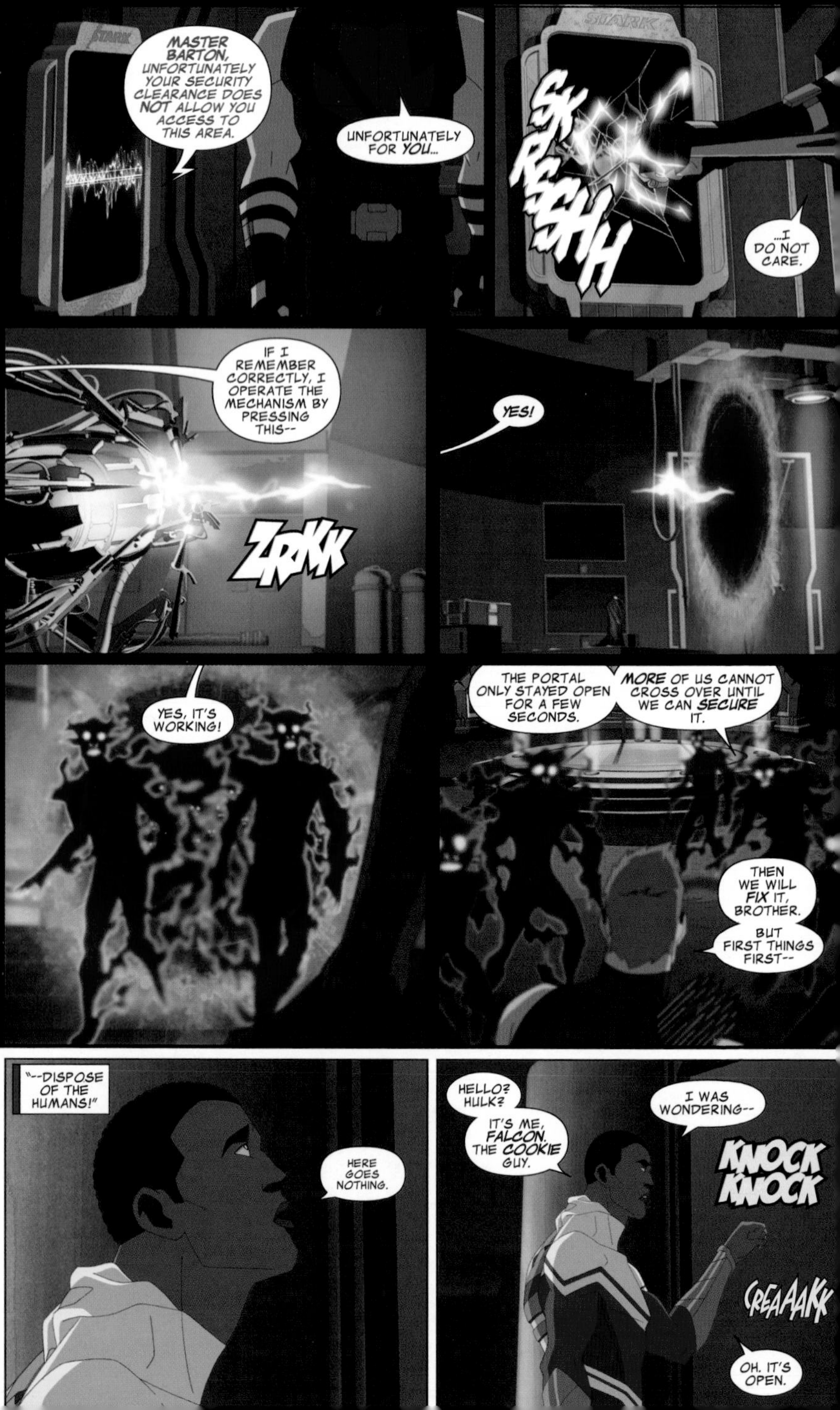
MASTER BARTON, UNFORTUNATELY YOUR SECURITY CLEARANCE DOES NOT ALLOW YOU ACCESS TO THIS AREA.
UNFORTUNATELY FOR YOU...
SKRESHH
...I DO NOT CARE.
IF I REMEMBER CORRECTLY, I OPERATE THE MECHANISM BY PRESSING THIS--
ZRKK
YES!
YES, IT'S WORKING!
THE PORTAL ONLY STAYED OPEN FOR A FEW SECONDS.
MORE OF US CANNOT CROSS OVER UNTIL WE CAN SECURE IT.
THEN WE WILL FIX IT, BROTHER.
BUT FIRST THINGS FIRST--
"--DISPOSE OF THE HUMANS!"
HERE GOES NOTHING.
HELLO? HULK?
IT'S ME, FALCON. THE COOKIE GUY.
I WAS WONDERING--
KNOCK KNOCK
CREAAAKK
OH. IT'S OPEN.

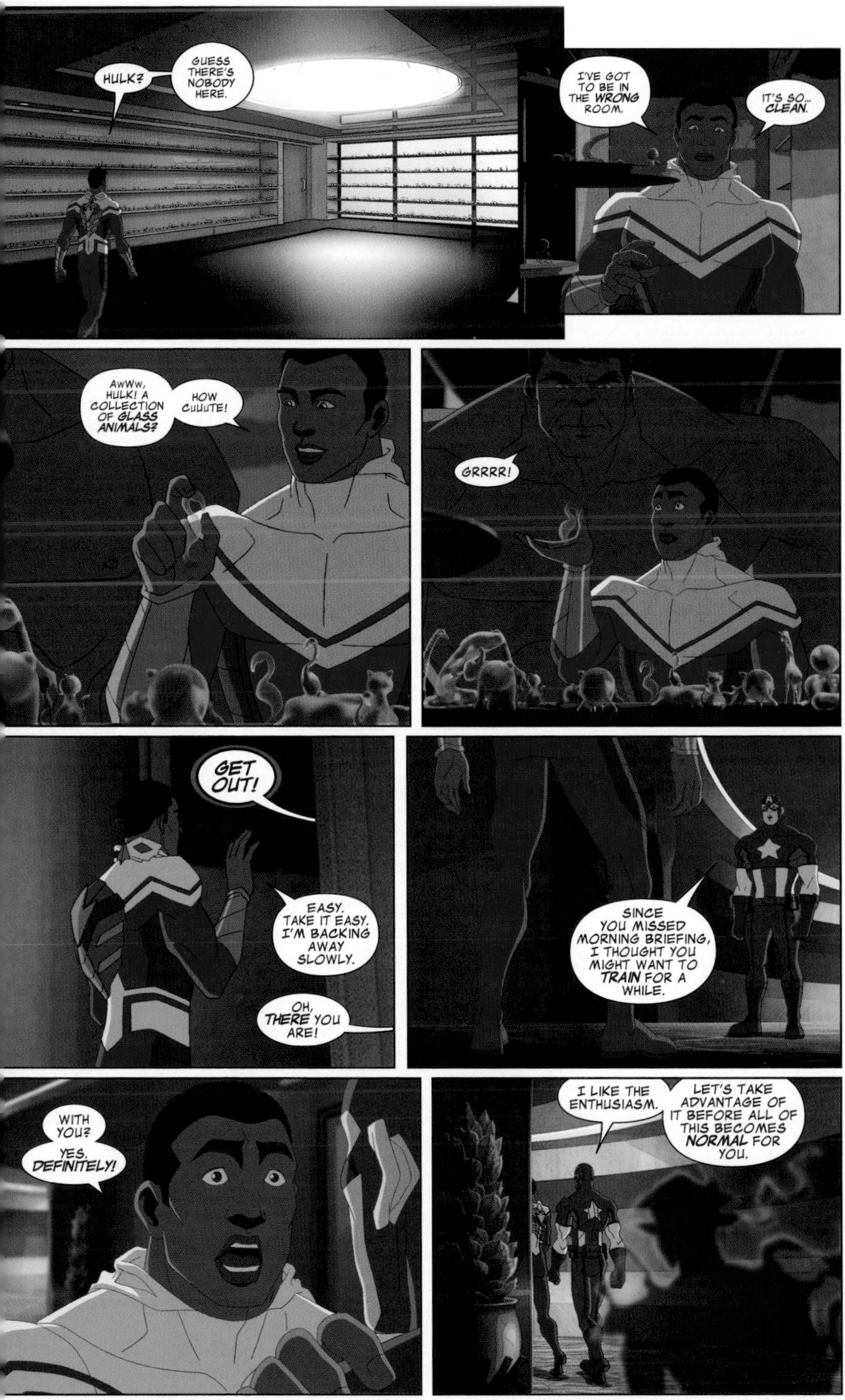
HULK?
GUESS THERE'S NOBODY HERE.
I'VE GOT TO BE IN THE WRONG ROOM.
IT'S SO... CLEAN.
AWWW, HULK! A COLLECTION OF GLASS ANIMALS?
HOW CUUUTE!
GRRRR!
GET OUT!
EASY. TAKE IT EASY. I'M BACKING AWAY SLOWLY.
OH, THERE YOU ARE!
SINCE YOU MISSED MORNING BRIEFING, I THOUGHT YOU MIGHT WANT TO TRAIN FOR A WHILE.
WITH YOU?
YES. DEFINITELY!
I LIKE THE ENTHUSIASM.
LET'S TAKE ADVANTAGE OF IT BEFORE ALL OF THIS BECOMES NORMAL FOR YOU.

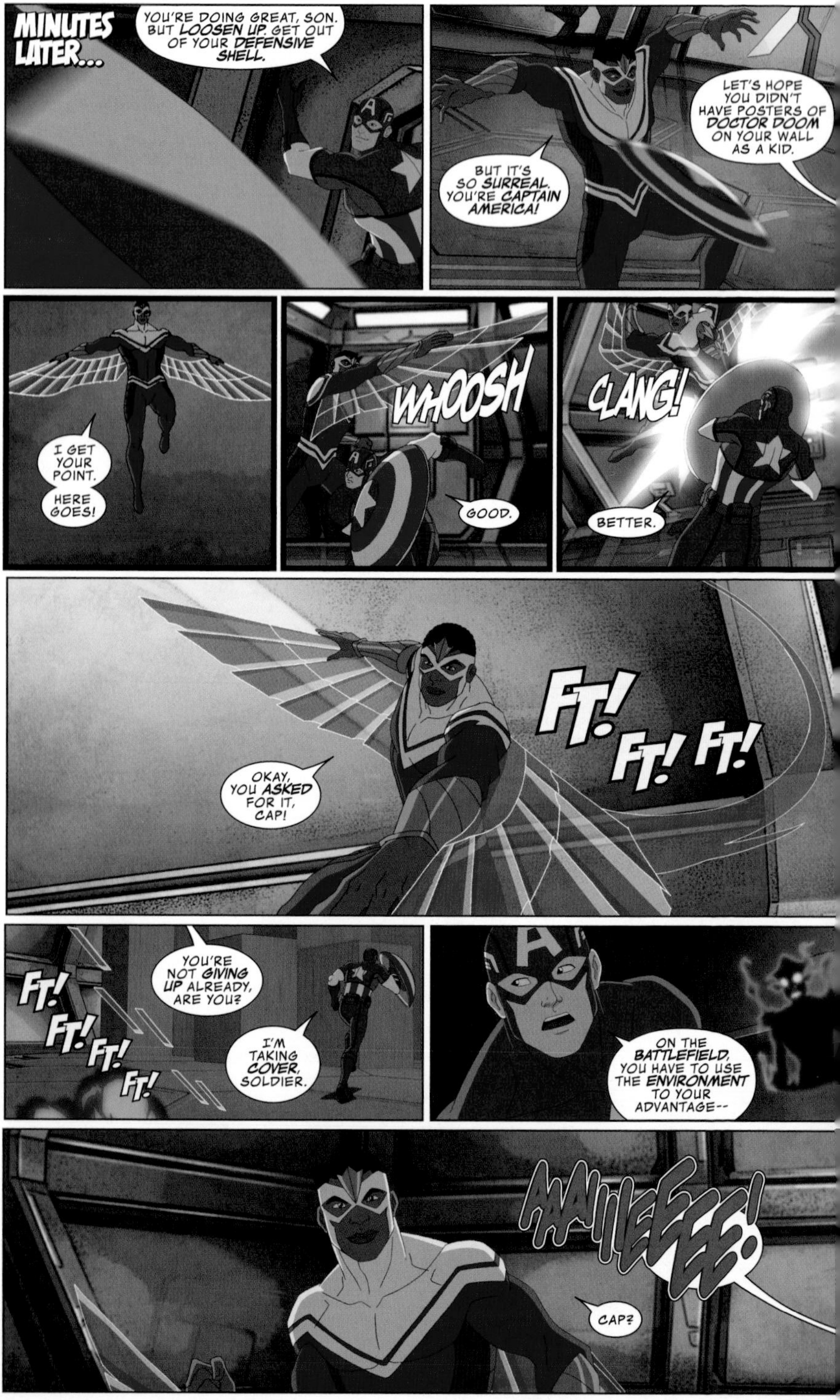
MINUTES LATER...
YOU'RE DOING GREAT, SON. BUT LOOSEN UP. GET OUT OF YOUR DEFENSIVE SHELL.
BUT IT'S SO SURREAL. YOU'RE CAPTAIN AMERICA!
LET'S HOPE YOU DIDN'T HAVE POSTERS OF DOCTOR DOOM ON YOUR WALL AS A KID.
I GET YOUR POINT.
HERE GOES!
WHOOSH
GOOD.
CLANG!
BETTER.
OKAY, YOU ASKED FOR IT, CAP!
FT! FT! FT!
FT! FT! FT! FT!
YOU'RE NOT GIVING UP ALREADY, ARE YOU?
I'M TAKING COVER, SOLDIER.
ON THE BATTLEFIELD, YOU HAVE TO USE THE ENVIRONMENT TO YOUR ADVANTAGE--
AAAIIIEEEE!
CAP?

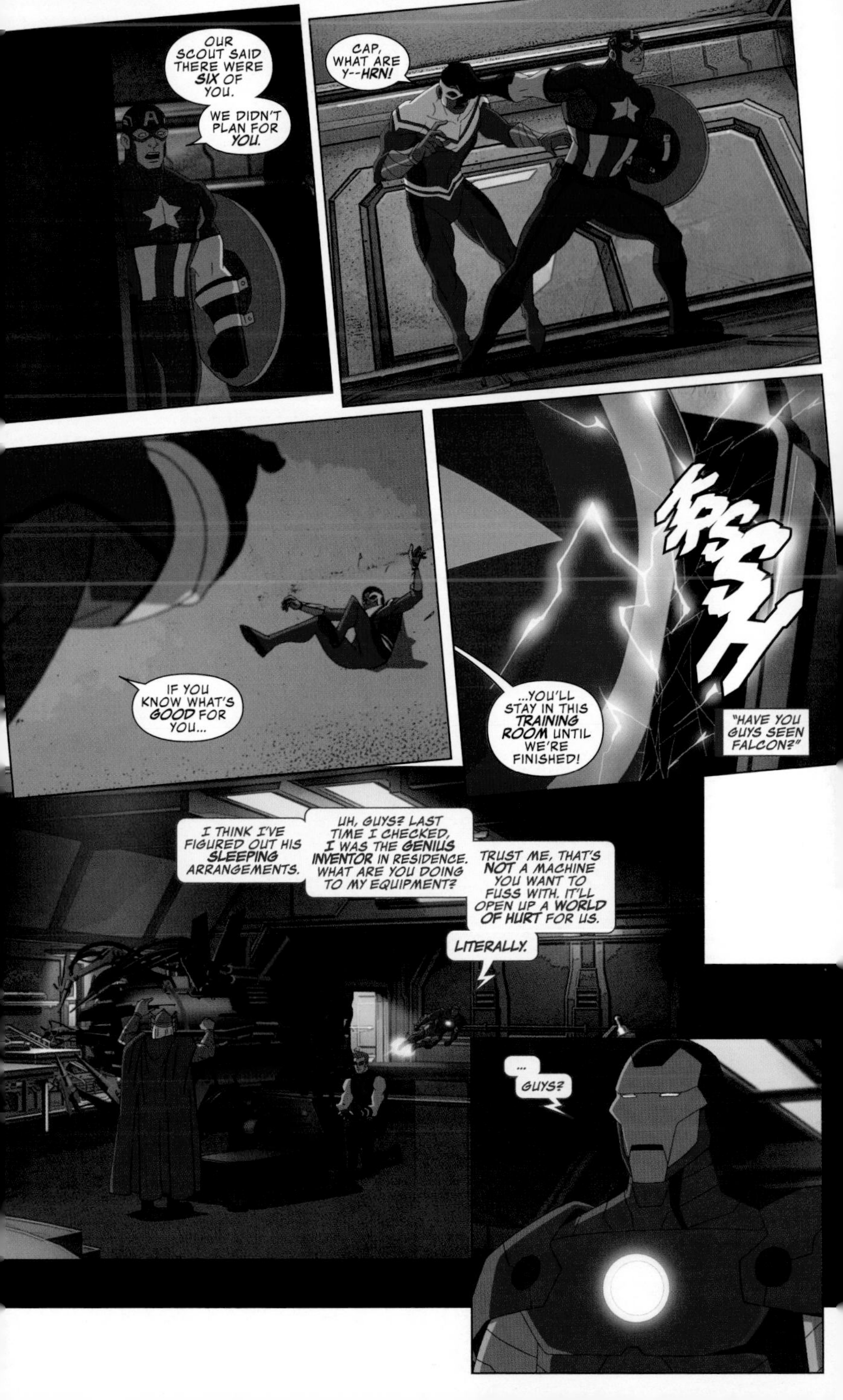
OUR SCOUT SAID THERE WERE SIX OF YOU.
WE DIDN'T PLAN FOR YOU.
CAP, WHAT ARE Y--HRN!
IF YOU KNOW WHAT'S GOOD FOR YOU...
...YOU'LL STAY IN THIS TRAINING ROOM UNTIL WE'RE FINISHED!
KRSSH
"HAVE YOU GUYS SEEN FALCON?"
I THINK I'VE FIGURED OUT HIS SLEEPING ARRANGEMENTS.
UH, GUYS? LAST TIME I CHECKED, I WAS THE GENIUS INVENTOR IN RESIDENCE. WHAT ARE YOU DOING TO MY EQUIPMENT?
TRUST ME, THAT'S NOT A MACHINE YOU WANT TO FUSS WITH. IT'LL OPEN UP A WORLD OF HURT FOR US.
LITERALLY.
... GUYS?

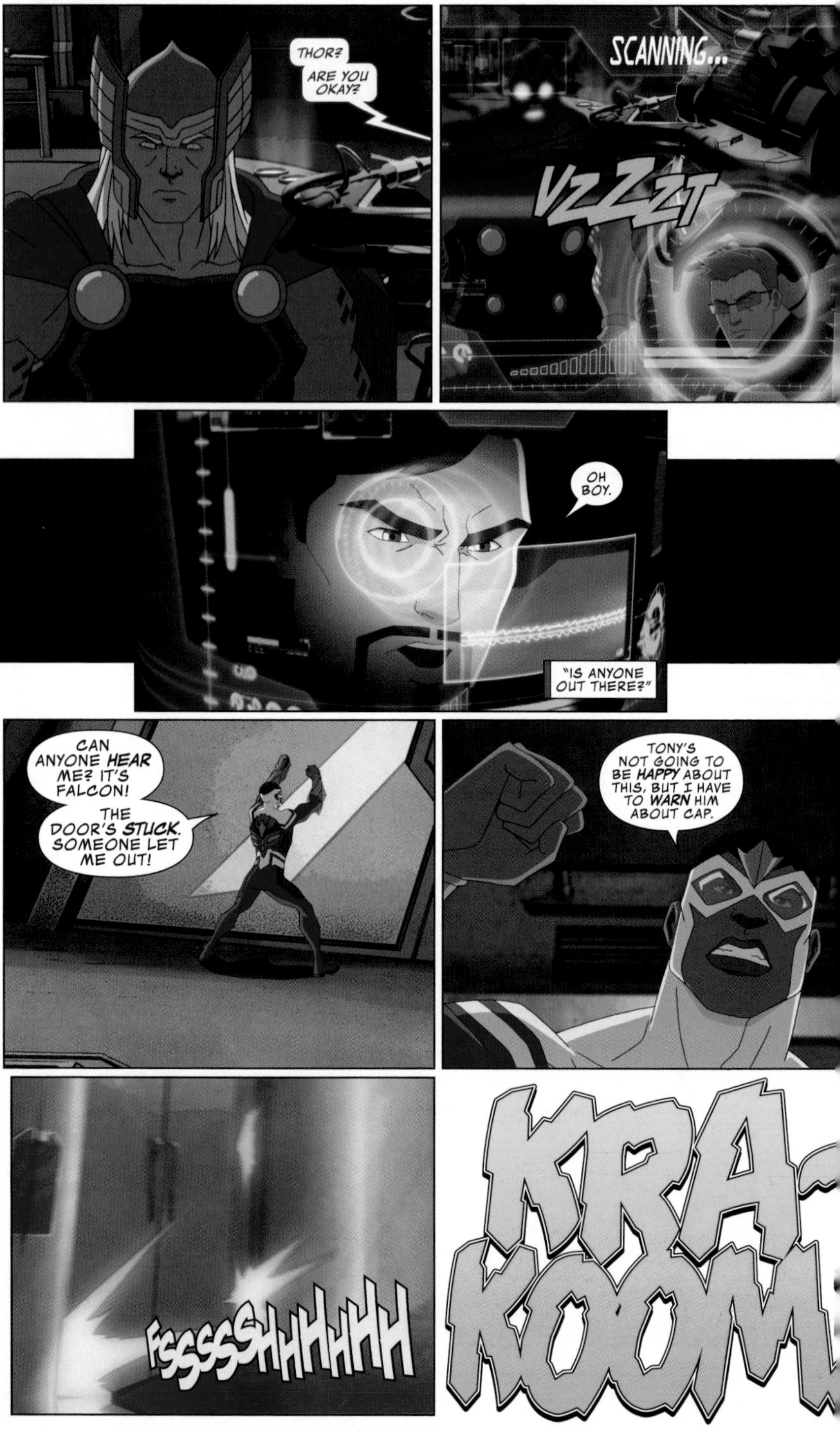

THOR? ARE YOU OKAY?
SCANNING...
VZZZT
OH BOY.
"IS ANYONE OUT THERE?"
CAN ANYONE HEAR ME? IT'S FALCON!
THE DOOR'S STUCK. SOMEONE LET ME OUT!
TONY'S NOT GOING TO BE HAPPY ABOUT THIS, BUT I HAVE TO WARN HIM ABOUT CAP.
FSSSSSHHHHHH
KRA-KOOM

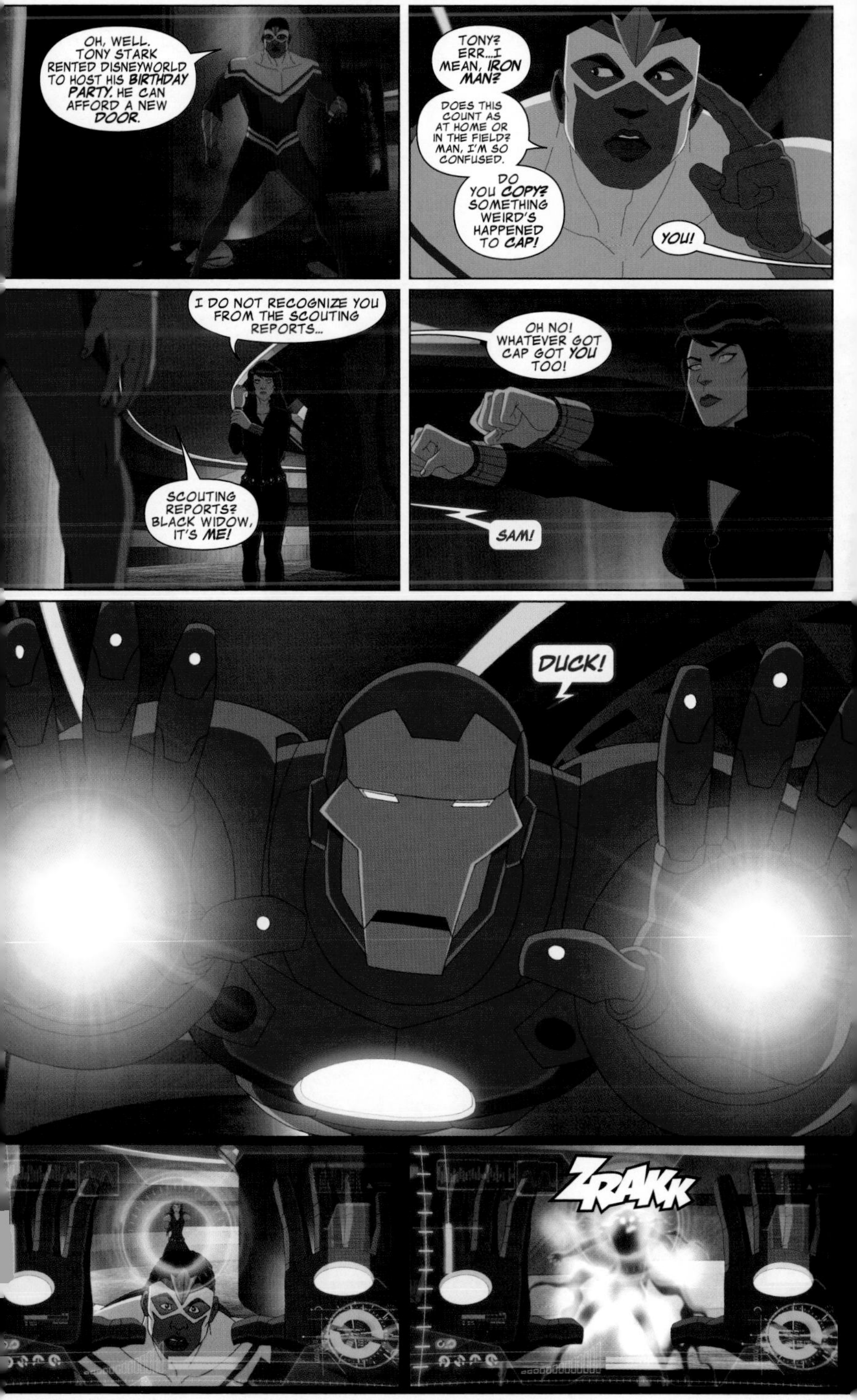

OH, WELL. TONY STARK RENTED DISNEYWORLD TO HOST HIS BIRTHDAY PARTY. HE CAN AFFORD A NEW DOOR.
TONY? ERR...I MEAN, IRON MAN?
DOES THIS COUNT AS AT HOME OR IN THE FIELD? MAN, I'M SO CONFUSED.
DO YOU COPY? SOMETHING WEIRD'S HAPPENED TO CAP!
YOU!
I DO NOT RECOGNIZE YOU FROM THE SCOUTING REPORTS...
SCOUTING REPORTS? BLACK WIDOW, IT'S ME!
OH NO! WHATEVER GOT CAP GOT YOU TOO!
SAM!
DUCK!
ZRAKK

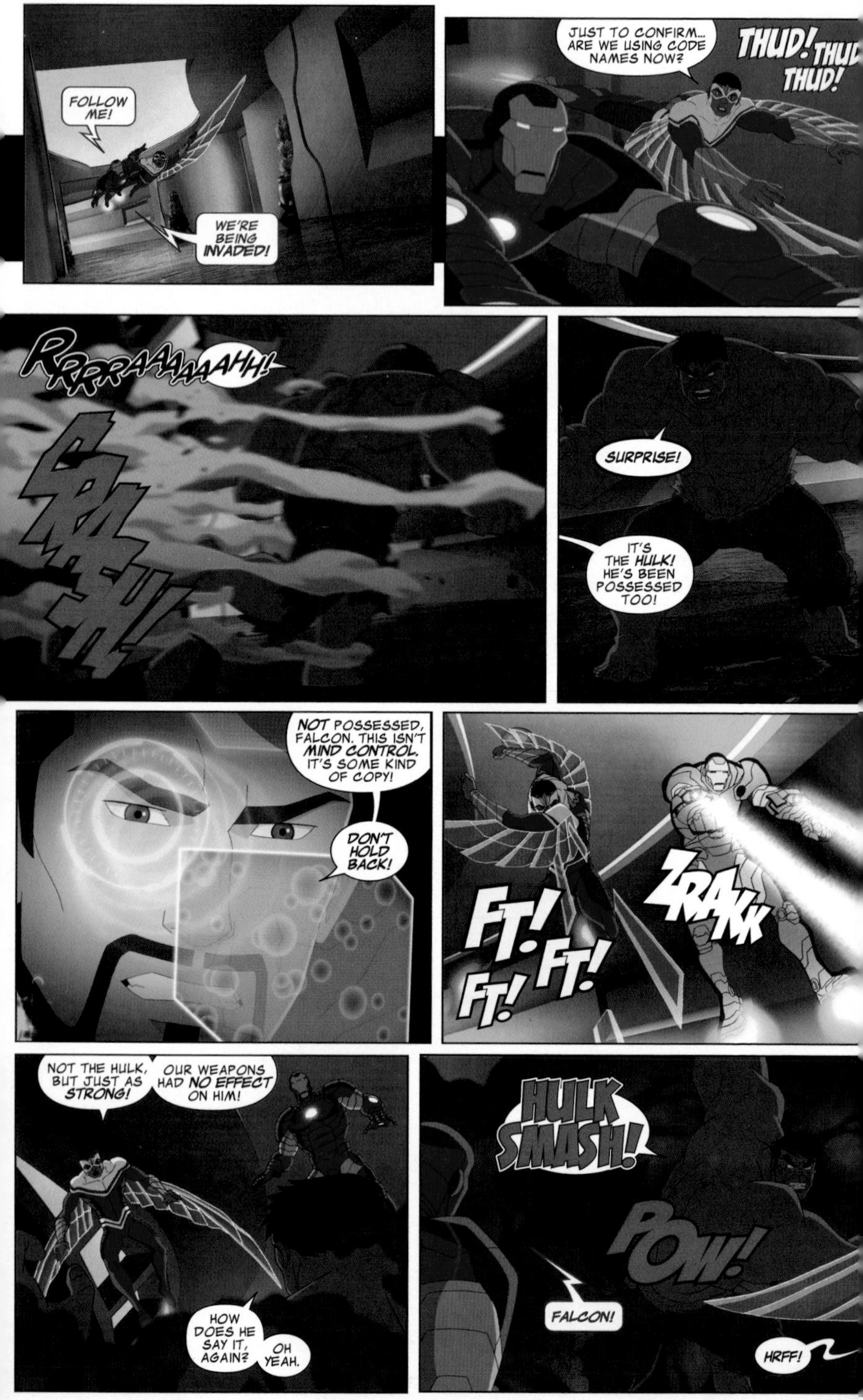
FOLLOW ME!
WE'RE BEING INVADED!
JUST TO CONFIRM... ARE WE USING CODE NAMES NOW?
THUD! THUD THUD!
RRRRAAAAAAAHH!
SURPRISE!
IT'S THE HULK! HE'S BEEN POSSESSED TOO!
NOT POSSESSED, FALCON. THIS ISN'T MIND CONTROL. IT'S SOME KIND OF COPY!
DON'T HOLD BACK!
FT! FT! FT!
ZRAKK
NOT THE HULK, BUT JUST AS STRONG!
OUR WEAPONS HAD NO EFFECT ON HIM!
HOW DOES HE SAY IT, AGAIN?
OH YEAH.
HULK SMASH!
POW!
FALCON!
HRFF!

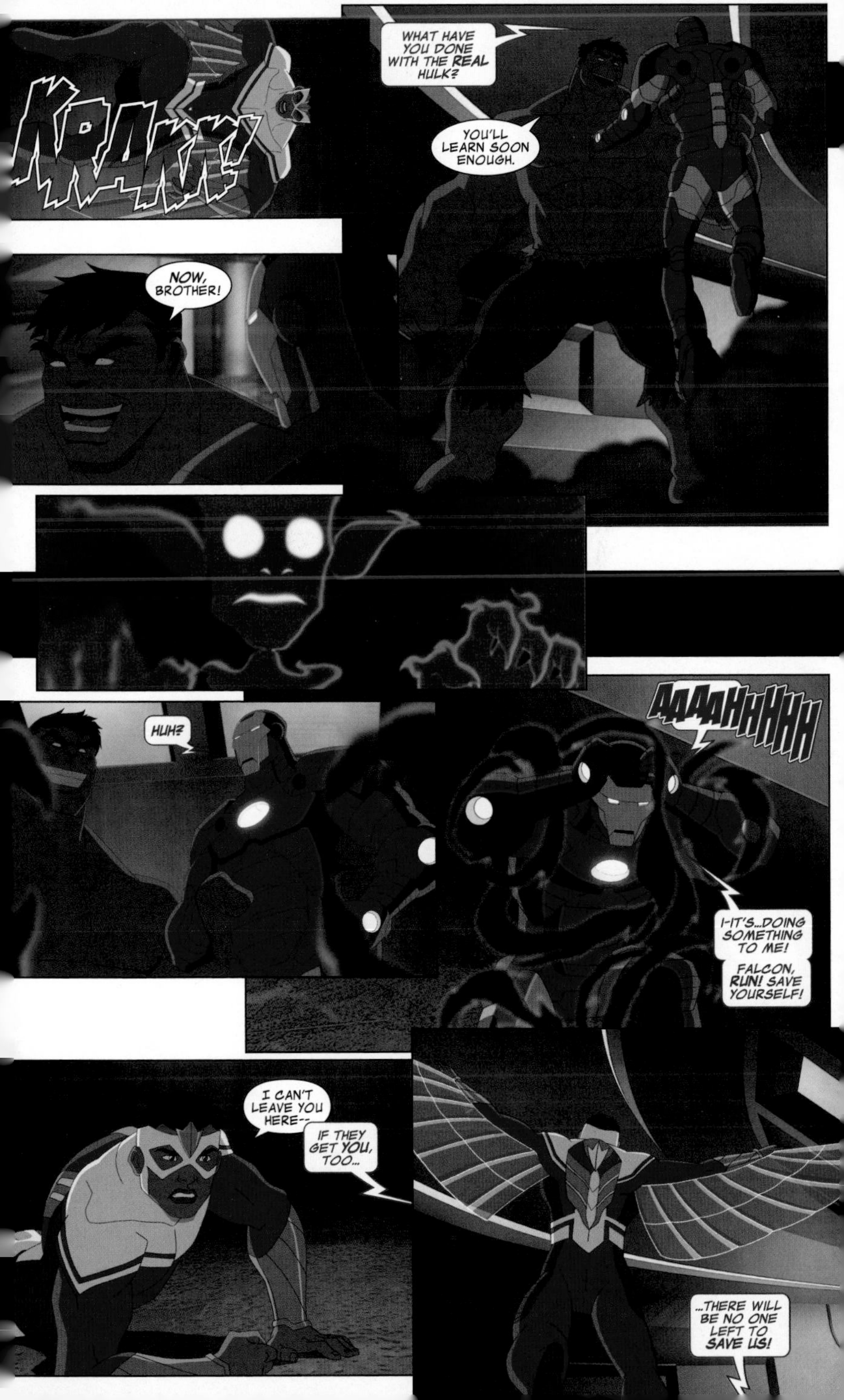

KRAKK!
WHAT HAVE YOU DONE WITH THE REAL HULK?
YOU'LL LEARN SOON ENOUGH.
NOW, BROTHER!
HUH?
AAAAHHHHH
I-IT'S...DOING SOMETHING TO ME!
FALCON, RUN! SAVE YOURSELF!
I CAN'T LEAVE YOU HERE--
IF THEY GET YOU, TOO...
...THERE WILL BE NO ONE LEFT TO SAVE US!

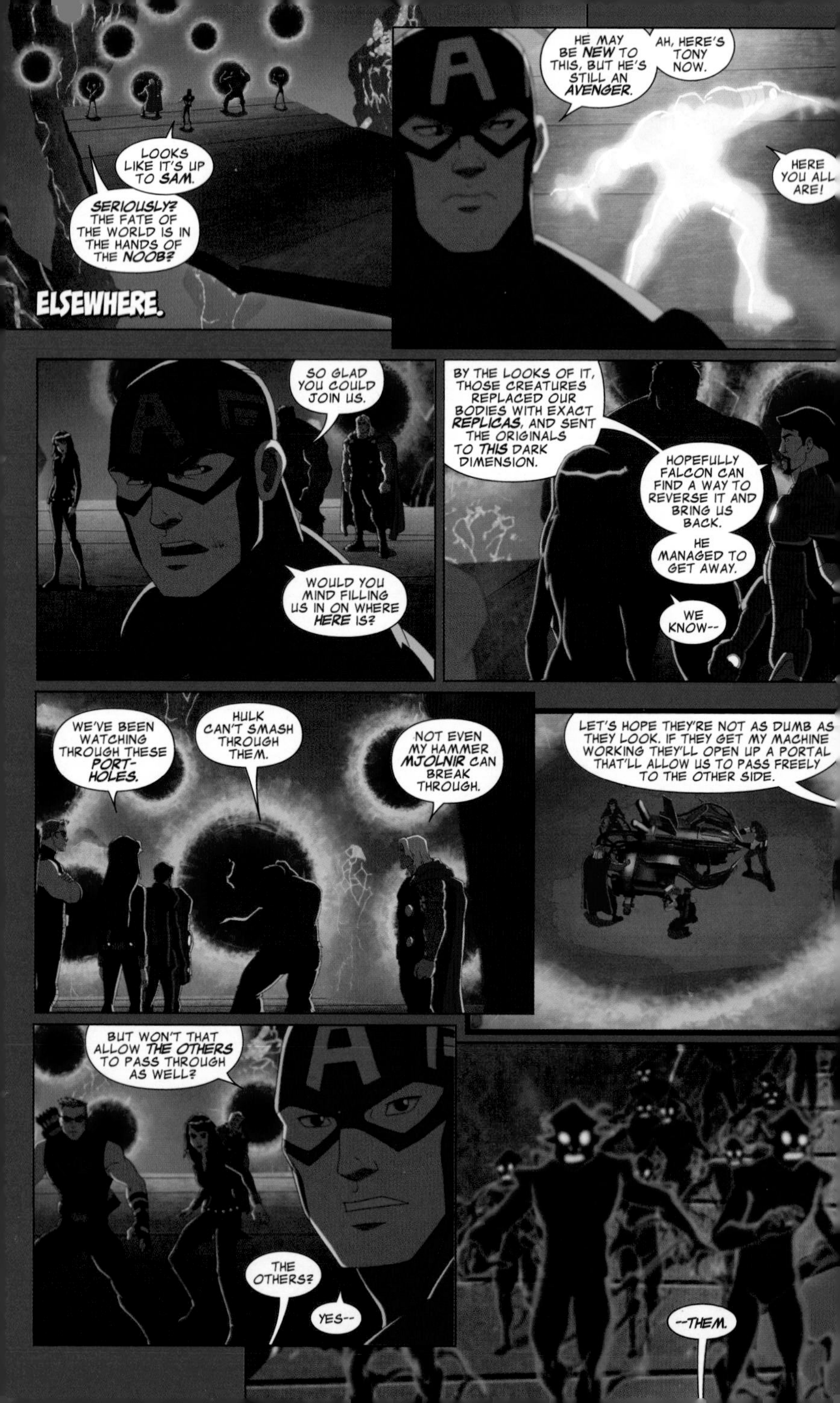
LOOKS LIKE IT'S UP TO SAM.
SERIOUSLY? THE FATE OF THE WORLD IS IN THE HANDS OF THE NOOB?
ELSEWHERE.
HE MAY BE NEW TO THIS, BUT HE'S STILL AN AVENGER.
AH, HERE'S TONY NOW.
HERE YOU ALL ARE!
SO GLAD YOU COULD JOIN US.
WOULD YOU MIND FILLING US IN ON WHERE HERE IS?
BY THE LOOKS OF IT, THOSE CREATURES REPLACED OUR BODIES WITH EXACT REPLICAS, AND SENT THE ORIGINALS TO THIS DARK DIMENSION.
HOPEFULLY FALCON CAN FIND A WAY TO REVERSE IT AND BRING US BACK.
HE MANAGED TO GET AWAY.
WE KNOW--
WE'VE BEEN WATCHING THROUGH THESE PORT-HOLES.
HULK CAN'T SMASH THROUGH THEM.
NOT EVEN MY HAMMER MJOLNIR CAN BREAK THROUGH.
LET'S HOPE THEY'RE NOT AS DUMB AS THEY LOOK. IF THEY GET MY MACHINE WORKING THEY'LL OPEN UP A PORTAL THAT'LL ALLOW US TO PASS FREELY TO THE OTHER SIDE.
BUT WON'T THAT ALLOW THE OTHERS TO PASS THROUGH AS WELL?
THE OTHERS?
YES--
--THEM.

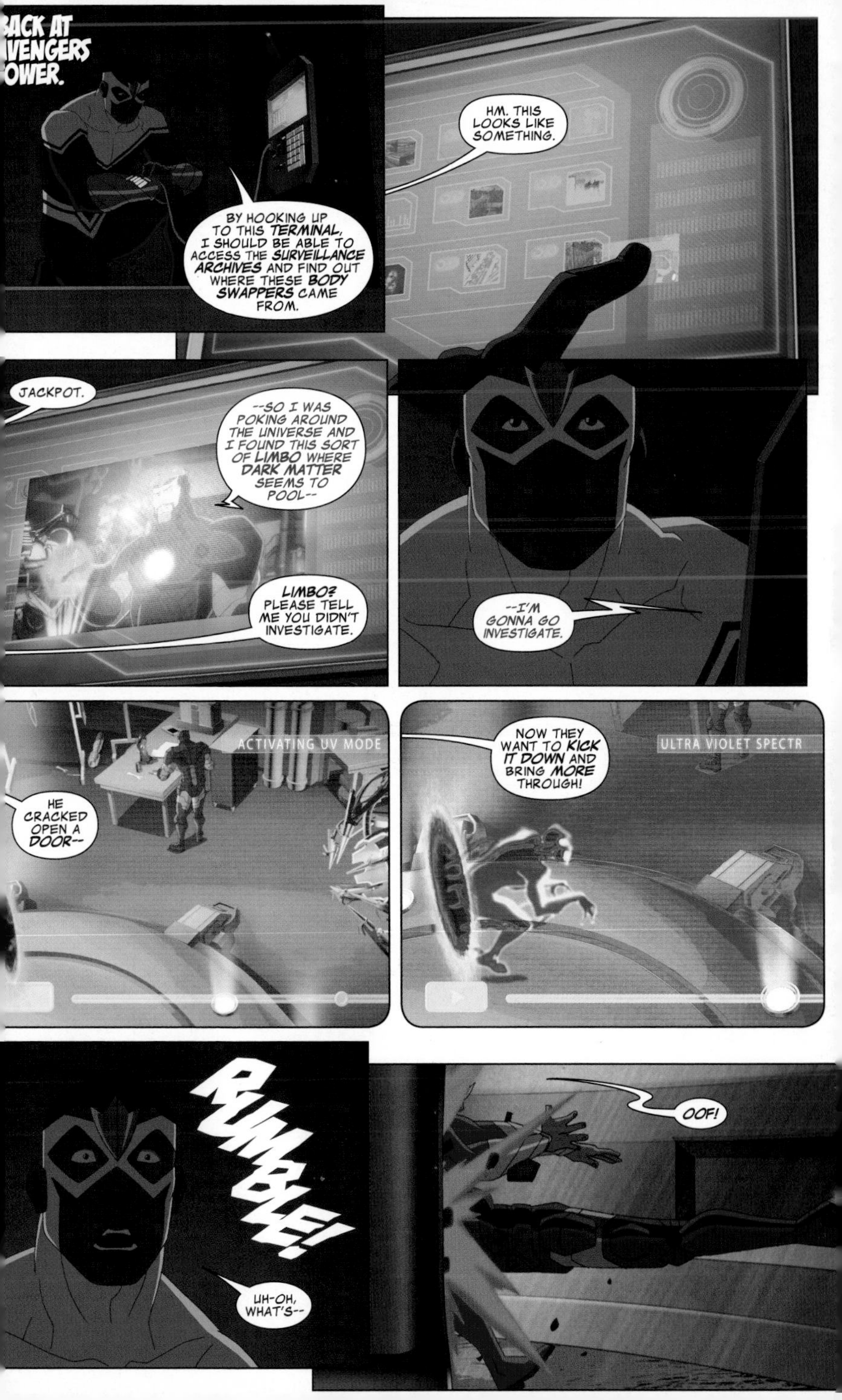

BACK AT AVENGERS TOWER.
BY HOOKING UP TO THIS TERMINAL, I SHOULD BE ABLE TO ACCESS THE SURVEILLANCE ARCHIVES AND FIND OUT WHERE THESE BODY SWAPPERS CAME FROM.
HM. THIS LOOKS LIKE SOMETHING.
JACKPOT.
--SO I WAS POKING AROUND THE UNIVERSE AND I FOUND THIS SORT OF LIMBO WHERE DARK MATTER SEEMS TO POOL--
LIMBO? PLEASE TELL ME YOU DIDN'T INVESTIGATE.
--I'M GONNA GO INVESTIGATE.
ACTIVATING UV MODE
HE CRACKED OPEN A DOOR--
ULTRA VIOLET SPECTR
NOW THEY WANT TO KICK IT DOWN AND BRING MORE THROUGH!
RUMBLE!
UH-OH, WHAT'S--
OOF!

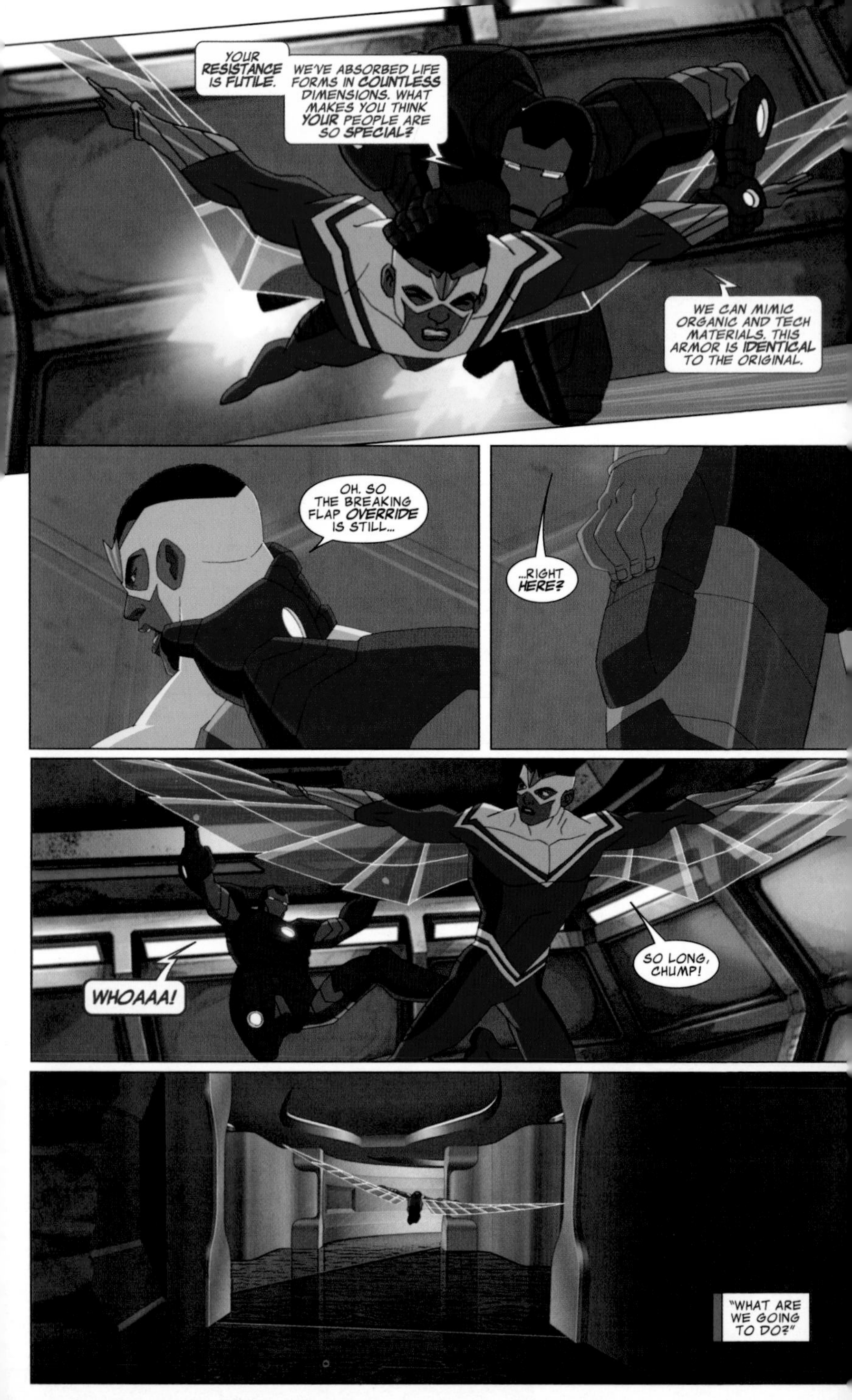

YOUR RESISTANCE IS FUTILE.
WE'VE ABSORBED LIFE FORMS IN COUNTLESS DIMENSIONS. WHAT MAKES YOU THINK YOUR PEOPLE ARE SO SPECIAL?
WE CAN MIMIC ORGANIC AND TECH MATERIALS. THIS ARMOR IS IDENTICAL TO THE ORIGINAL.
OH. SO THE BREAKING FLAP OVERRIDE IS STILL...
...RIGHT HERE?
WHOAAA!
SO LONG, CHUMP!
"WHAT ARE WE GOING TO DO?"

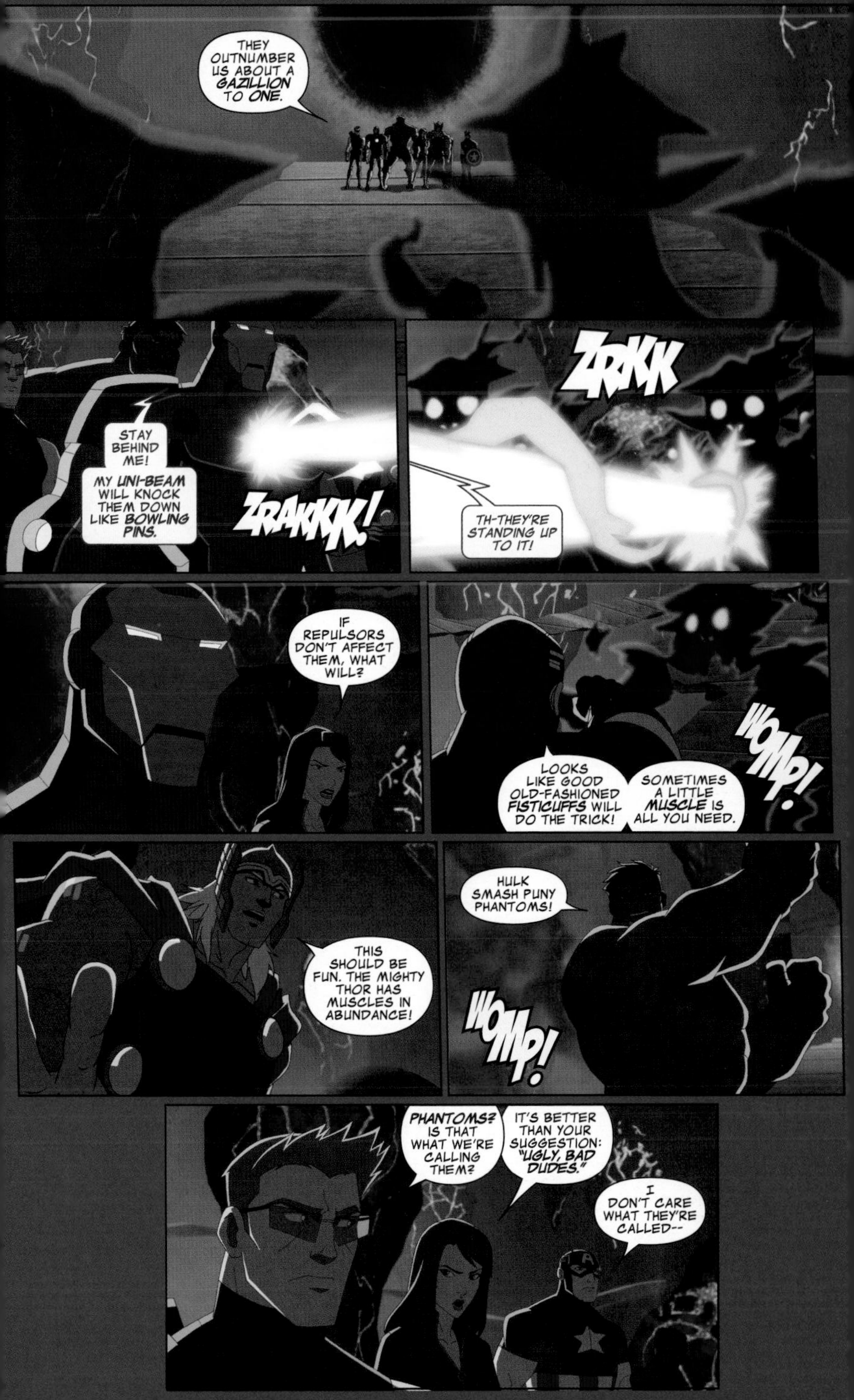
THEY OUTNUMBER US ABOUT A GAZILLION TO ONE.
STAY BEHIND ME!
MY UNI-BEAM WILL KNOCK THEM DOWN LIKE BOWLING PINS.
ZRAKKKK!
ZRKKK
TH-THEY'RE STANDING UP TO IT!
IF REPULSORS DON'T AFFECT THEM, WHAT WILL?
LOOKS LIKE GOOD OLD-FASHIONED FISTICUFFS WILL DO THE TRICK!
SOMETIMES A LITTLE MUSCLE IS ALL YOU NEED.
WOMP!
THIS SHOULD BE FUN. THE MIGHTY THOR HAS MUSCLES IN ABUNDANCE!
HULK SMASH PUNY PHANTOMS!
WOMP!
PHANTOMS? IS THAT WHAT WE'RE CALLING THEM?
IT'S BETTER THAN YOUR SUGGESTION: "UGLY, BAD DUDES."
I DON'T CARE WHAT THEY'RE CALLED--

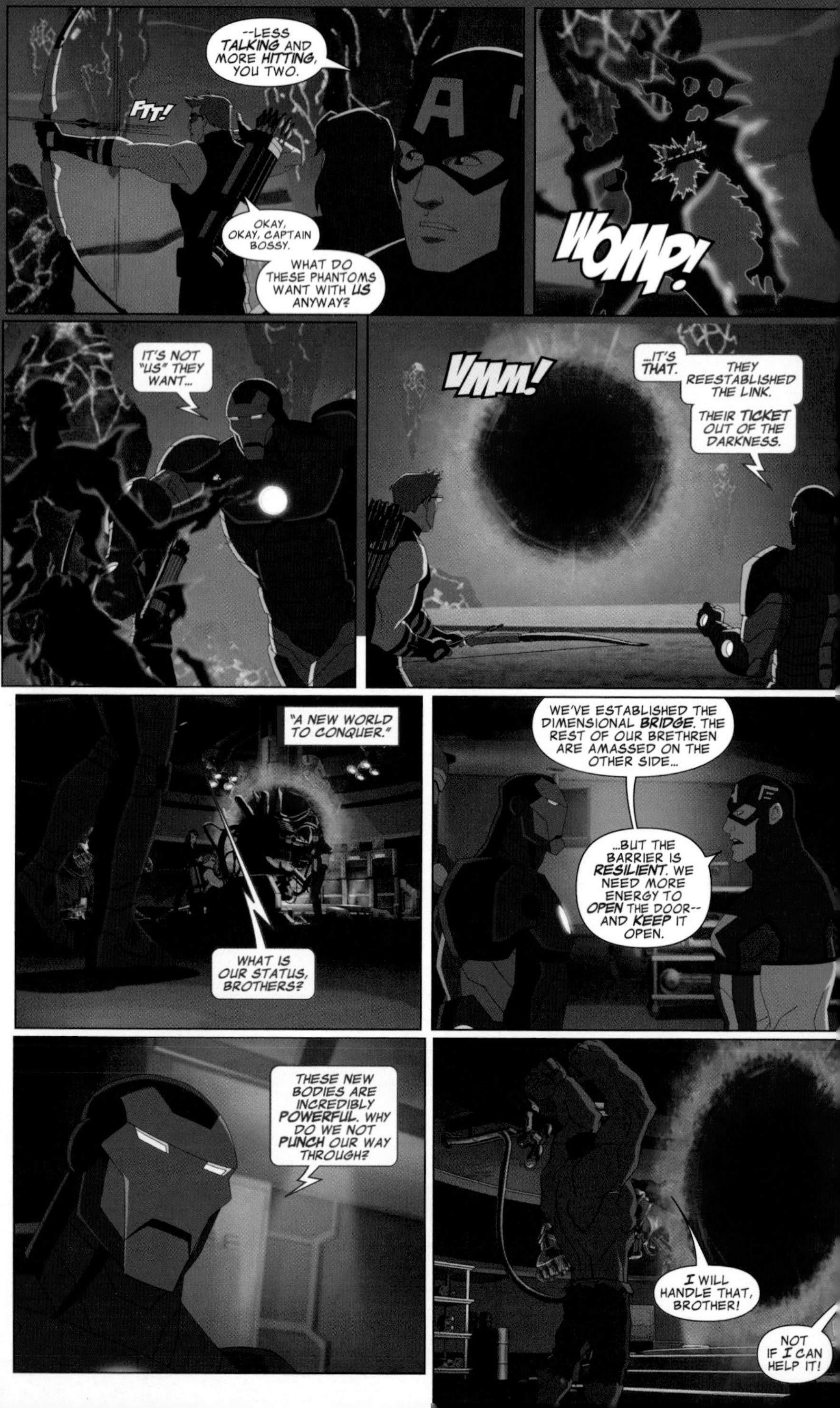
--LESS TALKING AND MORE HITTING, YOU TWO.
FTT!
OKAY, OKAY, CAPTAIN BOSSY.
WHAT DO THESE PHANTOMS WANT WITH US ANYWAY?
WOMP!
IT'S NOT "US" THEY WANT...
VMM!
...IT'S THAT.
THEY REESTABLISHED THE LINK.
THEIR TICKET OUT OF THE DARKNESS.
"A NEW WORLD TO CONQUER."
WHAT IS OUR STATUS, BROTHERS?
WE'VE ESTABLISHED THE DIMENSIONAL BRIDGE. THE REST OF OUR BRETHREN ARE AMASSED ON THE OTHER SIDE...
...BUT THE BARRIER IS RESILIENT. WE NEED MORE ENERGY TO OPEN THE DOOR--AND KEEP IT OPEN.
THESE NEW BODIES ARE INCREDIBLY POWERFUL. WHY DO WE NOT PUNCH OUR WAY THROUGH?
I WILL HANDLE THAT, BROTHER!
NOT IF I CAN HELP IT!

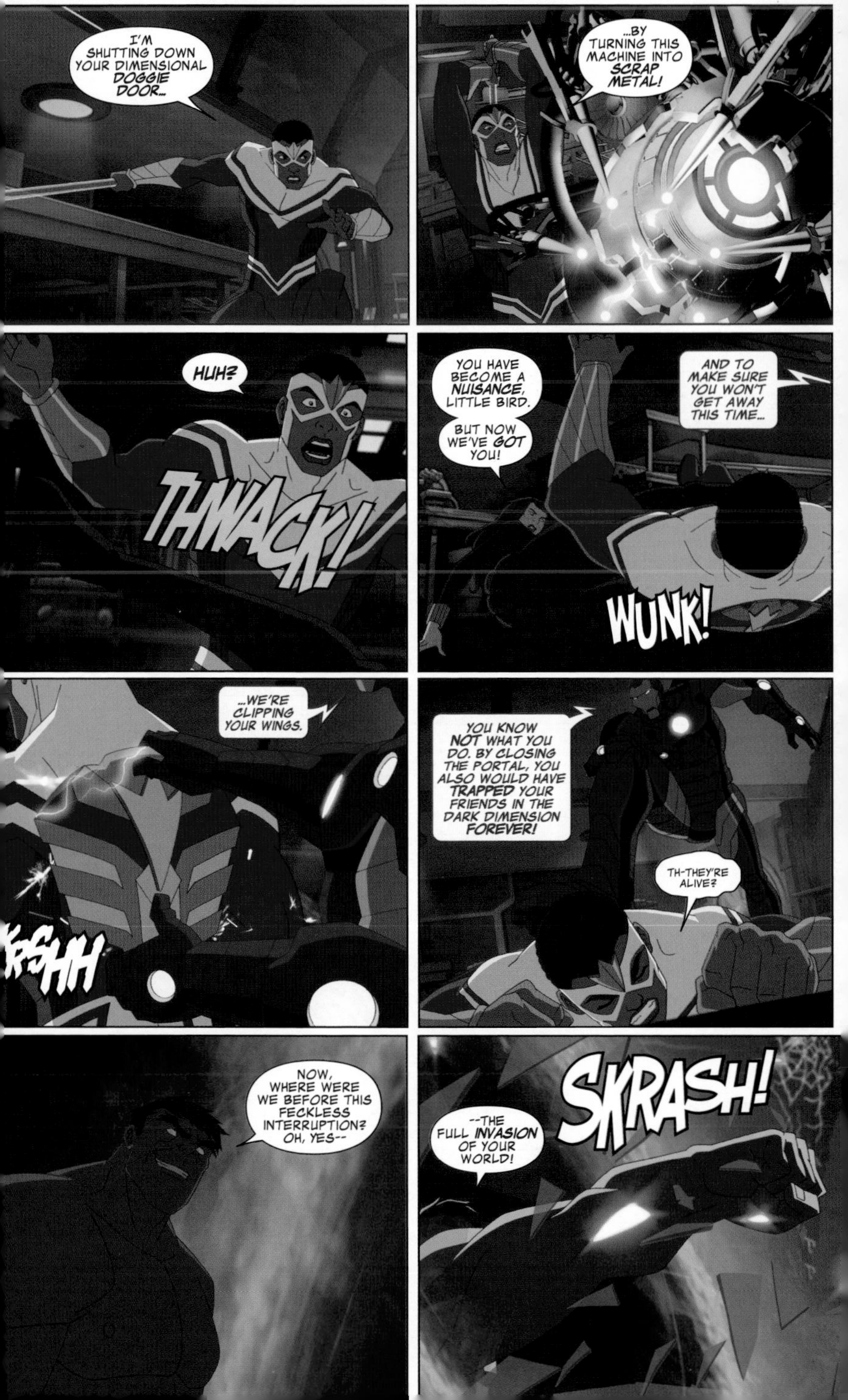
I'M SHUTTING DOWN YOUR DIMENSIONAL DOGGIE DOOR...
...BY TURNING THIS MACHINE INTO SCRAP METAL!
HUH?
THWACK!
YOU HAVE BECOME A NUISANCE, LITTLE BIRD.
BUT NOW WE'VE GOT YOU!
AND TO MAKE SURE YOU WON'T GET AWAY THIS TIME...
WUNK!
...WE'RE CLIPPING YOUR WINGS.
KRSHH
YOU KNOW NOT WHAT YOU DO. BY CLOSING THE PORTAL, YOU ALSO WOULD HAVE TRAPPED YOUR FRIENDS IN THE DARK DIMENSION FOREVER!
TH-THEY'RE ALIVE?
NOW, WHERE WERE WE BEFORE THIS FECKLESS INTERRUPTION? OH, YES--
SKRASH!
--THE FULL INVASION OF YOUR WORLD!

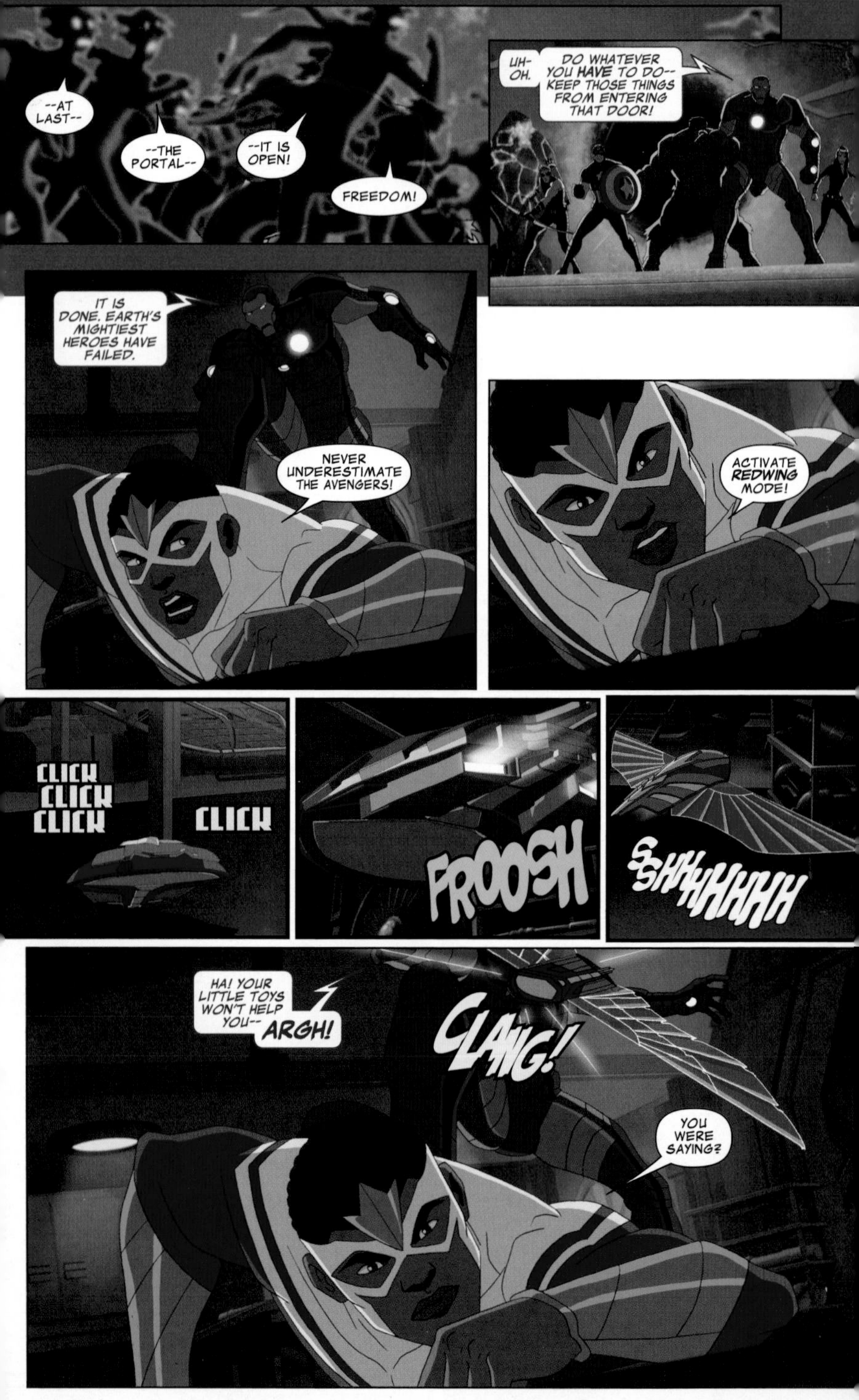
--AT LAST--
--THE PORTAL--
--IT IS OPEN!
FREEDOM!
UH-OH.
DO WHATEVER YOU HAVE TO DO-- KEEP THOSE THINGS FROM ENTERING THAT DOOR!
IT IS DONE. EARTH'S MIGHTIEST HEROES HAVE FAILED.
NEVER UNDERESTIMATE THE AVENGERS!
ACTIVATE REDWING MODE!
CLICK CLICK CLICK
CLICK
FROOSH
SSHHHHHHH
HA! YOUR LITTLE TOYS WON'T HELP YOU-- ARGH!
CLANG!
YOU WERE SAYING?

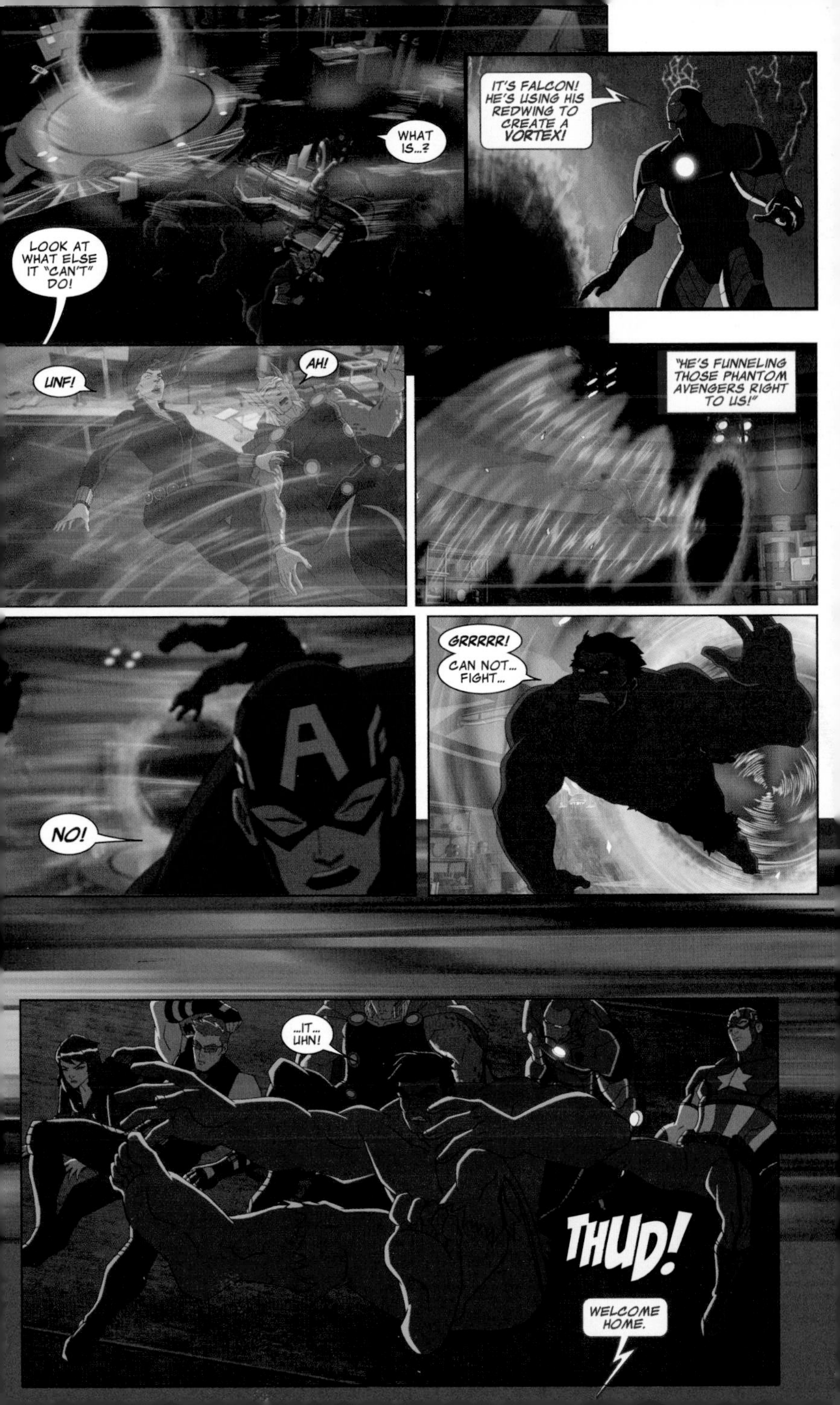
WHAT IS...?
IT'S FALCON! HE'S USING HIS REDWING TO CREATE A VORTEX!
LOOK AT WHAT ELSE IT "CAN'T" DO!
UNF!
AH!
"HE'S FUNNELING THOSE PHANTOM AVENGERS RIGHT TO US!"
NO!
GRRRRR!
CAN NOT... FIGHT...
...IT... UHN!
THUD!
WELCOME HOME.

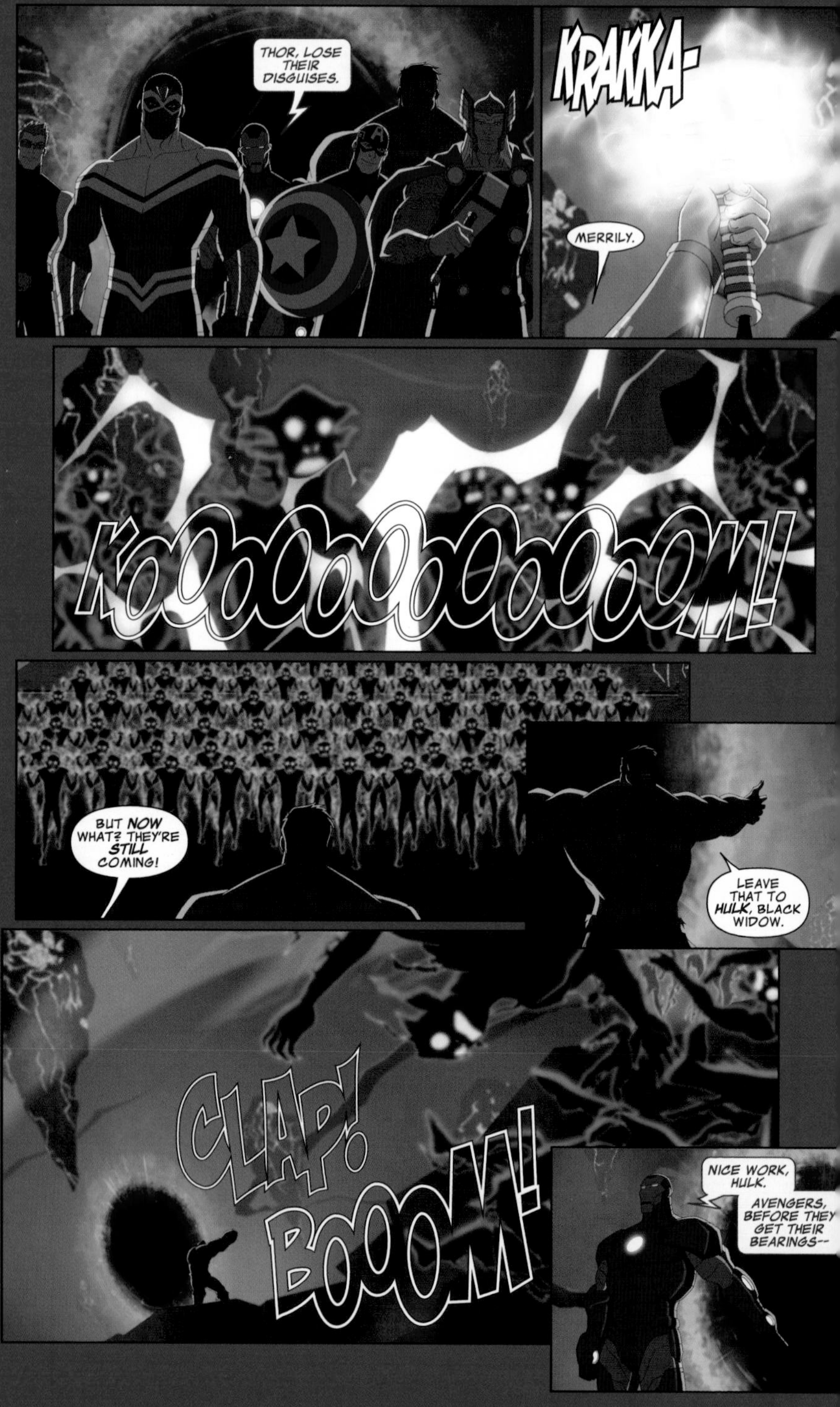
THOR, LOSE THEIR DISGUISES.
KRAKKA-
MERRILY.
KOOOOOOOOOOOOOM!
BUT NOW WHAT? THEY'RE STILL COMING!
LEAVE THAT TO HULK, BLACK WIDOW.
CLAP!
BOOOOM!
NICE WORK, HULK.
AVENGERS, BEFORE THEY GET THEIR BEARINGS--

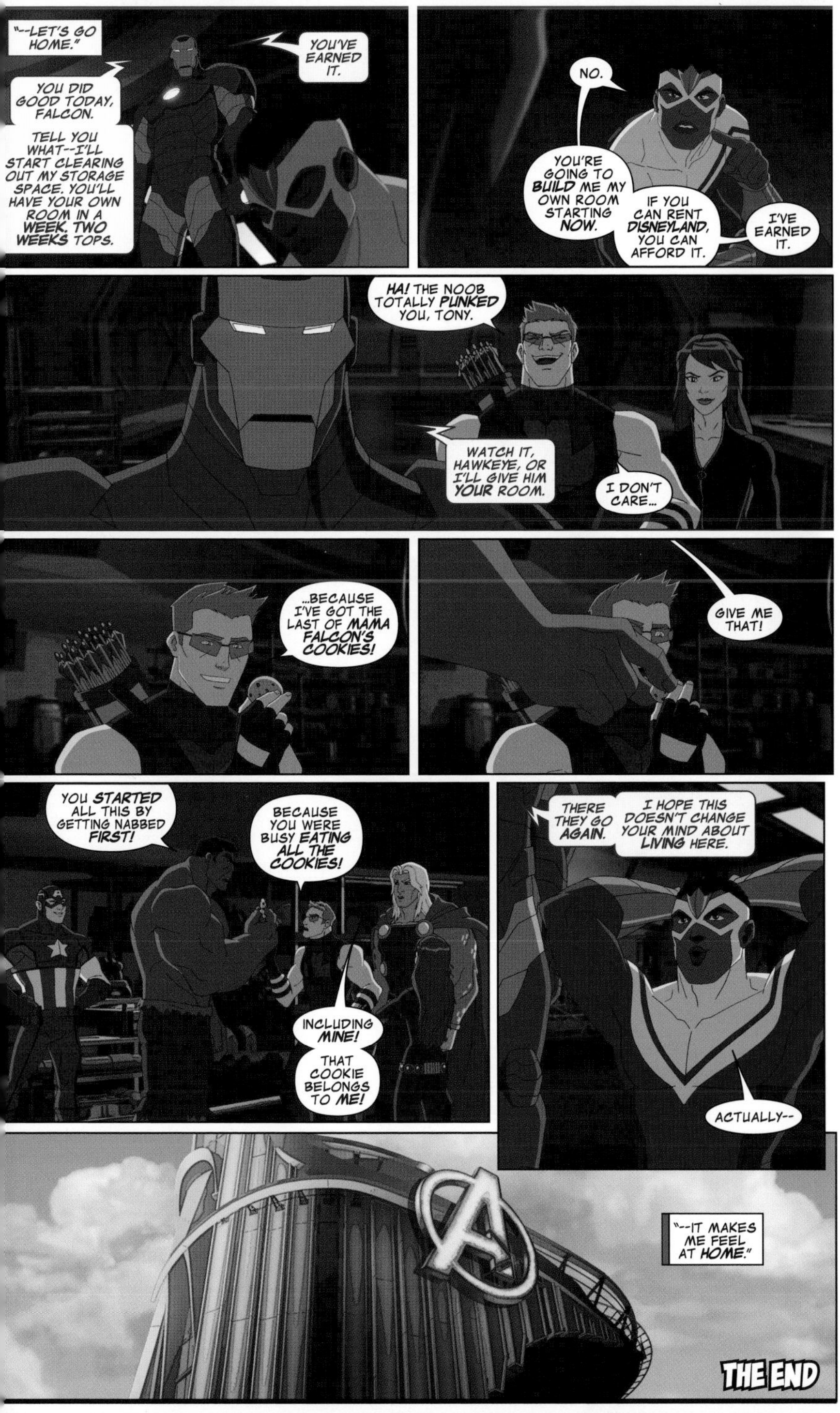
"--LET'S GO HOME."
YOU'VE EARNED IT.
YOU DID GOOD TODAY, FALCON.
TELL YOU WHAT--I'LL START CLEARING OUT MY STORAGE SPACE. YOU'LL HAVE YOUR OWN ROOM IN A WEEK. TWO WEEKS TOPS.
NO.
YOU'RE GOING TO BUILD ME MY OWN ROOM STARTING NOW.
IF YOU CAN RENT DISNEYLAND, YOU CAN AFFORD IT.
I'VE EARNED IT.
HA! THE NOOB TOTALLY PUNKED YOU, TONY.
WATCH IT, HAWKEYE, OR I'LL GIVE HIM YOUR ROOM.
I DON'T CARE...
...BECAUSE I'VE GOT THE LAST OF MAMA FALCON'S COOKIES!
GIVE ME THAT!
YOU STARTED ALL THIS BY GETTING NABBED FIRST!
BECAUSE YOU WERE BUSY EATING ALL THE COOKIES!
INCLUDING MINE!
THAT COOKIE BELONGS TO ME!
THERE THEY GO AGAIN.
I HOPE THIS DOESN'T CHANGE YOUR MIND ABOUT LIVING HERE.
ACTUALLY--
"--IT MAKES ME FEEL AT HOME."
THE END

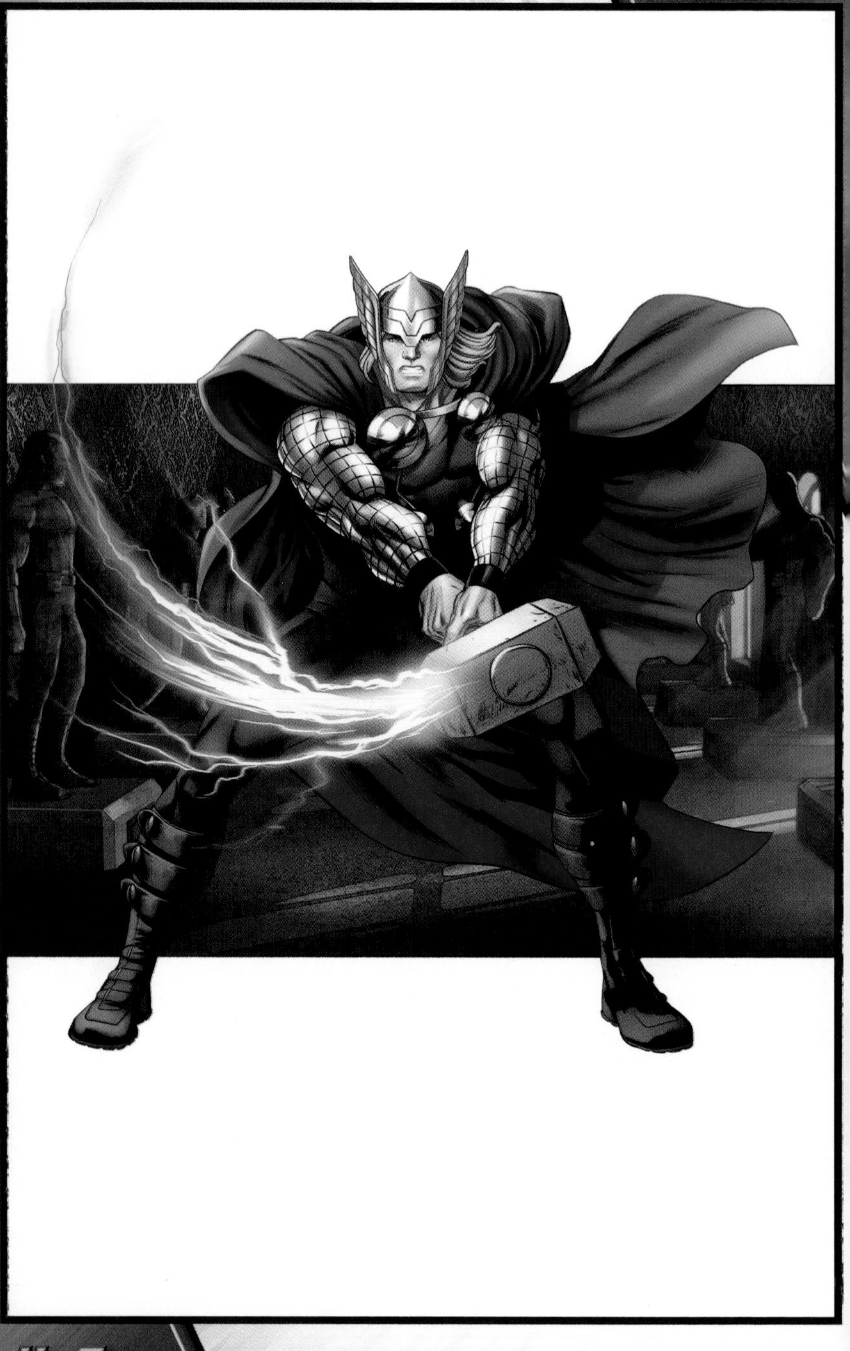

#4 BASED ON "THE SERPENT OF DOOM"

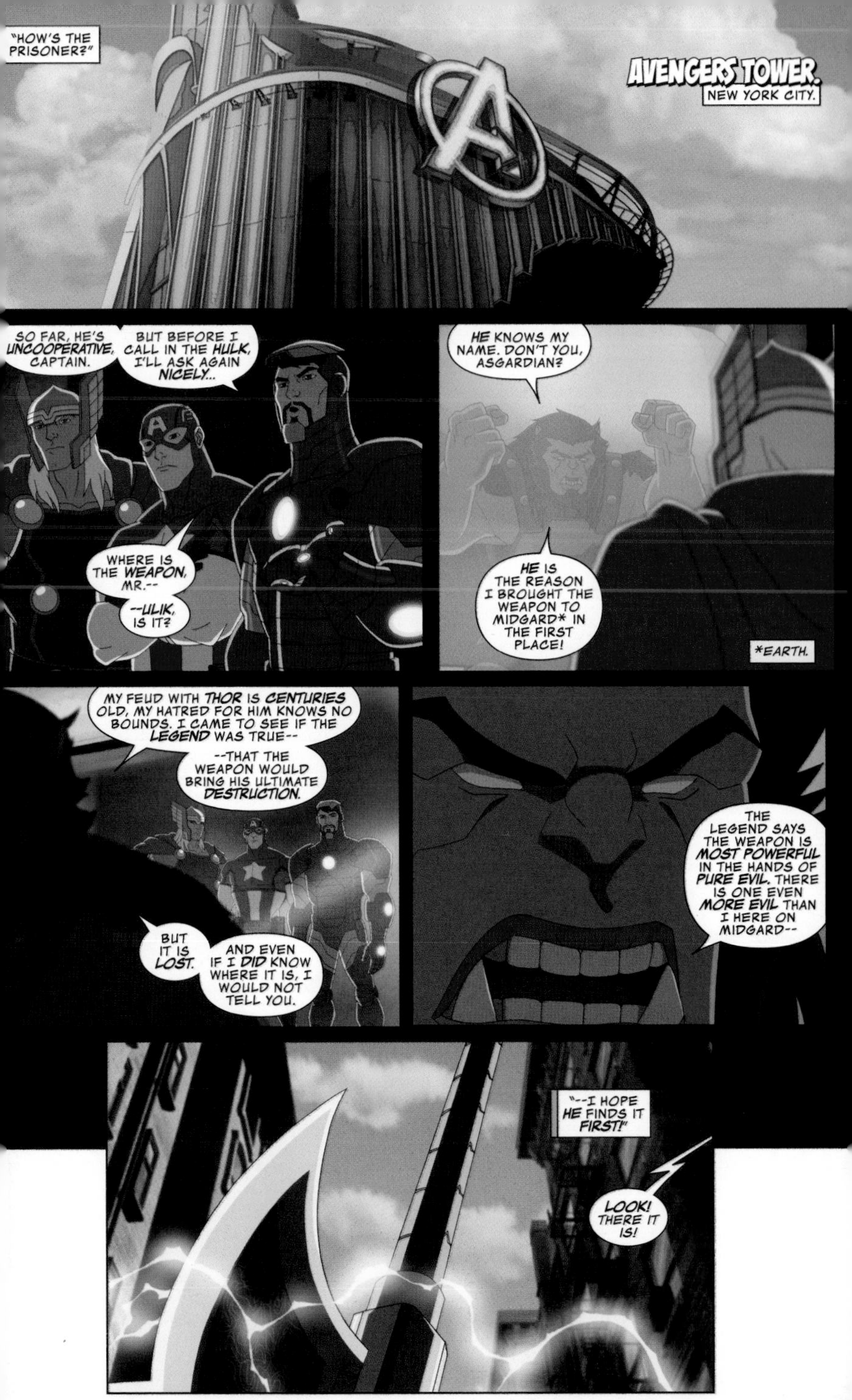
"HOW'S THE PRISONER?"
AVENGERS TOWER.
NEW YORK CITY.
SO FAR, HE'S UNCOOPERATIVE, CAPTAIN.
BUT BEFORE I CALL IN THE HULK, I'LL ASK AGAIN NICELY...
WHERE IS THE WEAPON, MR.--
--ULIK, IS IT?
HE KNOWS MY NAME. DON'T YOU, ASGARDIAN?
HE IS THE REASON I BROUGHT THE WEAPON TO MIDGARD* IN THE FIRST PLACE!
*EARTH.
MY FEUD WITH THOR IS CENTURIES OLD, MY HATRED FOR HIM KNOWS NO BOUNDS. I CAME TO SEE IF THE LEGEND WAS TRUE--
--THAT THE WEAPON WOULD BRING HIS ULTIMATE DESTRUCTION.
BUT IT IS LOST.
AND EVEN IF I DID KNOW WHERE IT IS, I WOULD NOT TELL YOU.
THE LEGEND SAYS THE WEAPON IS MOST POWERFUL IN THE HANDS OF PURE EVIL. THERE IS ONE EVEN MORE EVIL THAN I HERE ON MIDGARD--
"--I HOPE HE FINDS IT FIRST!"
LOOK! THERE IT IS!

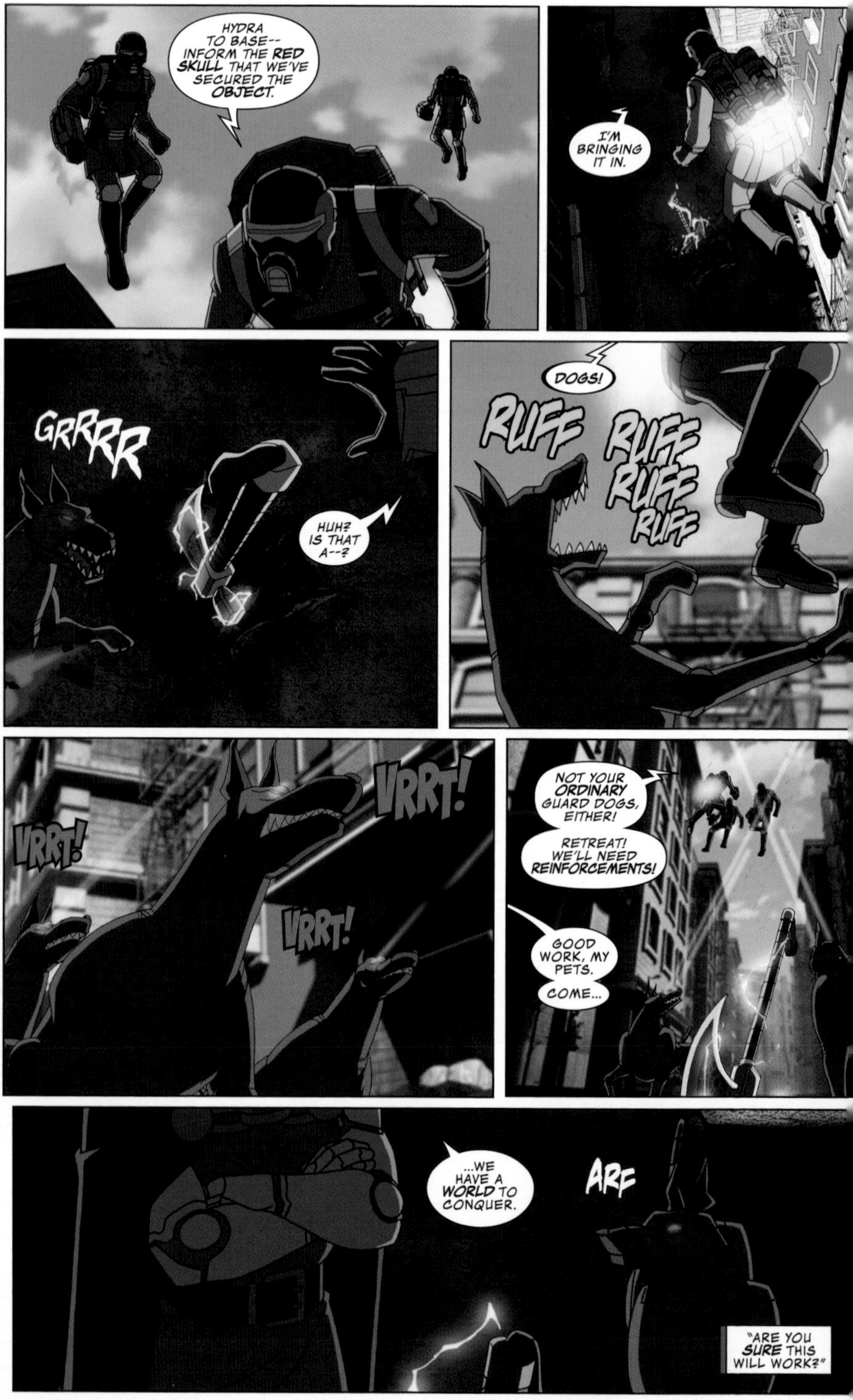

HYDRA TO BASE-- INFORM THE RED SKULL THAT WE'VE SECURED THE OBJECT.
I'M BRINGING IT IN.
GRRRR
HUH? IS THAT A--?
DOGS!
RUFF
RUFF RUFF RUFF
VRRT!
VRRT!
VRRT!
NOT YOUR ORDINARY GUARD DOGS, EITHER!
RETREAT! WE'LL NEED REINFORCEMENTS!
GOOD WORK, MY PETS.
COME...
...WE HAVE A WORLD TO CONQUER.
ARF
"ARE YOU SURE THIS WILL WORK?"

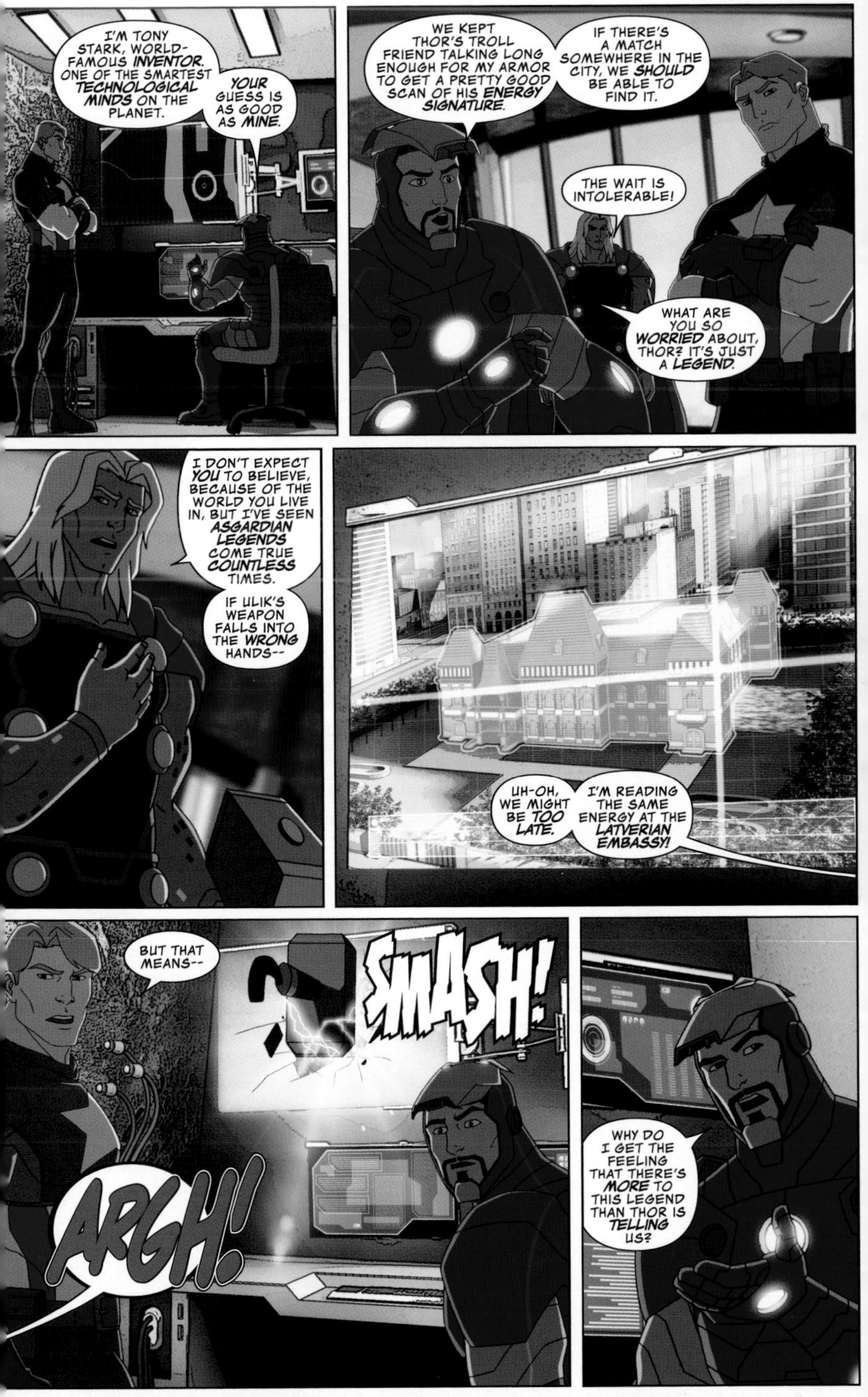
I'M TONY STARK, WORLD-FAMOUS INVENTOR. ONE OF THE SMARTEST TECHNOLOGICAL MINDS ON THE PLANET.
YOUR GUESS IS AS GOOD AS MINE.
WE KEPT THOR'S TROLL FRIEND TALKING LONG ENOUGH FOR MY ARMOR TO GET A PRETTY GOOD SCAN OF HIS ENERGY SIGNATURE.
IF THERE'S A MATCH SOMEWHERE IN THE CITY, WE SHOULD BE ABLE TO FIND IT.
THE WAIT IS INTOLERABLE!
WHAT ARE YOU SO WORRIED ABOUT, THOR? IT'S JUST A LEGEND.
I DON'T EXPECT YOU TO BELIEVE, BECAUSE OF THE WORLD YOU LIVE IN, BUT I'VE SEEN ASGARDIAN LEGENDS COME TRUE COUNTLESS TIMES.
IF ULIK'S WEAPON FALLS INTO THE WRONG HANDS--
I'M READING THE SAME ENERGY AT THE LATVERIAN EMBASSY!
UH-OH, WE MIGHT BE TOO LATE.
BUT THAT MEANS--
SMASH!
ARGH!
WHY DO I GET THE FEELING THAT THERE'S MORE TO THIS LEGEND THAN THOR IS TELLING US?

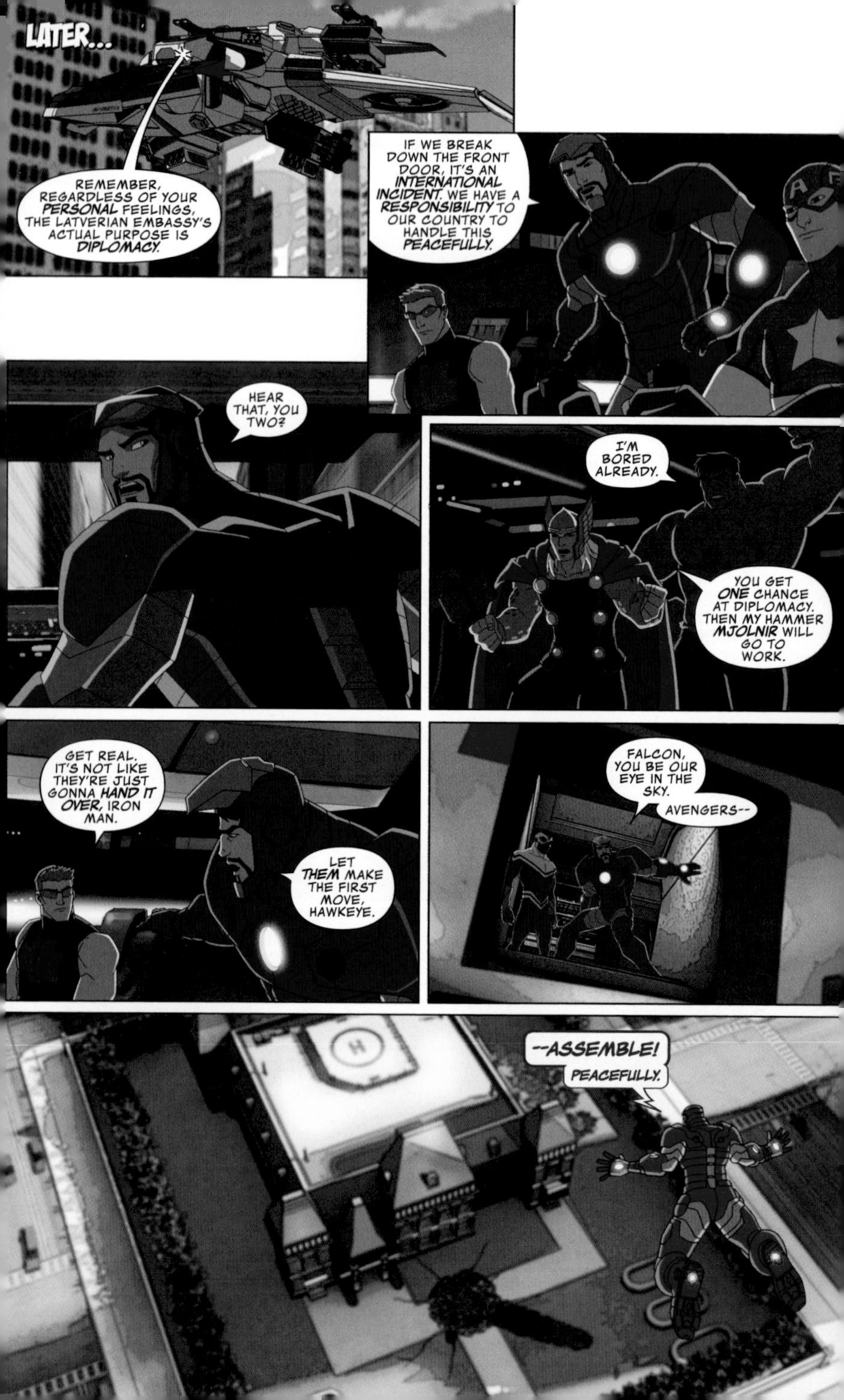
LATER...
REMEMBER, REGARDLESS OF YOUR PERSONAL FEELINGS, THE LATVERIAN EMBASSY'S ACTUAL PURPOSE IS DIPLOMACY.
IF WE BREAK DOWN THE FRONT DOOR, IT'S AN INTERNATIONAL INCIDENT. WE HAVE A RESPONSIBILITY TO OUR COUNTRY TO HANDLE THIS PEACEFULLY.
HEAR THAT, YOU TWO?
I'M BORED ALREADY.
YOU GET ONE CHANCE AT DIPLOMACY. THEN MY HAMMER MJOLNIR WILL GO TO WORK.
GET REAL. IT'S NOT LIKE THEY'RE JUST GONNA HAND IT OVER, IRON MAN.
LET THEM MAKE THE FIRST MOVE, HAWKEYE.
FALCON, YOU BE OUR EYE IN THE SKY.
AVENGERS--
--ASSEMBLE!
PEACEFULLY.

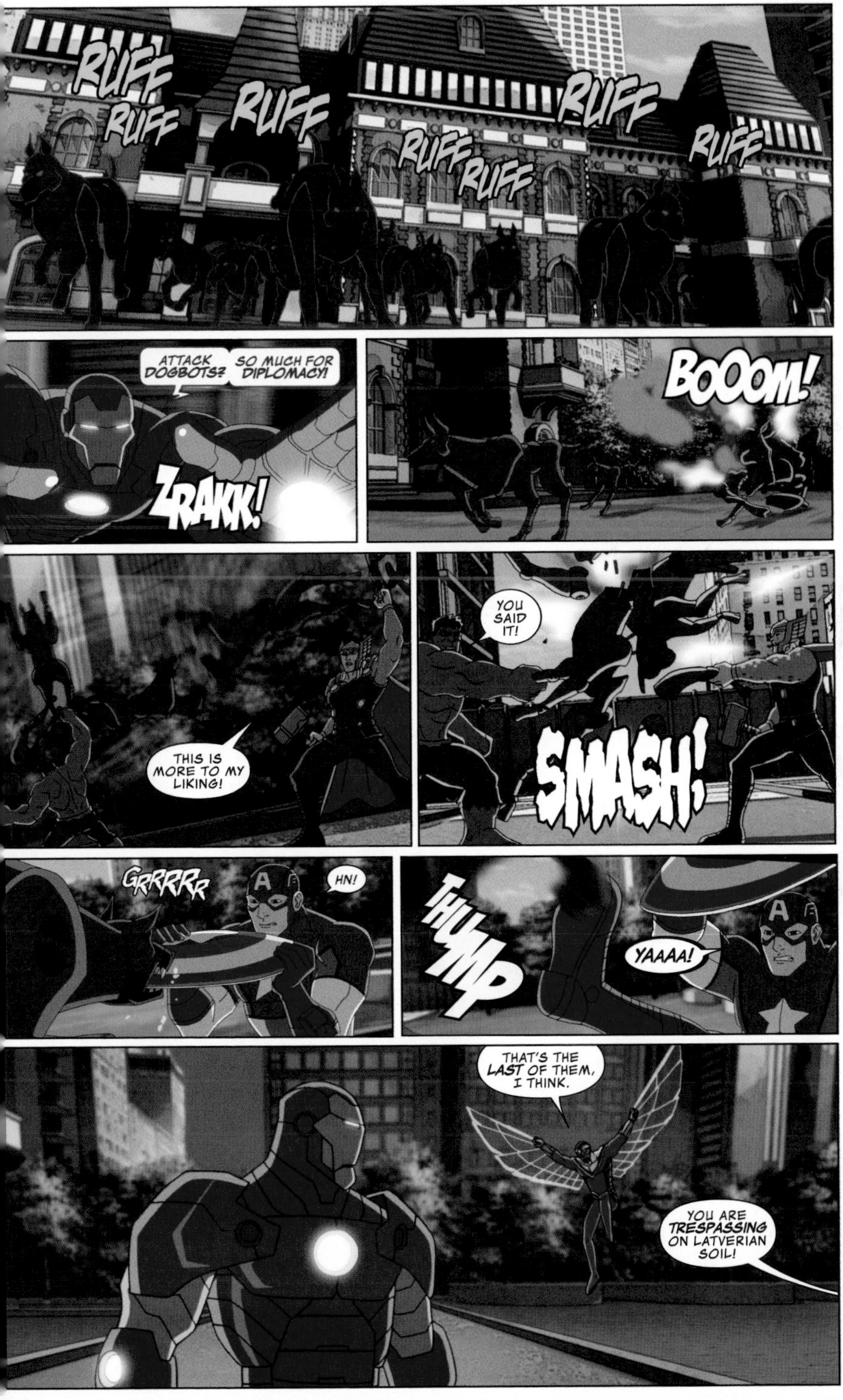
RUFF RUFF
RUFF
RUFF RUFF
RUFF
RUFF
ATTACK DOGBOTS?
SO MUCH FOR DIPLOMACY!
ZRAKK!
BOOOM!
THIS IS MORE TO MY LIKING!
YOU SAID IT!
SMASH!
GRRRRR
HN!
THUMP
YAAAA!
THAT'S THE LAST OF THEM, I THINK.
YOU ARE TRESPASSING ON LATVERIAN SOIL!

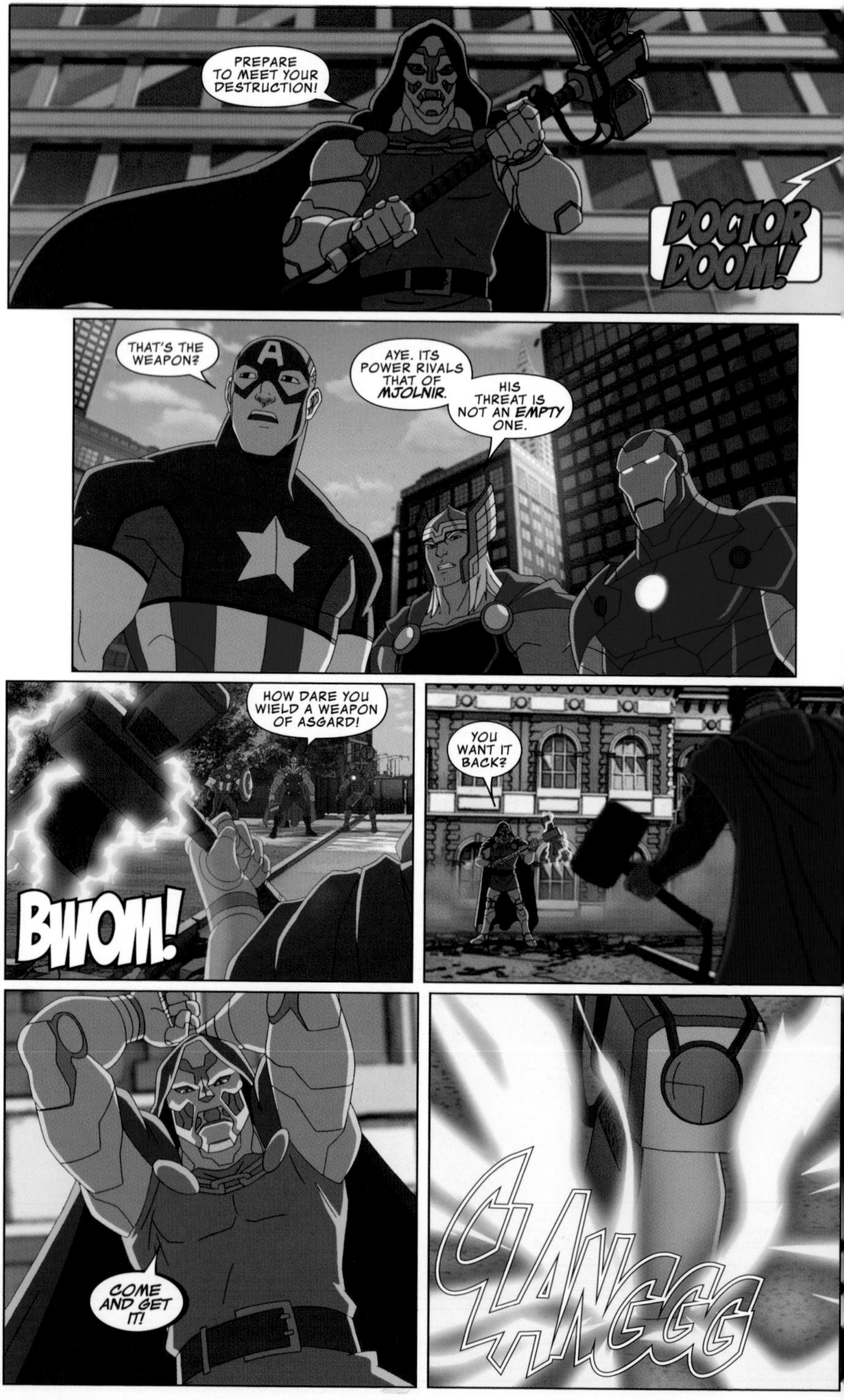
PREPARE TO MEET YOUR DESTRUCTION!
DOCTOR DOOM!
THAT'S THE WEAPON?
AYE. ITS POWER RIVALS THAT OF MJOLNIR.
HIS THREAT IS NOT AN EMPTY ONE.
HOW DARE YOU WIELD A WEAPON OF ASGARD!
BWOM!
YOU WANT IT BACK?
COME AND GET IT!
CLANGGG

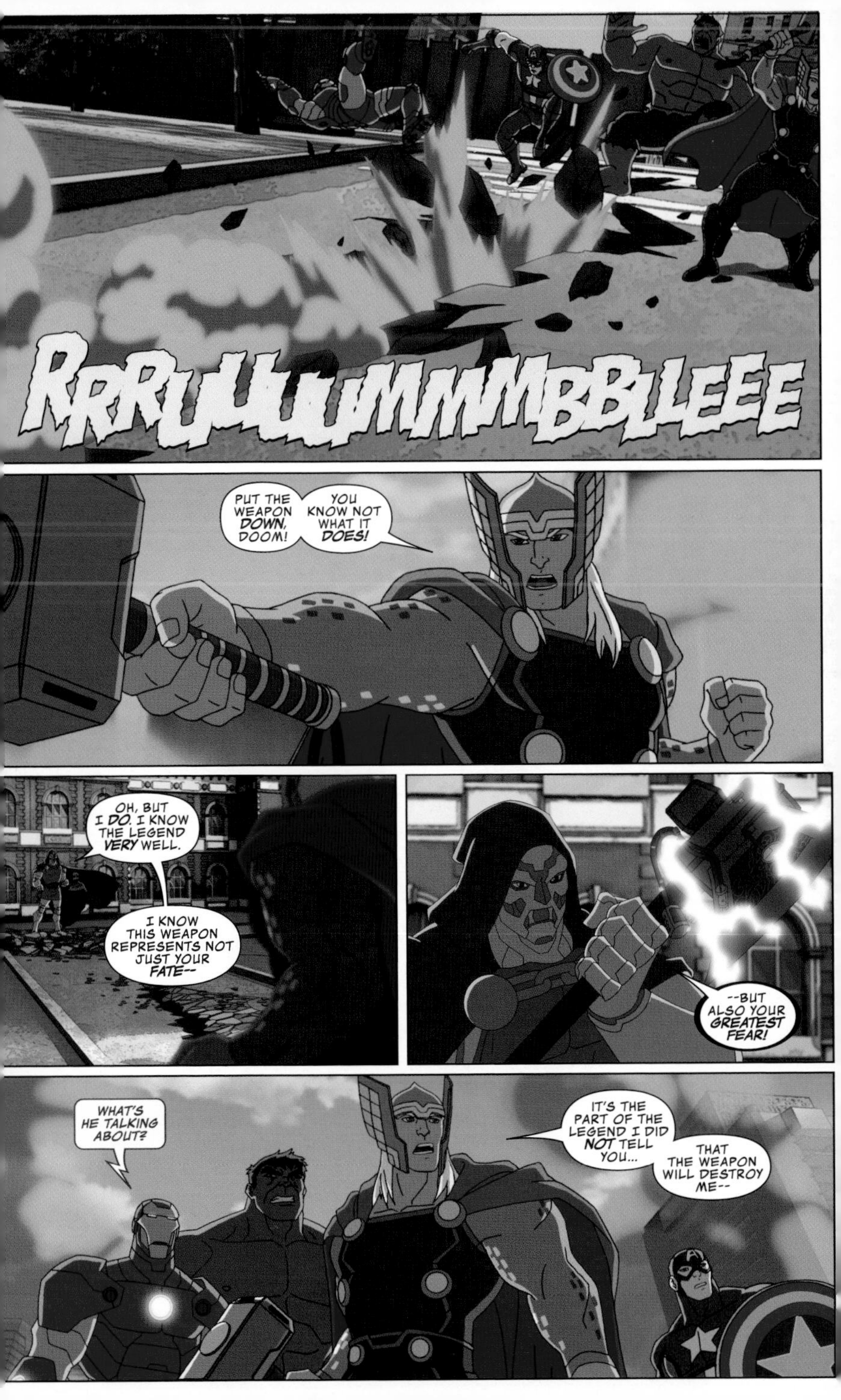
RRRUUUUMMMMBBLLEEE
PUT THE WEAPON DOWN, DOOM!
YOU KNOW NOT WHAT IT DOES!
OH, BUT I DO. I KNOW THE LEGEND VERY WELL.
I KNOW THIS WEAPON REPRESENTS NOT JUST YOUR FATE--
--BUT ALSO YOUR GREATEST FEAR!
WHAT'S HE TALKING ABOUT?
IT'S THE PART OF THE LEGEND I DID NOT TELL YOU...
THAT THE WEAPON WILL DESTROY ME--

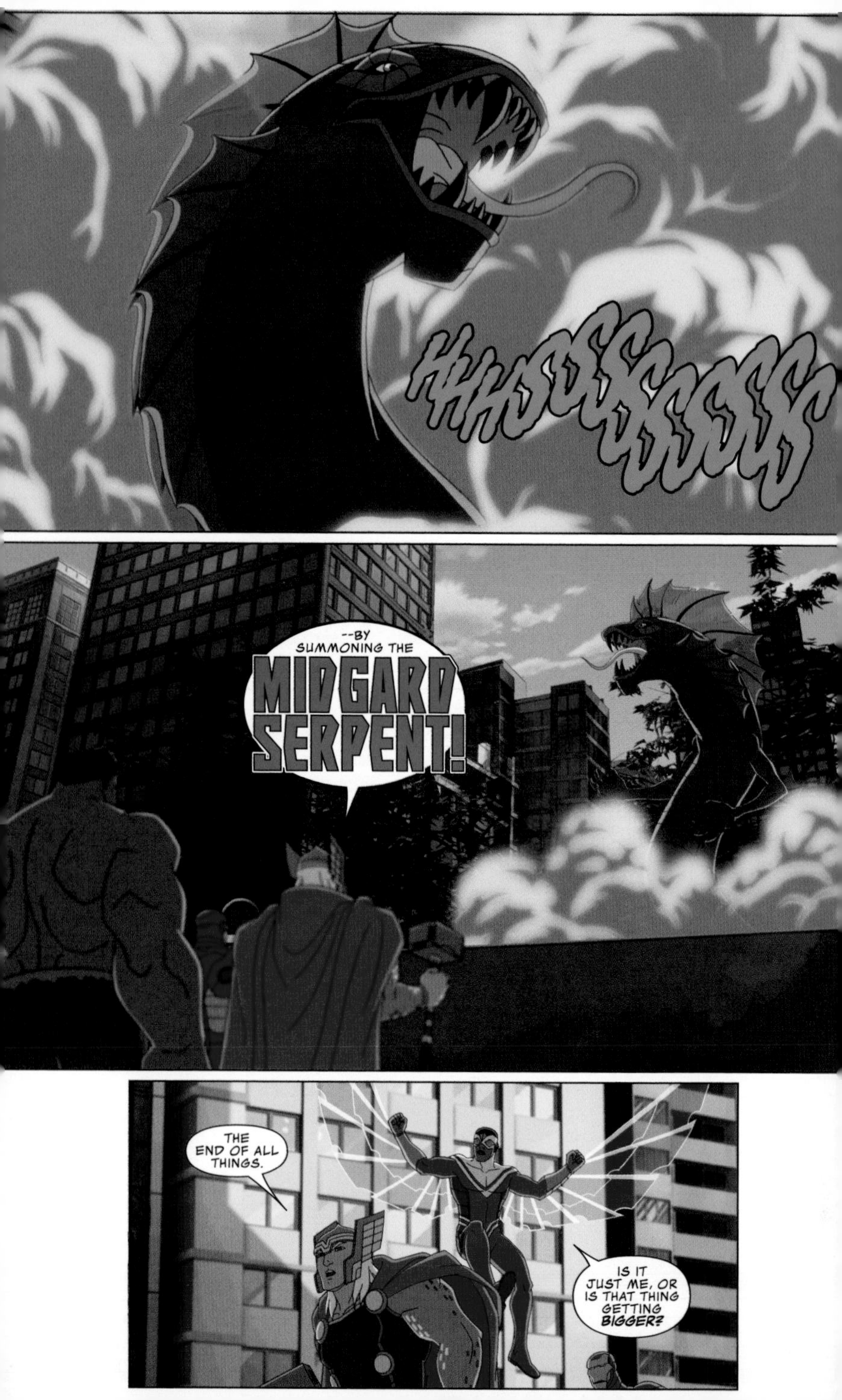
HHSSSSSSSS
--BY SUMMONING THE MIDGARD SERPENT!
THE END OF ALL THINGS.
IS IT JUST ME, OR IS THAT THING GETTING BIGGER?

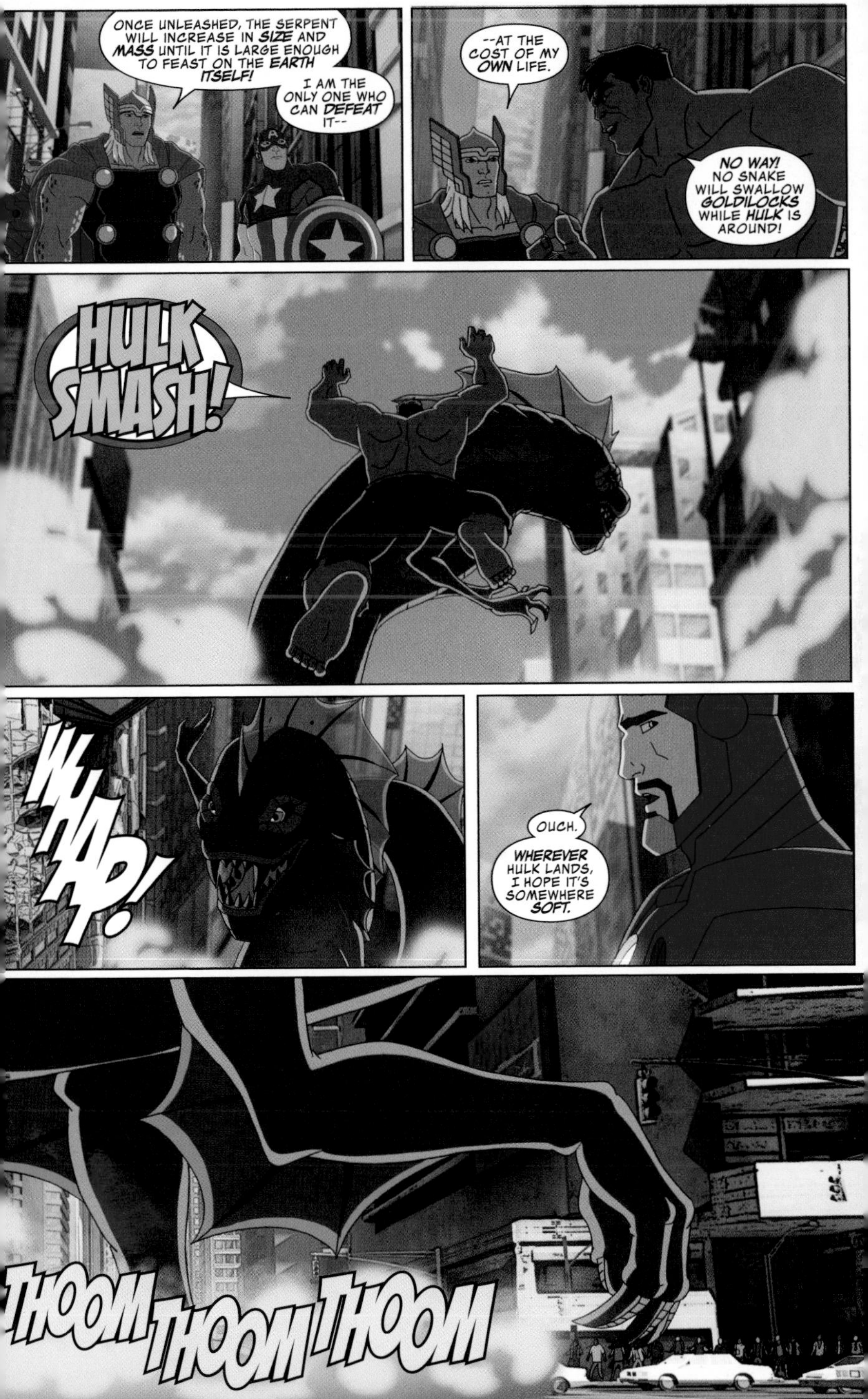

ONCE UNLEASHED, THE SERPENT WILL INCREASE IN SIZE AND MASS UNTIL IT IS LARGE ENOUGH TO FEAST ON THE EARTH ITSELF!
I AM THE ONLY ONE WHO CAN DEFEAT IT--
--AT THE COST OF MY OWN LIFE.
NO WAY! NO SNAKE WILL SWALLOW GOLDILOCKS WHILE HULK IS AROUND!
HULK SMASH!
WHAP!
OUCH.
WHEREVER HULK LANDS, I HOPE IT'S SOMEWHERE SOFT.
THOOM THOOM THOOM

AAAHHH!

RUN!

IT'LL CRUSH US ALL!

HAWKEYE, HELP ME GET THE **CIVILIANS** TO SAFETY!

SURE THING, **CAP!**

BUT WHERE IS IT **SAFE** WHEN THE SNAKE'S AS BIG AS THE **CITY?**

FALCON, GO FIND WHERE THE HULK LANDED.

WITHOUT HIS **STRENGTH,** WE DON'T STAND A CHANCE.

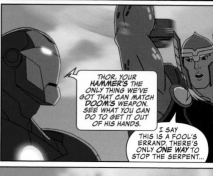

THOR, YOUR **HAMMER'S** THE ONLY THING WE'VE GOT THAT CAN MATCH **DOOM'S** WEAPON. SEE WHAT YOU CAN DO TO GET IT OUT OF HIS HANDS.

I SAY THIS IS A **FOOL'S** ERRAND. THERE'S ONLY **ONE WAY** TO STOP THE SERPENT...

...BUT IF MY **FINAL ACT** IS TO TAKE DOWN **VICTOR VON DOOM--**

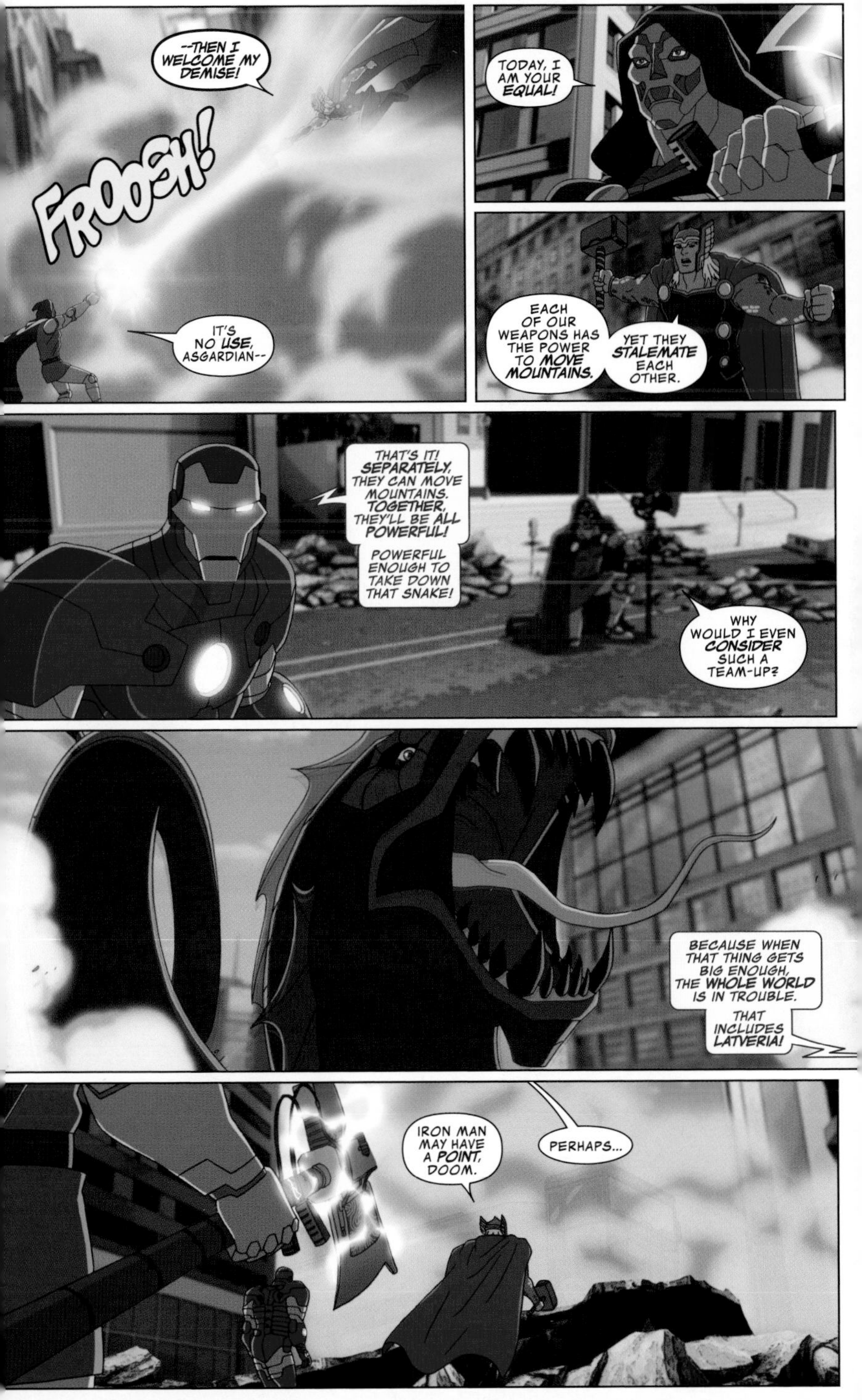
--THEN I WELCOME MY DEMISE!
FROOSH!
IT'S NO USE, ASGARDIAN--
TODAY, I AM YOUR EQUAL!
EACH OF OUR WEAPONS HAS THE POWER TO MOVE MOUNTAINS.
YET THEY STALEMATE EACH OTHER.
THAT'S IT! SEPARATELY, THEY CAN MOVE MOUNTAINS. TOGETHER, THEY'LL BE ALL POWERFUL!
POWERFUL ENOUGH TO TAKE DOWN THAT SNAKE!
WHY WOULD I EVEN CONSIDER SUCH A TEAM-UP?
BECAUSE WHEN THAT THING GETS BIG ENOUGH, THE WHOLE WORLD IS IN TROUBLE.
THAT INCLUDES LATVERIA!
IRON MAN MAY HAVE A POINT, DOOM.
PERHAPS...

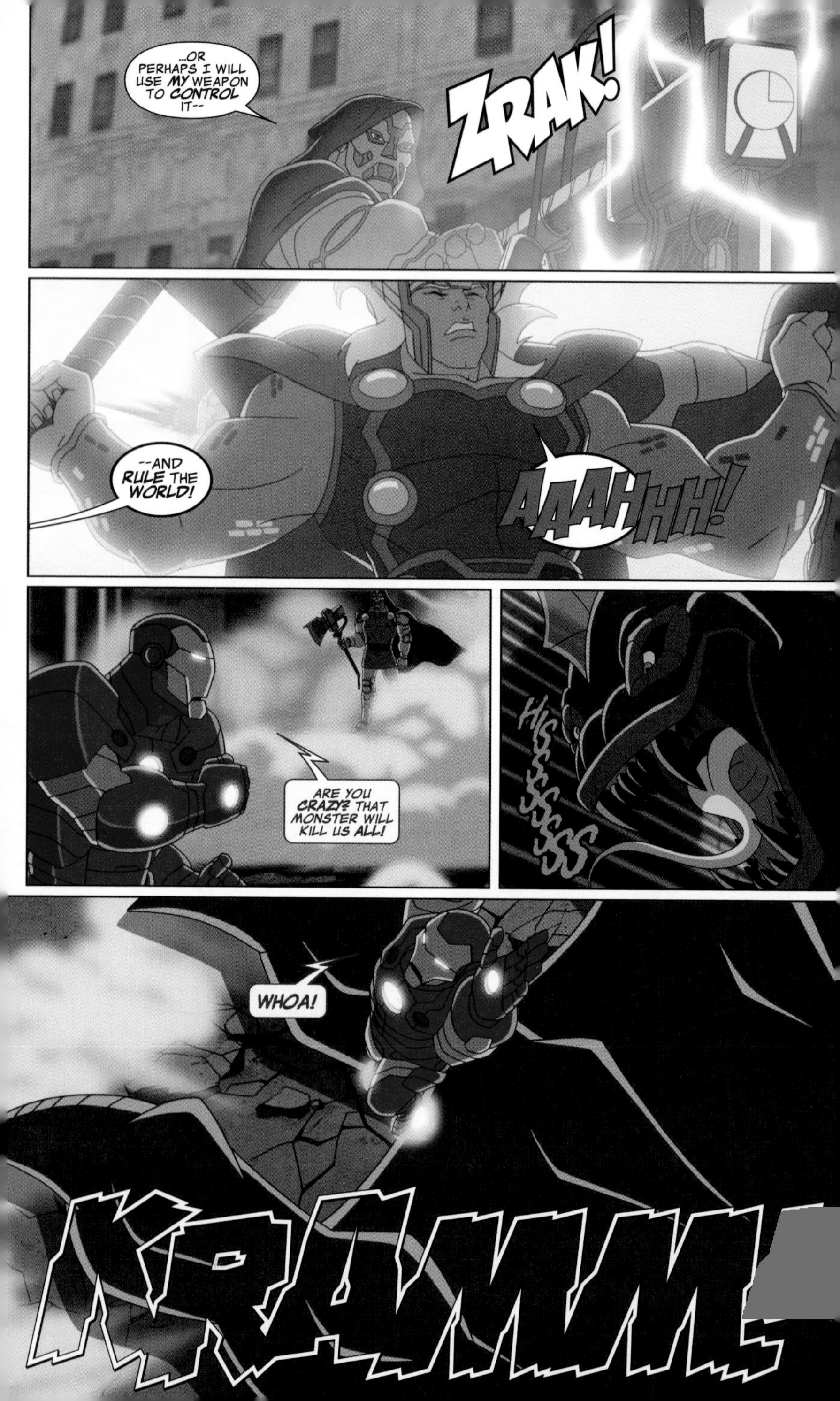

...OR PERHAPS I WILL USE MY WEAPON TO CONTROL IT--
ZRAK!
--AND RULE THE WORLD!
AAAHHH!
ARE YOU CRAZY? THAT MONSTER WILL KILL US ALL!
HISSSSSSSS
WHOA!
KRUMM

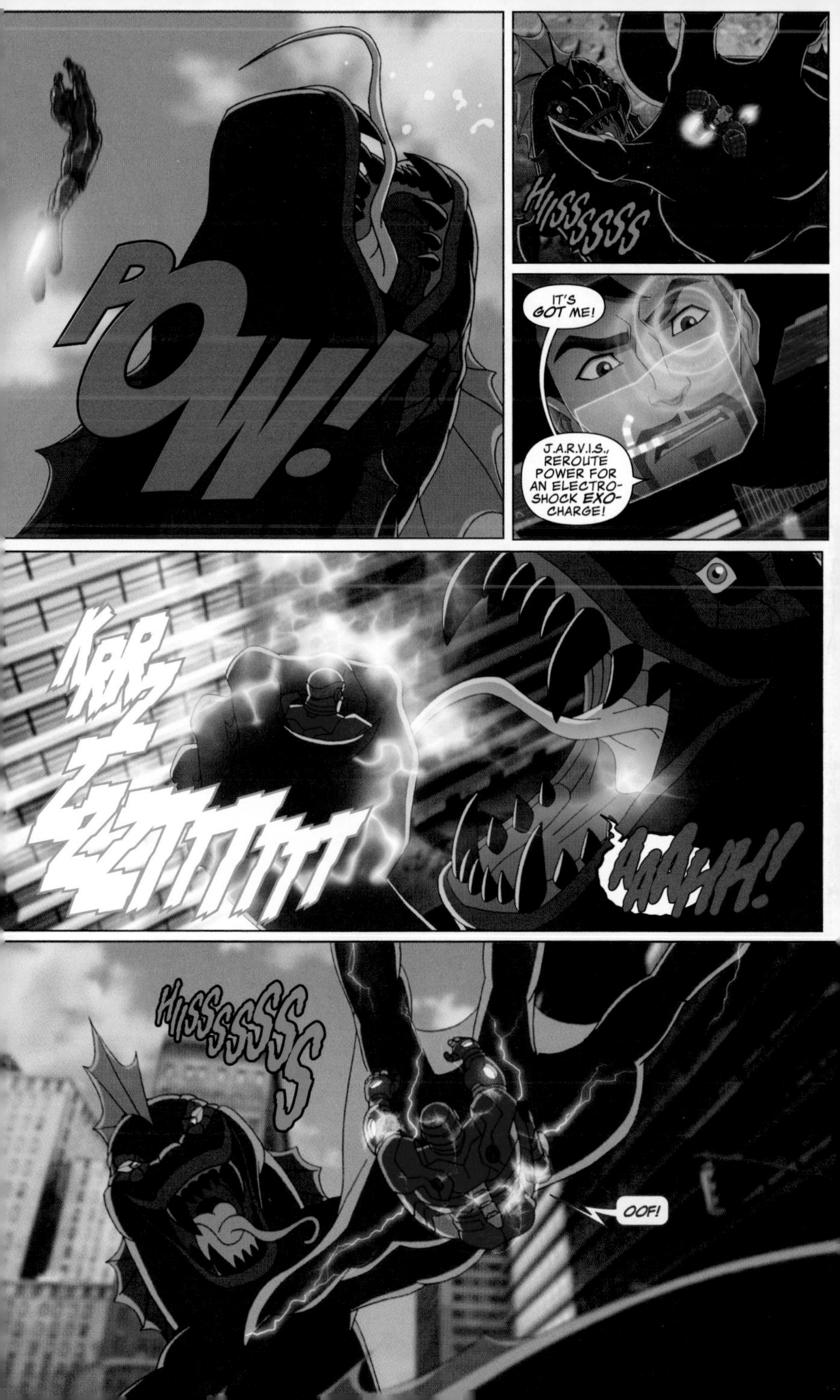
POW!
HIISSSSSSS
IT'S GOT ME!
J.A.R.V.I.S., REROUTE POWER FOR AN ELECTRO-SHOCK EXO-CHARGE!
KRRZZZZTTTTTTT
AAAHH!
HIISSSSSSSS
OOF!

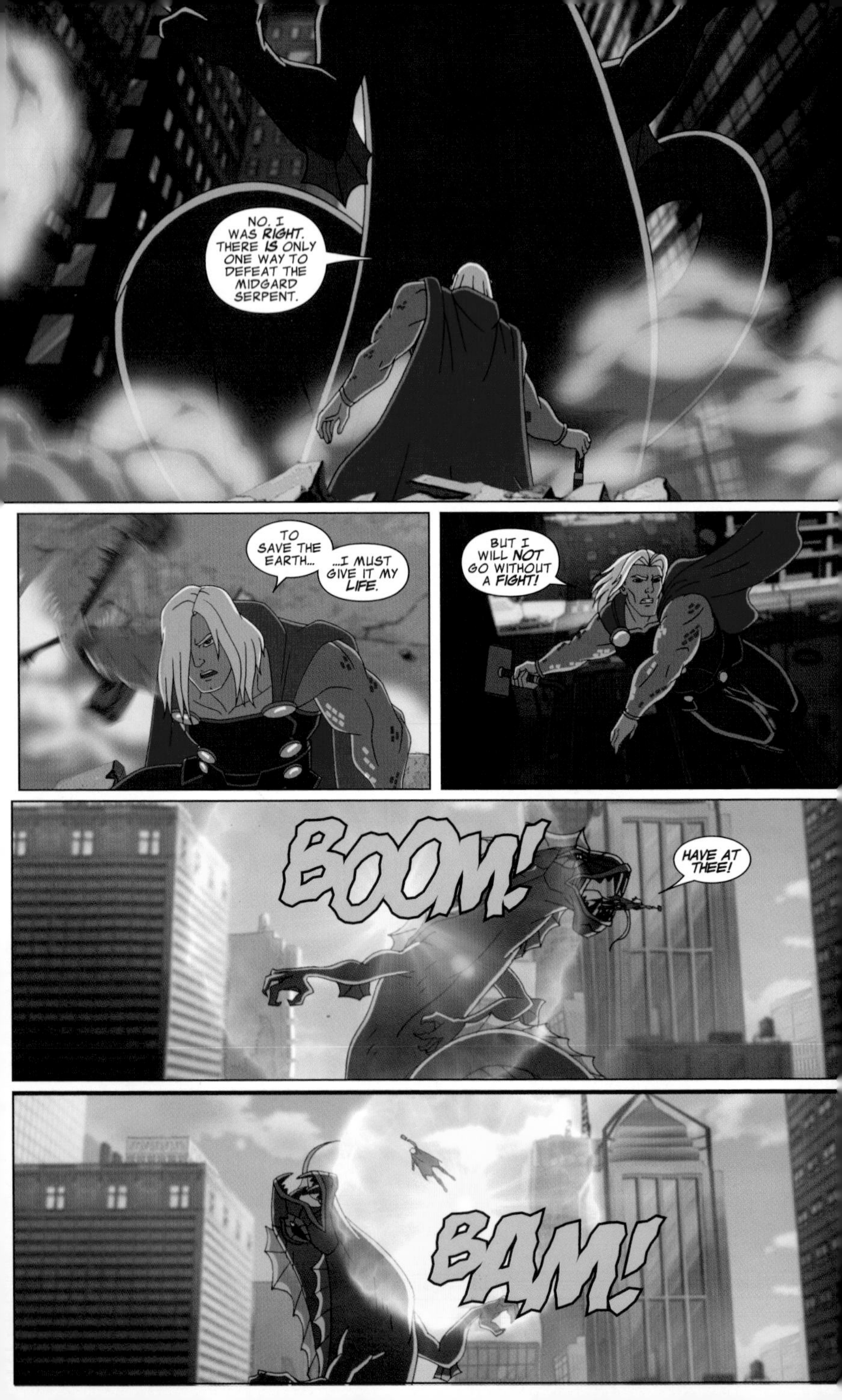

NO. I WAS RIGHT. THERE IS ONLY ONE WAY TO DEFEAT THE MIDGARD SERPENT.
TO SAVE THE EARTH...
...I MUST GIVE IT MY LIFE.
BUT I WILL NOT GO WITHOUT A FIGHT!
BOOM!
HAVE AT THEE!
BAM!

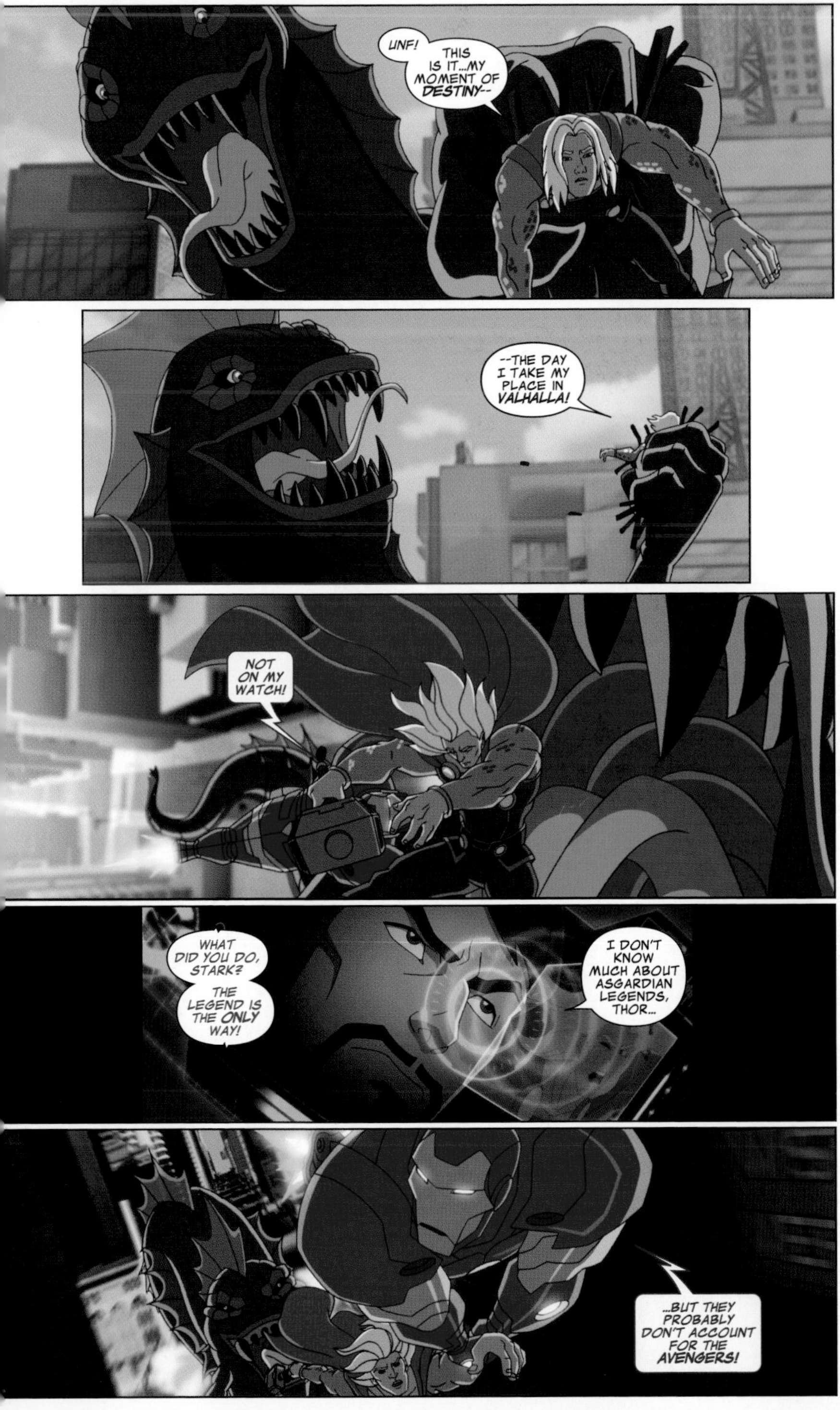
UNF!
THIS IS IT...MY MOMENT OF DESTINY--
--THE DAY I TAKE MY PLACE IN VALHALLA!
NOT ON MY WATCH!
WHAT DID YOU DO, STARK?
THE LEGEND IS THE ONLY WAY!
I DON'T KNOW MUCH ABOUT ASGARDIAN LEGENDS, THOR...
...BUT THEY PROBABLY DON'T ACCOUNT FOR THE AVENGERS!

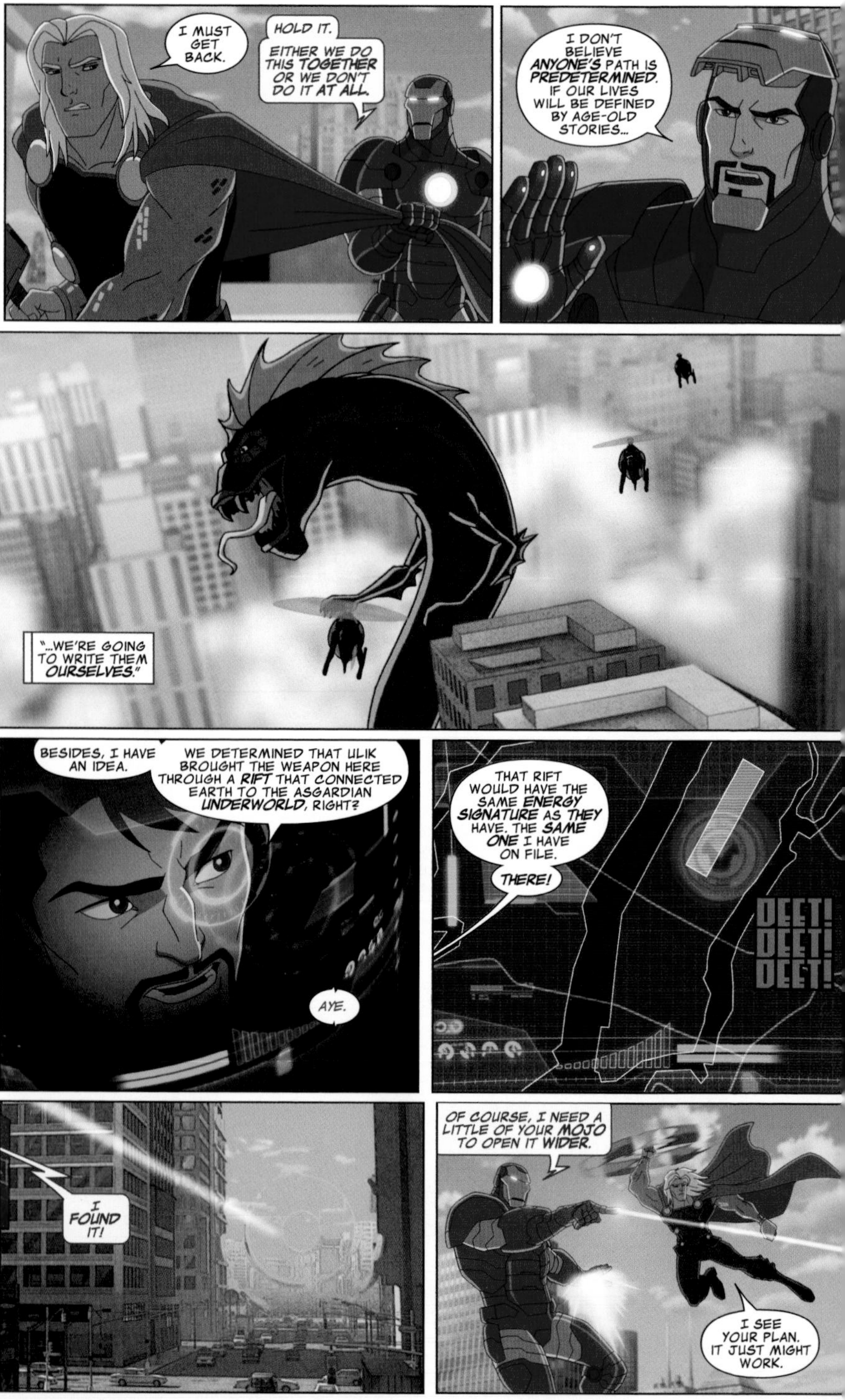
I MUST GET BACK.
HOLD IT.
EITHER WE DO THIS TOGETHER OR WE DON'T DO IT AT ALL.
I DON'T BELIEVE ANYONE'S PATH IS PREDETERMINED. IF OUR LIVES WILL BE DEFINED BY AGE-OLD STORIES...
"...WE'RE GOING TO WRITE THEM OURSELVES."
BESIDES, I HAVE AN IDEA.
WE DETERMINED THAT ULIK BROUGHT THE WEAPON HERE THROUGH A RIFT THAT CONNECTED EARTH TO THE ASGARDIAN UNDERWORLD, RIGHT?
AYE.
THAT RIFT WOULD HAVE THE SAME ENERGY SIGNATURE AS THEY HAVE. THE SAME ONE I HAVE ON FILE.
THERE!
DEET! DEET! DEET!
I FOUND IT!
OF COURSE, I NEED A LITTLE OF YOUR MOJO TO OPEN IT WIDER.
I SEE YOUR PLAN. IT JUST MIGHT WORK.

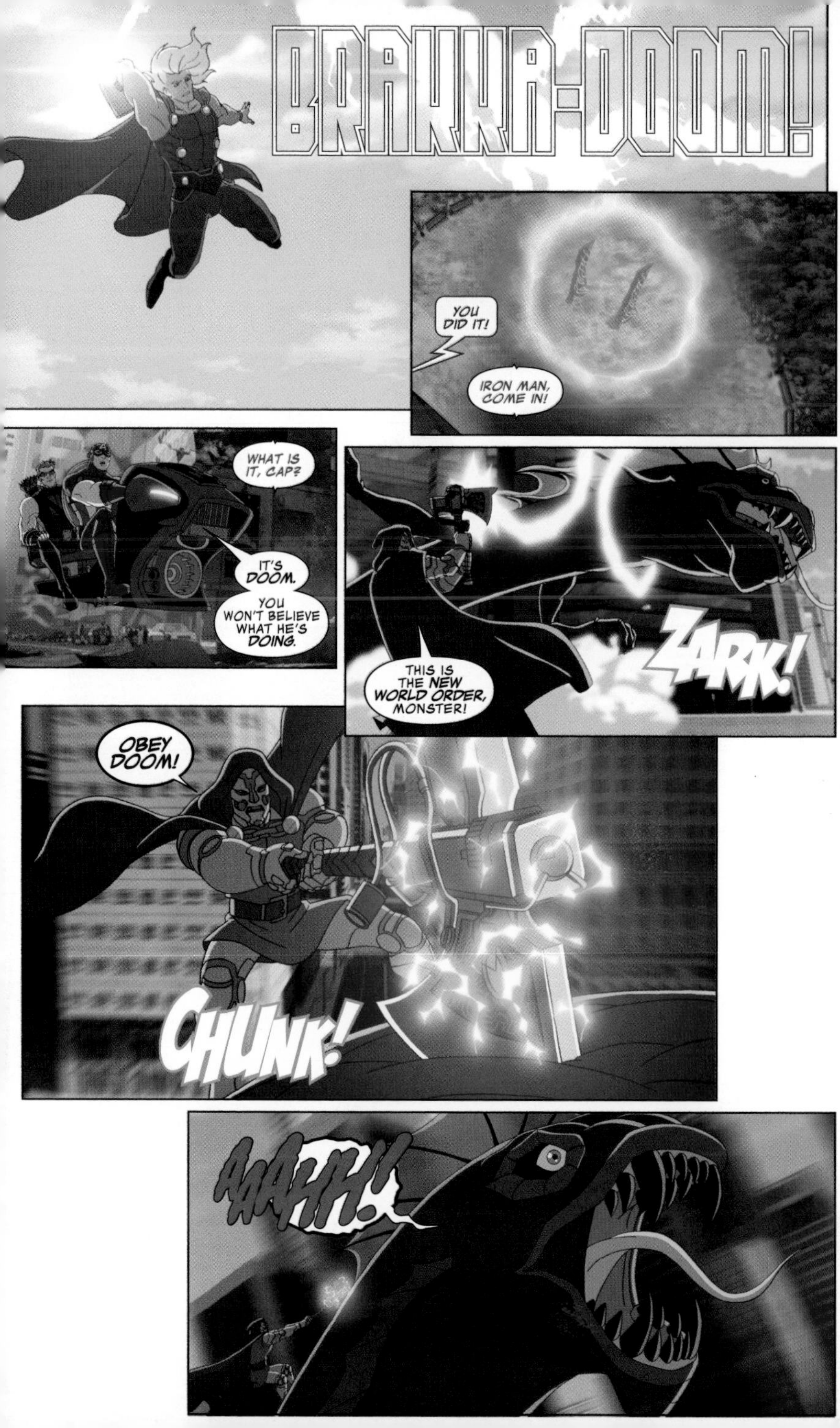
BRAKKA-DOOM!
YOU DID IT!
IRON MAN, COME IN!
WHAT IS IT, CAP?
IT'S DOOM.
YOU WON'T BELIEVE WHAT HE'S DOING.
THIS IS THE NEW WORLD ORDER, MONSTER!
ZARK!
OBEY DOOM!
CHUNK!
AAAHH!!

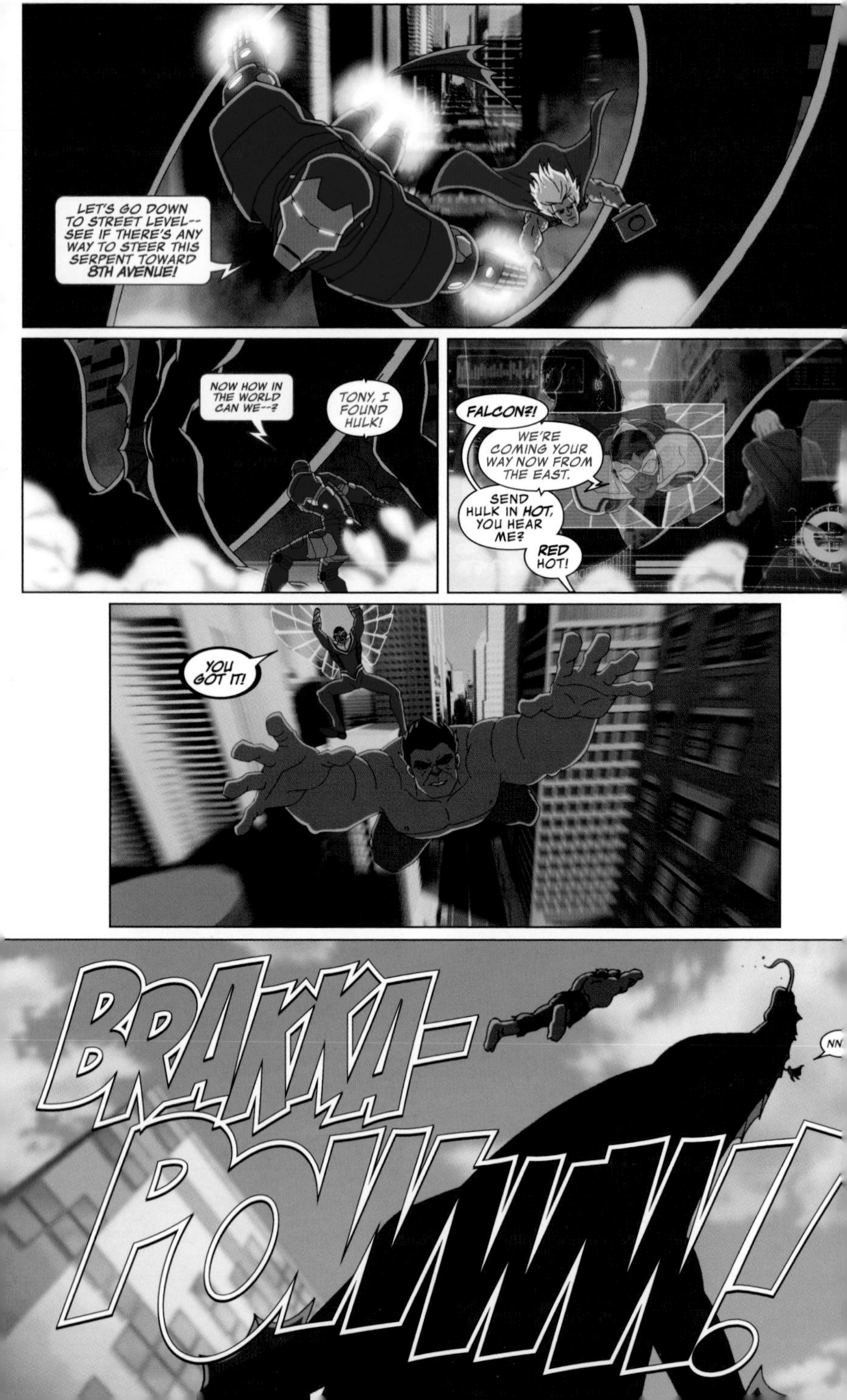
LET'S GO DOWN TO STREET LEVEL-- SEE IF THERE'S ANY WAY TO STEER THIS SERPENT TOWARD 8TH AVENUE!
NOW HOW IN THE WORLD CAN WE--?
TONY, I FOUND HULK!
FALCON?!
WE'RE COMING YOUR WAY NOW FROM THE EAST.
SEND HULK IN HOT, YOU HEAR ME?
RED HOT!
YOU GOT IT!
BRAKKA-KOWWWW!
NN

W-WHAT IS THAT DOWN BELOW?

THE WEAPON! IT'S *STUCK!*

I WILL NOT *LEAVE* IT! I WILL *NOT*--

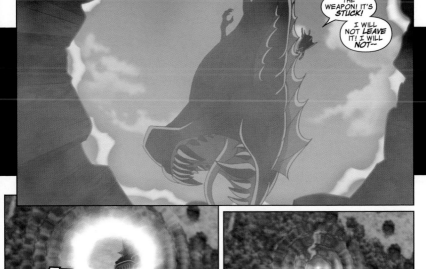

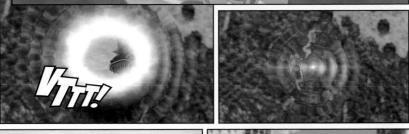

VTTT!

THE *RIFT!* IT *CLOSES* BEHIND THEM!

IT NEEDS JUST *ONE LAST* STRIKE OF MJOLNIR'S *MAGIC*--

--SO THAT IT *NEVER* OPENS *AGAIN!*

KRA KKKK

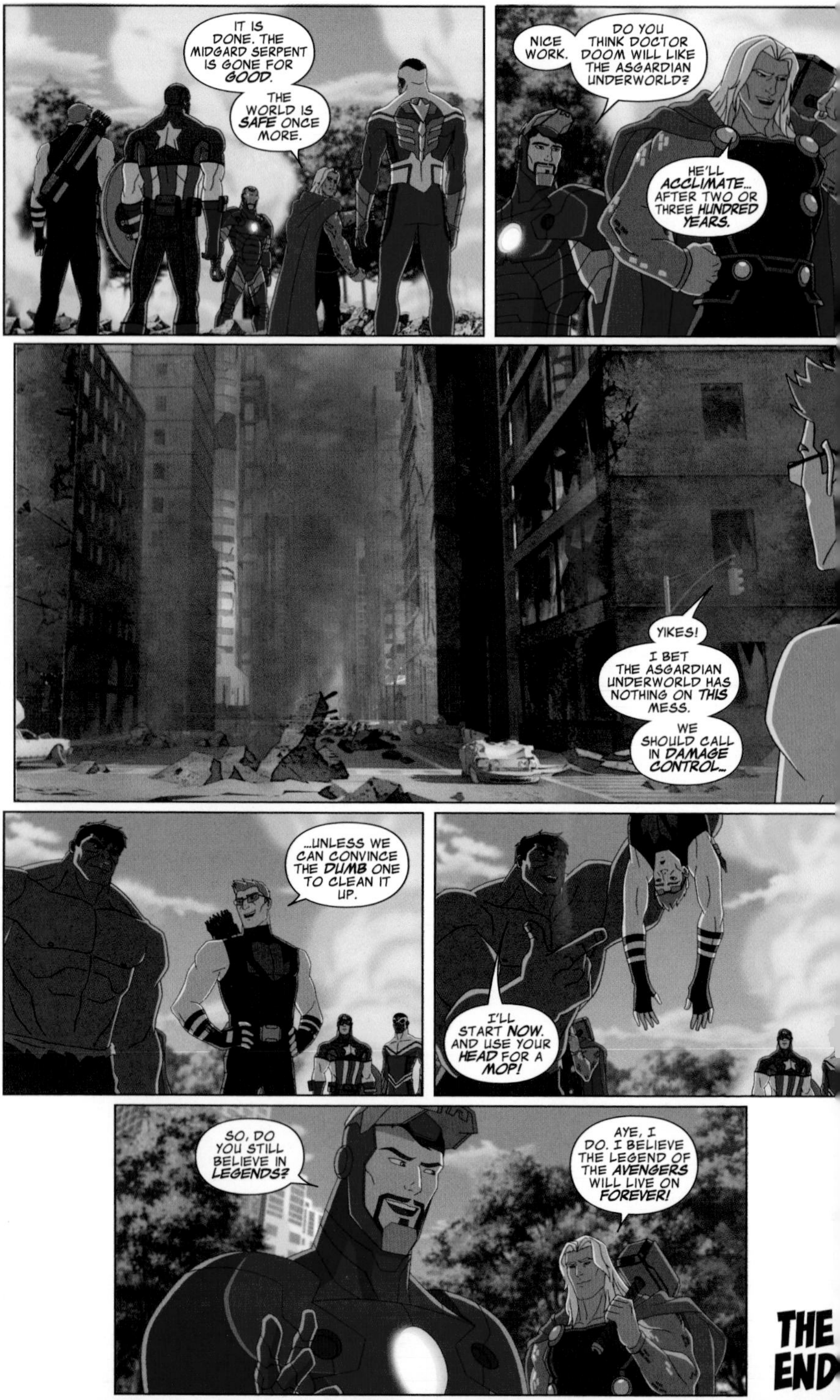
IT IS DONE. THE MIDGARD SERPENT IS GONE FOR GOOD.
THE WORLD IS SAFE ONCE MORE.
NICE WORK.
DO YOU THINK DOCTOR DOOM WILL LIKE THE ASGARDIAN UNDERWORLD?
HE'LL ACCLIMATE... AFTER TWO OR THREE HUNDRED YEARS.
YIKES!
I BET THE ASGARDIAN UNDERWORLD HAS NOTHING ON THIS MESS.
WE SHOULD CALL IN DAMAGE CONTROL...
...UNLESS WE CAN CONVINCE THE DUMB ONE TO CLEAN IT UP.
I'LL START NOW. AND USE YOUR HEAD FOR A MOP!
SO, DO YOU STILL BELIEVE IN LEGENDS?
AYE, I DO. I BELIEVE THE LEGEND OF THE AVENGERS WILL LIVE ON FOREVER!
THE END

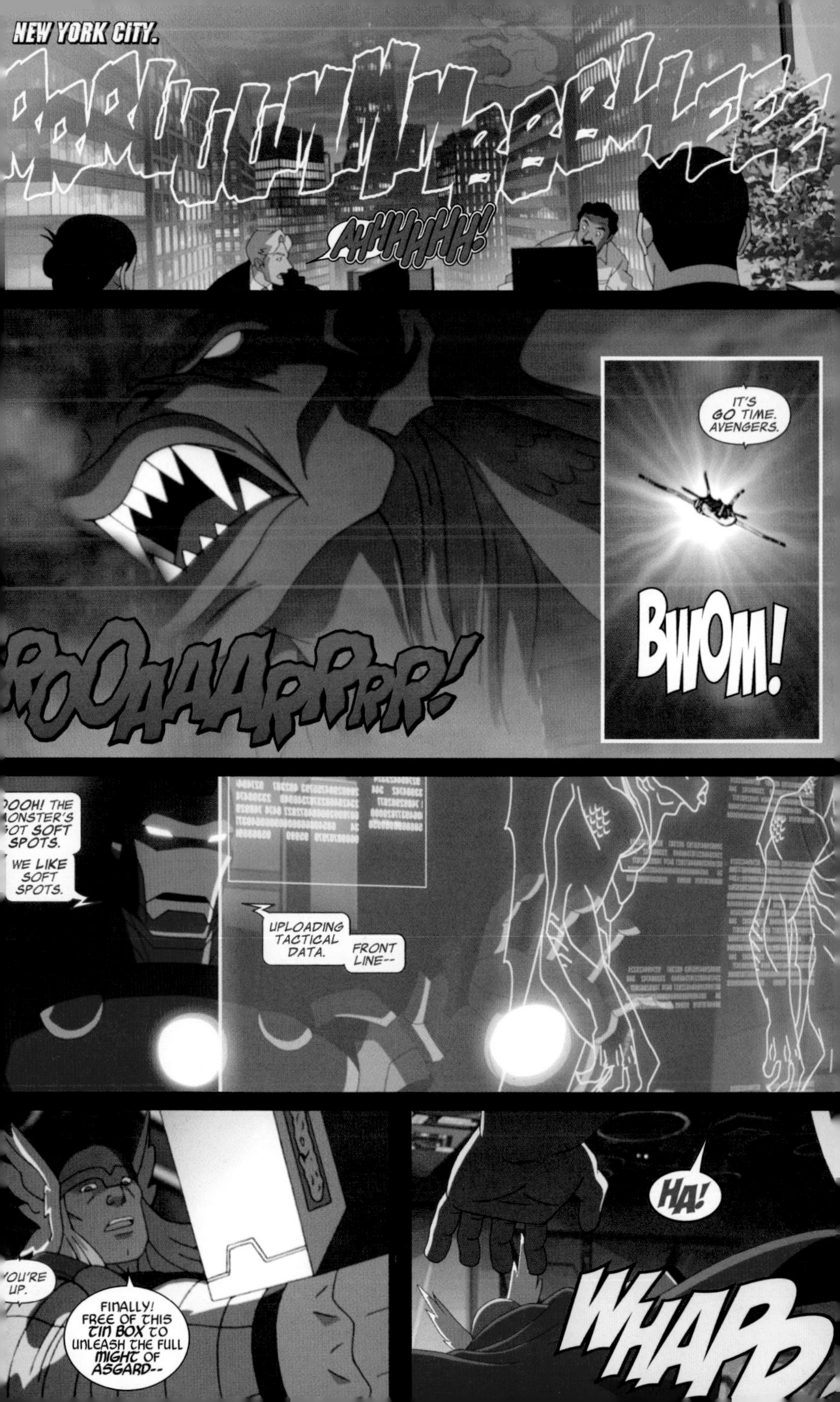

NEW YORK CITY.
AHHHHHH!
IT'S GO TIME. AVENGERS.
BWOM!
ROOAAARRRR!
OOOH! THE MONSTER'S GOT SOFT SPOTS.
WE LIKE SOFT SPOTS.
UPLOADING TACTICAL DATA.
FRONT LINE--
YOU'RE UP.
FINALLY! FREE OF THIS TIN BOX TO UNLEASH THE FULL MIGHT OF ASGARD--
HA!
WHAP

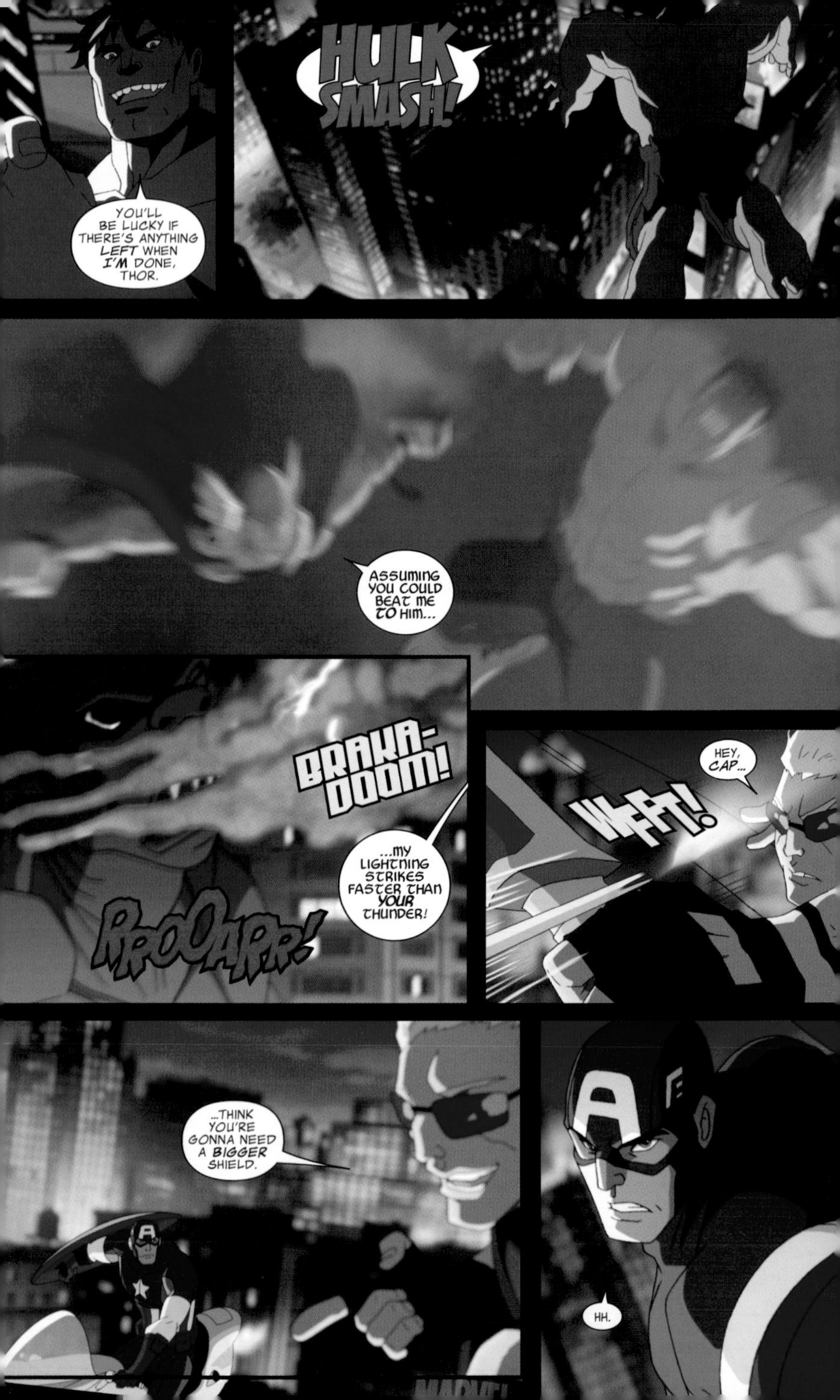

HULK SMASH!
YOU'LL BE LUCKY IF THERE'S ANYTHING LEFT WHEN I'M DONE, THOR.
ASSUMING YOU COULD BEAT ME TO HIM...
BRAKA-DOOM!
...MY LIGHTNING STRIKES FASTER THAN YOUR THUNDER!
RROOARR!
HEY, CAP...
WFFT!
...THINK YOU'RE GONNA NEED A BIGGER SHIELD.
HH.

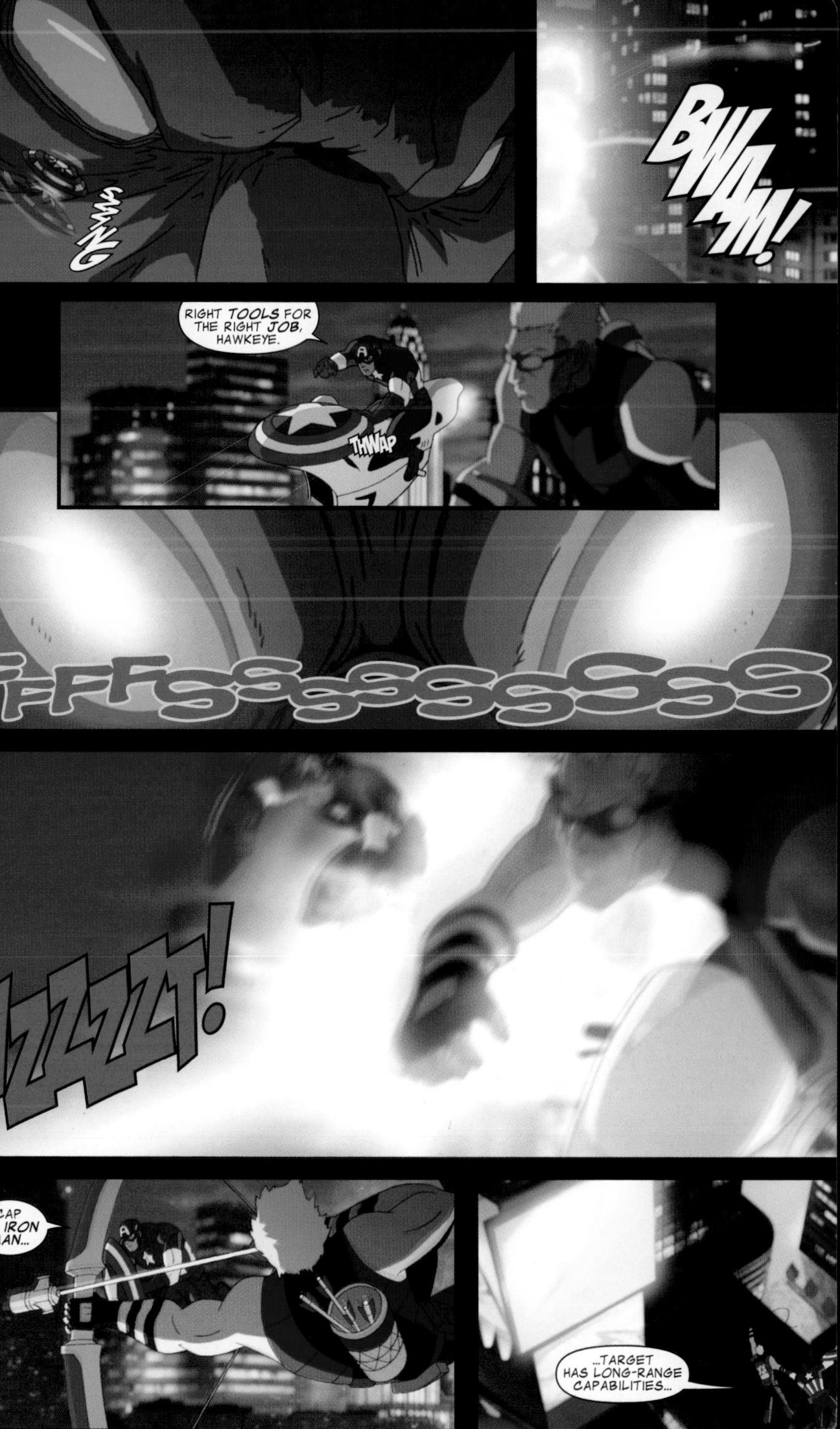

SSSSSNG
BWAAM!
RIGHT TOOLS FOR THE RIGHT JOB, HAWKEYE.
THWAP
FFFSSSSSSSSSS
ZZZZT!
CAP IRON AN...
...TARGET HAS LONG-RANGE CAPABILITIES...

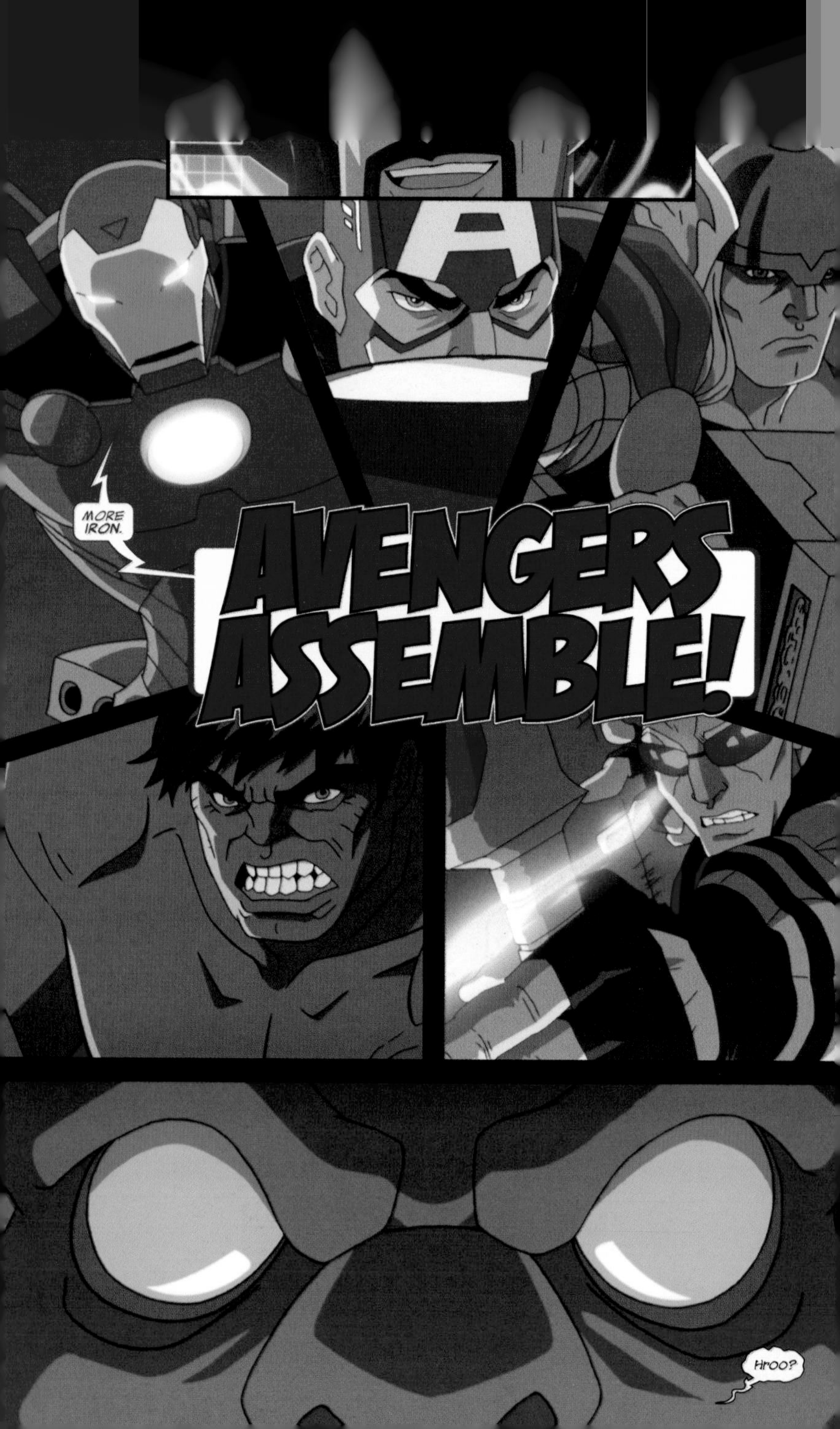

MORE IRON.
AVENGERS ASSEMBLE!
Hroo?

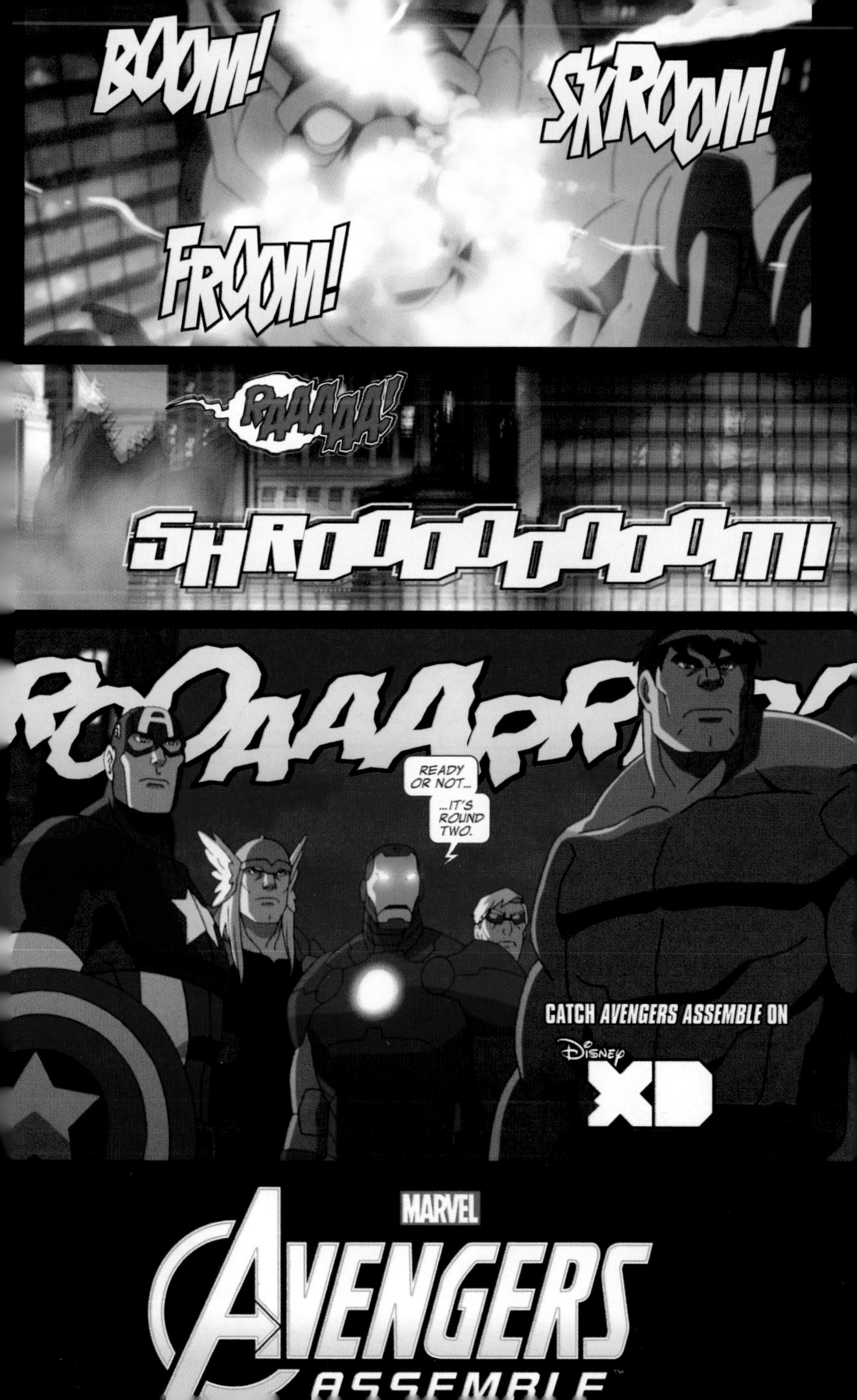
BOOM!
SKROOM!
FROOM!
RAAAAA!
SHROOOOOOM!
READY OR NOT...
...IT'S ROUND TWO.
CATCH AVENGERS ASSEMBLE ON
DISNEY XD
MARVEL
AVENGERS ASSEMBLE

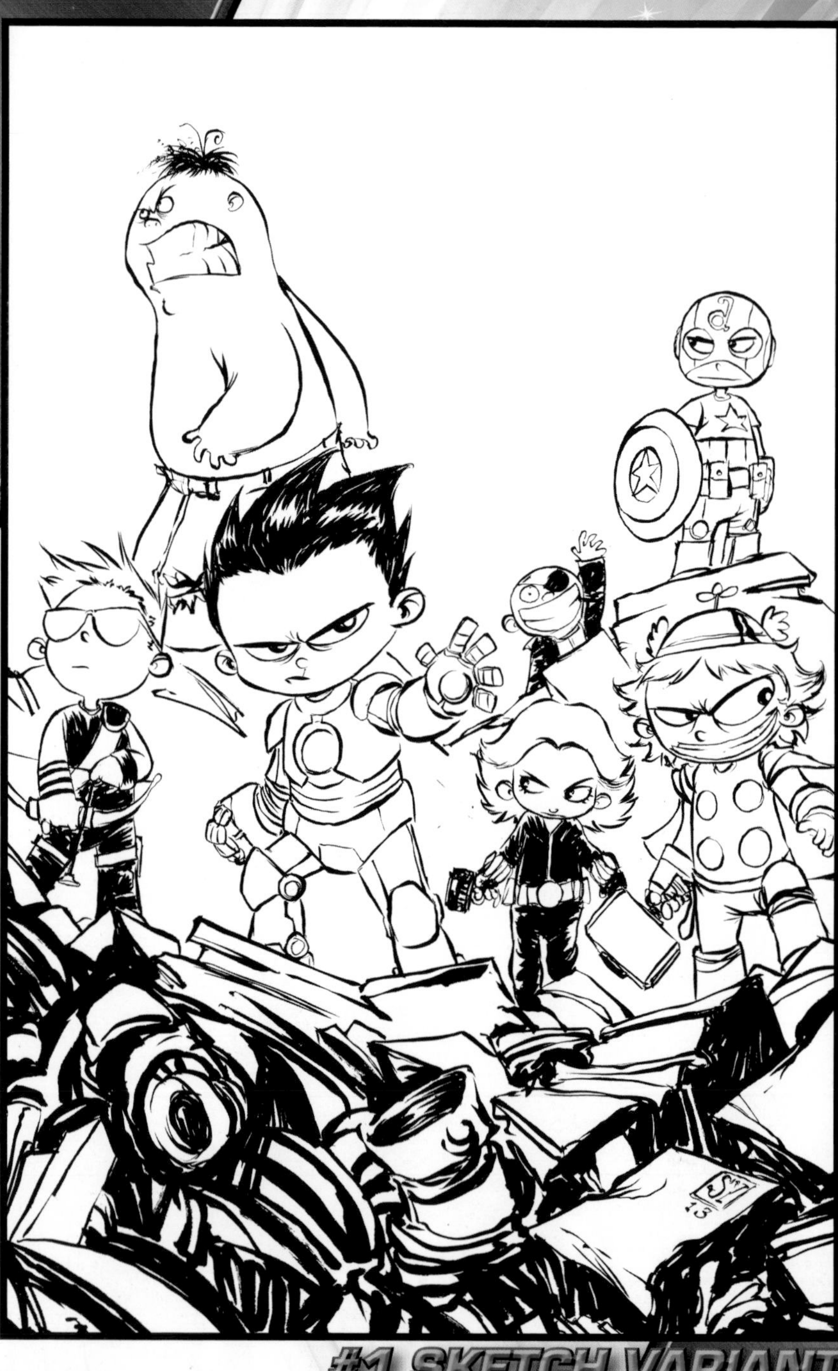

SY
13

#1 SKETCH VARIANT
by Skottie Young

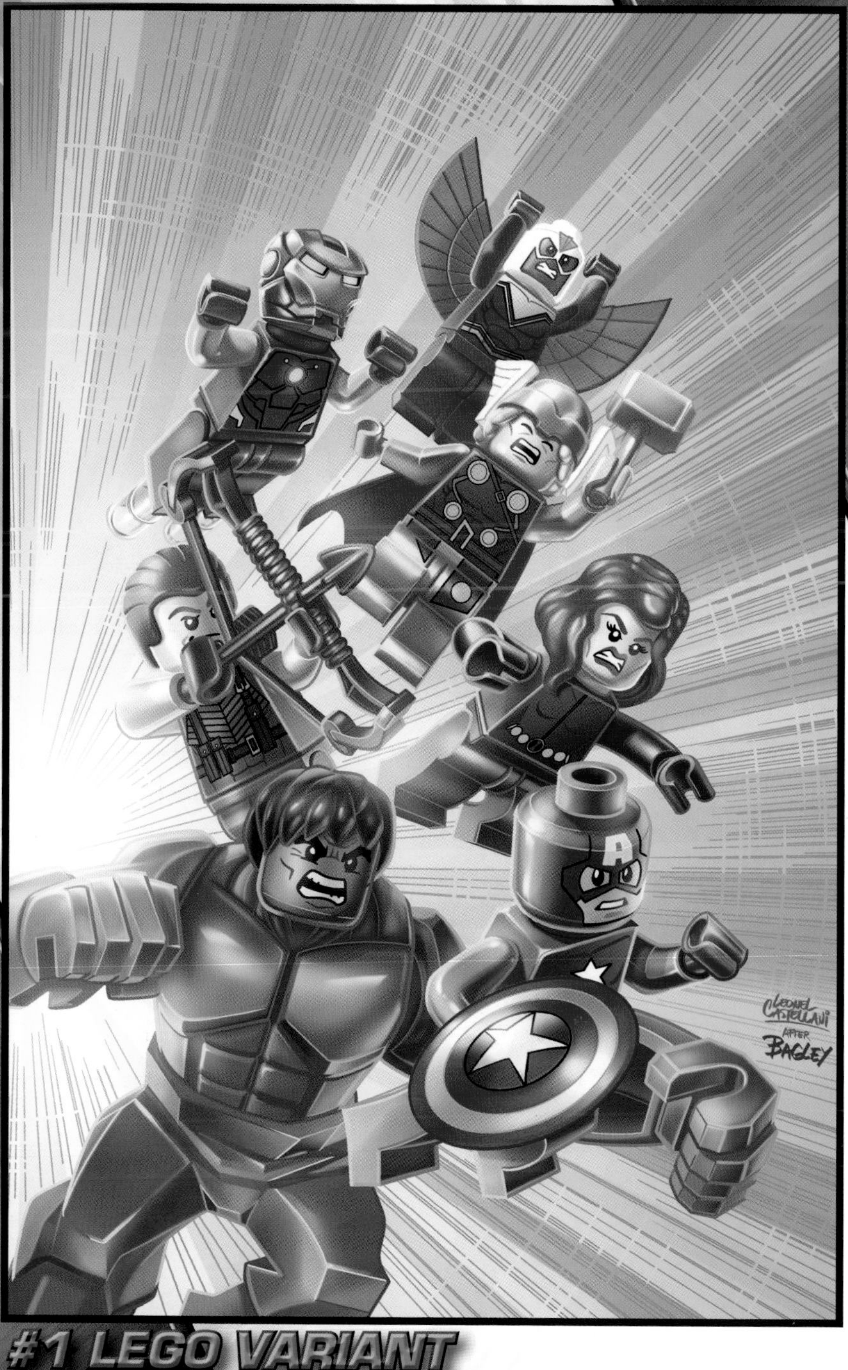
LEONEL CASTELLANI
AFTER
BAGLEY

#1 LEGO VARIANT
by Leonel Castellani

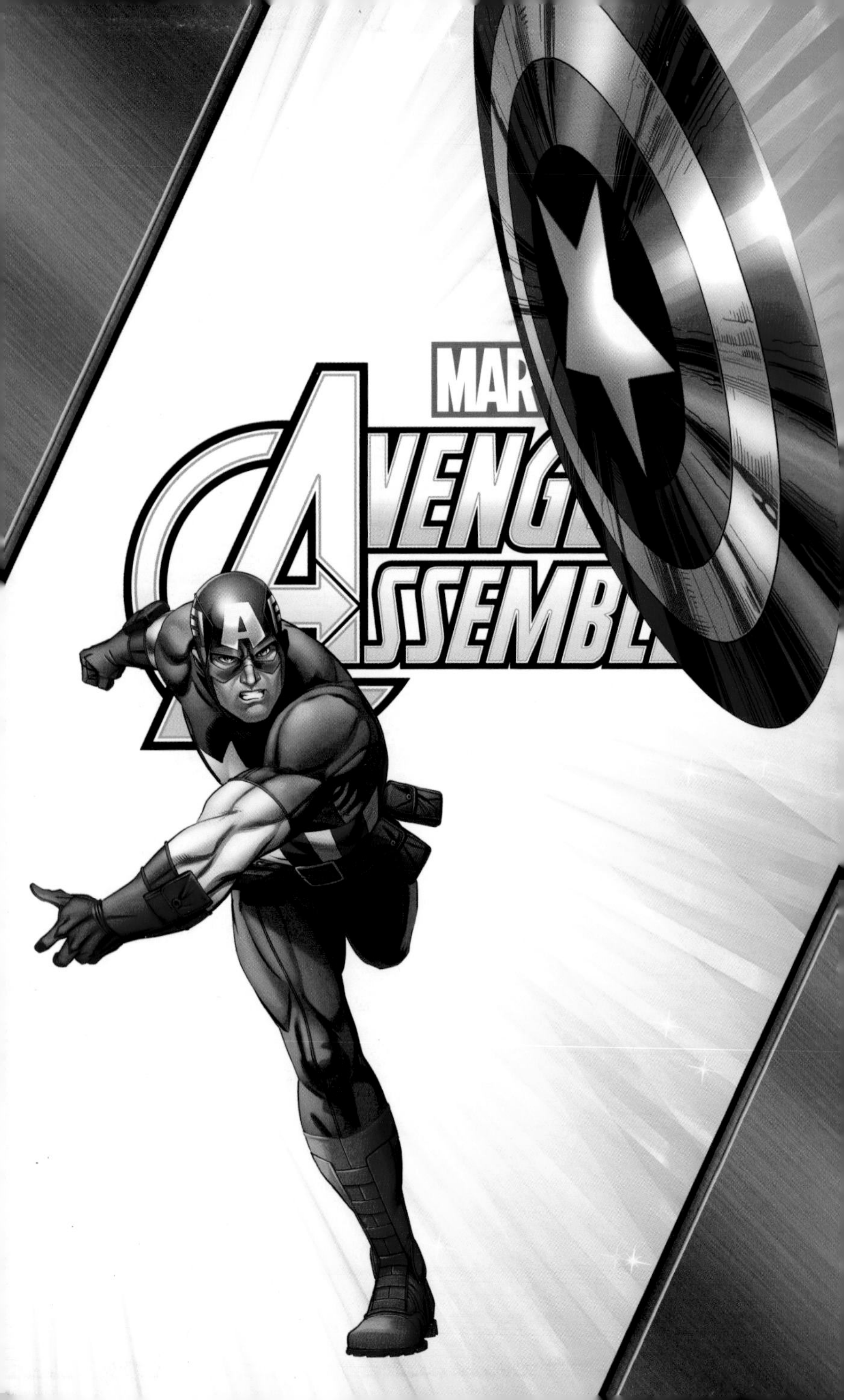